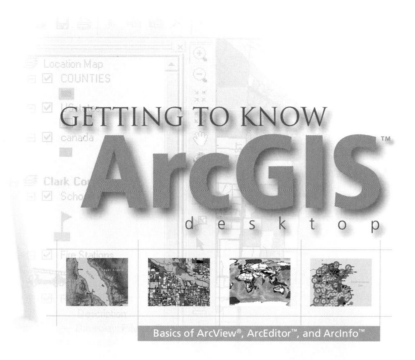

GETTING TO KNOW
ArcGIS™
desktop

Basics of ArcView®, ArcEditor™, and ArcInfo™

Tim Ormsby | Eileen Napoleon | Robert Burke | Carolyn Groessl | Laura Feaster

ESRI PRESS

REDLANDS, CALIFORNIA

First printing June 2001. Second printing September 2001. Third printing October 2002. Fourth printing January 2003. Fifth printing September 2003.

Printed in the United States of America.

Library of Congress Cataloging-in-Publication Data
Getting to know ArcGIS desktop : basics of ArcView, ArcEditor, and ArcInfo /
Tim Ormsby ... [et al.].
　　　p.　cm.
　　ISBN 1-879102-89-7 (pbk., 2 CD)
　　　1. ArcGIS.　2. Geographic information systems.　3. Graphical user
　　interfaces (Computer systems).　I. Ormsby, Tim.　II. Title.
　　G70.212.G489　2001
　　910'.285—dc21　　　　　　　　　　　　　　　　2001003387

Published by ESRI, 380 New York Street, Redlands, California 92373-8100.

Books from ESRI Press are available to resellers worldwide through Independent Publishers Group (IPG). For information on volume discounts, or to place an order, call IPG at 1-800-888-4741 in the United States, or at 312-337-0747 outside the United States.

CONTENTS

ACKNOWLEDGMENTS

ESRI thanks the following people and groups for contributing data and images to this book.

Maps of rainfall, elevation, soils, and growing seasons for North and South America (chapter 1) are based on data provided by DATA+ and the Russian Academy of Sciences.

Maps of elevation, hillshade, and temperature for the Mojave Desert (chapter 5) are based on data provided by the United States Department of Defense Mojave Desert Ecosystem Program.

Satellite image and map of Mission Bay, San Diego, California (chapter 5), provided by the United States Geological Survey.

African diamond mine, river, and wildlife layers (chapters 5 and 6) provided by DATA+ and the Russian Academy of Sciences.

State of Louisiana layers (chapter 9), including nonhazardous waste pits, parish boundaries, and navigable waterways, provided by David Gisclair of the Louisiana Oil Spill Coordinator's Office, Baton Rouge, Louisiana.

City of Riverside layers (chapter 10), including neighborhoods, places, buildings, and zoning, provided by the City of Riverside GIS Department.

City of Riverside census tract layer (chapter 10) provided by the United States Census Bureau.

City of Riverside freeways layer (chapter 10) provided by Geographic Data Technology, Inc. Copyright 1990–1998 Geographic Data Technology, Inc. All rights reserved.

Tongass National Forest, Alaska, stream and forest stand layers (chapters 11 and 12) provided by the United States Forest Service, Tongass National Forest, Ketchikan Area.

Population attributes for U.S. states and cities (chapter 13) provided by the United States Census Bureau.

City of Manhattan, Kansas, and Riley County, Kansas, layers (chapters 14, 15, and 16), including parcels, water lines, water valves, fire hydrants, and air photo, provided by Dan Oldehoeft, City of Manhattan, Kansas, and John Cowan, Riley County, Kansas.

Satellite image of Crater Lake (chapter 15) provided by the United States Geological Survey. Web address: tahoe.usgs.gov/craterlake/space.shtml

Atlanta streets layer (chapter 17) provided by Geographic Data Technology, Inc. Copyright 1990–1998 Geographic Data Technology, Inc. All rights reserved.

Typhoon Etang latitude and longitude coordinates (chapter 18) provided by the United States Department of Defense Joint Typhoon Warning Center. Web address: www.npmoc.navy.mil/jtwc.html

Tiger reserve layers for India (chapter 18) provided by the World Wildlife Fund. Web address: www.worldwildlife.org

Thanks to our editor, Michael Karman, *il miglior fabbro*.

Thanks also to Jonell Alvi for additional writing; to Judy Boyd, Tom Brenneman, Nick Frunzi, Christian Harder, Makram Murad, Gillian Silvertand, Damian Spangrud, Thad Tilton, and Randy Worch for technical reviews and advice; and to Prashant Hedao and Brian Parr for data acquisition.

Getting to Know ArcGIS Desktop: Basics of ArcView, ArcEditor, and ArcInfo is the latest software workbook from ESRI. Like its predecessors, *Getting to Know ArcView GIS* and *Extending ArcView GIS*, this is a practical book that teaches how to use the software through exercises and color graphics. Concepts are explained at the beginning of each chapter and as needed throughout.

ArcGIS™ Desktop is the collective name for three products, ArcView® 8.x, ArcEditor™ 8.x, and ArcInfo™ 8.x. These products have the same interface and share much of their functionality. ArcEditor does everything ArcView does and goes beyond it; ArcInfo goes beyond ArcEditor. *Getting to Know ArcGIS Desktop* does not cover features unique to ArcEditor or ArcInfo, but because the three products have the same foundation, the book is an introduction to all three.

If you are new to ArcGIS Desktop software, and even if you have some experience, this book will be useful to you. If you are an ArcView 3 user, you will find some familiar elements in the new software, but a great deal that is different—beginning with the interface. ArcView 8 is not an updated version of ArcView 3, but a different product.

This book comes with two CDs. One has a fully functional copy of ArcView 8 software that expires 180 days after you install it; the other has exercise data. You need to install both CDs to do the exercises in the book. (If you already have a copy of ArcView, ArcEditor, or ArcInfo, you need only to install the data.) Appendix B tells you how to install the software and data.

Getting to Know ArcGIS Desktop is not a GIS textbook. If you have no GIS background, chapter 1 explains some concepts that will better prepare you for the exercises, but the book's purpose is to teach software, not theory. It is designed for practical uses, such as classroom lab work or on-the-job training.

The book has two introductory chapters and seventeen exercise chapters. Each exercise chapter contains two to four exercises that show you how to accomplish a particular GIS task in a realistic context. Many different tasks are covered, including symbolizing and labeling maps, classifying data, querying maps, analyzing spatial relationships, setting map projections, building spatial databases, editing data, geocoding addresses, and making map layouts. An online exercise teaches you how to use Geography Network[SM], a Web site where you can bring maps and data from the Internet to ArcView.

You can save your work at the end of each exercise, but every new exercise is another starting point, with the maps and data you need already prepared for you. It is recommended that you follow the chapters in order—especially because tools and functions used frequently in early chapters may not be explained again in later ones. The exercises will work no matter which chapter you start with. We estimate it will take one to two hours to complete a chapter.

Getting to Know ArcGIS Desktop is an introductory book. While it doesn't teach you everything about ArcView 8, it teaches you much of what you'll need to know to complete your own GIS projects.

Introducing GIS

For a long time, people have studied the world using models such as maps and globes. In the last thirty years or so, it has become possible to put these models inside computers—more sophisticated models into smaller computers every year. These computer models, along with the tools for analyzing them, make up a geographic information system (GIS).

In a GIS, you can study not just this map or that map, but every possible map. With the right data, you can see whatever you want—land, elevation, climate zones, forests, political boundaries, population density, per capita income, land use, energy consumption, mineral resources, and a thousand other things—in whatever part of the world interests you.

The map of the world, below, shows countries, cities, rivers, lakes, and the ocean.

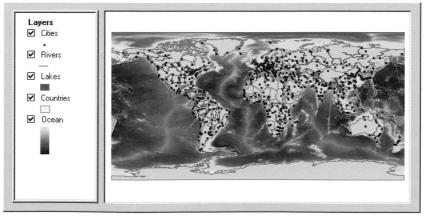

The map has a legend (or table of contents) on the left and a display area on the right.

A GIS map contains layers

On a paper map, you can't peel cities away from countries, or countries away from the ocean, but on a GIS map you can. A GIS map is made up of *layers,* or collections of geographic objects that are alike. To make a map, you can add as many layers as you want.

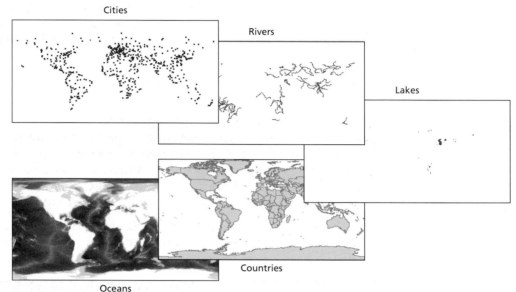

This world map is made up of five layers. It could have many more.

Layers may contain features or surfaces

In this map, the Cities layer includes many different cities and the Rivers layer many different rivers. The same is true of the Lakes and Countries layers. Each geographic object in a layer—each city, river, lake, or country—is called a feature.

Not all layers contain features. The Oceans layer is not a collection of geographic objects the way the others are. It is a single, continuous expanse that changes from one location to another according to the depth of the water. A geographic expanse of this kind is called a surface.

Features have shape and size

Geographic objects have an endless variety of shapes. All of them, however, can be represented as one of three geometrical forms—a polygon, a line, or a point.

Polygons represent things large enough to have boundaries, such as countries, lakes, and tracts of land. Lines represent things too narrow to be polygons, such as rivers, roads, and pipelines. Points are used for things too small to be polygons, such as cities, schools, and fire hydrants. (The same object may be represented by a polygon in one layer and a line or a point in a different layer, depending on how large it is presented.)

Polygons, lines, and points collectively are called vector data.

Surfaces have numeric values rather than shapes

Unlike countries or rivers, things such as elevation, slope, temperature, rainfall, and wind speed have no distinct shape. What they have instead are measurable values for any particular location on the earth's surface. (Wherever you go, for instance, you are either at sea level or a number of meters above or below it.) Geographic phenomena like these are easier to represent as surfaces than as features.

The most common kind of surface is a raster, a matrix of identically sized square cells. Each cell represents a unit of surface area—for example, 10 square meters—and contains a measured or estimated value for that location.

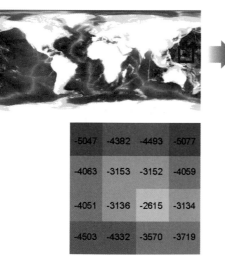

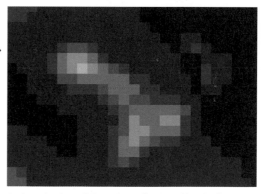

A close look at this raster of ocean depth shows that it is composed of square cells. Each cell holds a numeric value.

The world is not divided neatly into features and surfaces. Many things can be looked at either way. For example, polygons are often used to mark the boundaries of different vegetation types in a region, but this implies that the change from one type to another is more abrupt than it probably is. Vegetation can also be represented as a raster surface, where each cell value stands for the presence of a type of vegetation.

Features have locations

If you were asked to find Helsinki, Finland, on a map of the world, it probably wouldn't take you very long. But suppose Helsinki wasn't shown on the map. Could you make a pencil mark where it ought to go?

Now suppose you could lay a fine grid over the world map and you knew that Helsinki was a certain number of marks up from and to the right of a given starting point. It would be easy to put your pencil on the right spot. A grid of this kind is called a coordinate system, and it's what a GIS uses to put features in their proper places on a map.

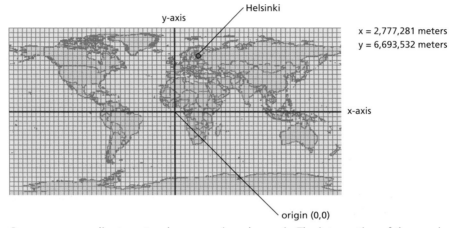

On a map, a coordinate system has an x-axis and a y-axis. The intersection of the axes is called the origin. Feature locations are specified by their distance from the origin in meters, feet, or a similar unit of measure.

The location of a point feature on a map is defined by a pair of x,y coordinates. A straight line needs two pairs of coordinates—one at the beginning and one at the end. If the line bends, like a river, there must be a pair of coordinates at every location where the line changes direction. The same holds true for a polygon, which is simply a line that returns to its starting point.

Features can be displayed at different sizes

On a GIS map, you can zoom in to see features at closer range. As you do so, the scale of the map changes.

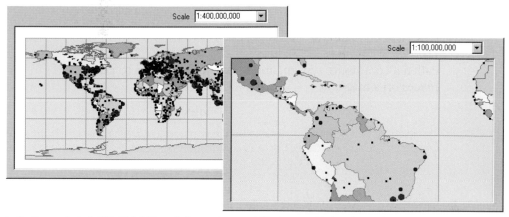

Left: the scale is 1:400,000,000 and the entire world is shown. Right: the scale is 1:100,000,000 and you see part of South America and Central America.

Scale, commonly expressed as a ratio, is the relationship between the size of features on a map and the size of the corresponding places in the world. If the scale of a map is 1:100,000,000, it means that features on the map are one hundred million times smaller than their true size.

Zooming in gives you a closer view of features within a smaller area. The amount of detail in the features does not change, however. A river has the same bends, and a coastline the same crenulations, whether you are zoomed in and can discern them or are zoomed out and cannot.

How much detail features have depends on the layer you use. Just as a paper map of the world generalizes the shape of Brazil more than a map of South America does, so different GIS layers can contain more feature detail or less.

Features are linked to information

There is more to a feature than its shape and location. There is everything else that might happen to be known about it. For a country, this might include its population, capital, system of government, leading imports and exports, average rainfall, mineral resources, and many other things. For a road, it might be its speed limit, the number of lanes it has, whether it is paved or unpaved, and whether it is one-way or two-way. There is a great deal of information to be had about any feature, from a humble length of sewer pipe to an ocean.

Information about the features in a layer is stored in a table. The table has a record (row) for each feature in the layer and a field (column) for each category of information. These categories are called *attributes*.

Shape	OID	NAME	ENERGY PERCAP	NET MIGRATION	URBAN PCT	GREENHOUSE
Polygon	186	Romania	84.12	-0.60	58.21	27.52
Polygon	189	Russia	179.76	1.02	77.68	405.04
Polygon	190	Rwanda	1.64	-2.46	6.16	0.20
Polygon	245	Samoa	11.93	-11.59	21.67	0.04
Polygon	200	San Marino	-99.00	11.62	96.30	-99.00
Polygon	221	Sao Tome and Principe	8.14	-3.62	46.26	0.02
Polygon	191	Saudi Arabia	206.86	1.36	85.74	63.82
Polygon	196	Senegal	5.92	0.00	47.00	1.02
Polygon	204	Serbia and Montenegro	67.32	6.26	59.86	15.25
Polygon	194	Seychelles	93.24	-6.30	58.44	0.14
Polygon	199	Sierra Leone	2.56	10.61	36.65	0.24
Polygon	201	Singapore	334.36	26.80	100.00	25.93
Polygon	132	Slovakia	135.18	0.53	61.11	11.60
Polygon	198	Slovenia	154.45	1.75	52.62	4.48
Polygon	28	Solomon Islands	5.69	0.00	19.59	0.04
Polygon	202	Somalia	1.21	0.00	27.49	0.16

Record: 0   Show: All Selected   Records (0 out of 252 Selected.)   Options

The attribute table for a layer of countries includes each feature's shape, ID number, and name, among other things.

Features on a GIS map are linked to the information in their attribute table. If you highlight China on a map, you can bring up all the information stored about it in the attribute table for countries. If you highlight a record in the table, you see the corresponding feature on the map.

Shape	OID	NAME	ENERGY PERCAP	NET MIGRATION	URBAN PCT	GREENHOUS
Polygon	50	Central African Republic	1.48	-1.42	41.19	0.08
Polygon	37	Chad	0.34	0.00	23.79	0.05
Polygon	42	Chile	59.69	0.00	84.60	14.29
Polygon	41	China	29.46	-0.40	34.34	740.38
Polygon	124	Christmas Island	-99.00	-99.00	-99.00	-99.00
Polygon	44	Cocos (Keeling) Islands	-99.00	-99.00	-99.00	-99.00
Polygon	47	Colombia	31.30	-0.33	74.94	17.58
Polygon	46	Comoros	2.23	0.00	33.14	0.02
Polygon	40	Congo, Democratic Republic of	2.60	0.82	30.28	0.49
Polygon	39	Congo, Republic of	7.39	0.00	62.56	1.87

Record: 48   Show: All Selected   Records (1 out of 252 Selected.)   Options

The link between features and their attributes makes it possible to ask questions about the information in an attribute table and display the answer on the map.

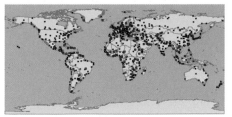

Which cities are national capitals?

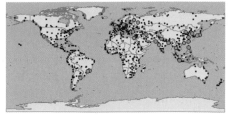

Which cities have populations over five million?

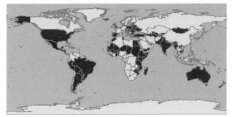

Which countries are net importers of goods?

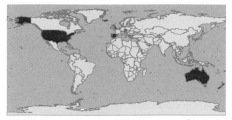

Which countries are net importers of goods and have per capita GDP of $10,000 or more?

Similarly, you can use attributes to create *thematic maps*, maps in which colors or other symbols are applied to features to indicate their attributes.

Energy consumption per capita

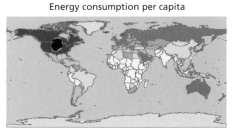

The darker the shade of brown, the more energy is used per person in each country.

Migration

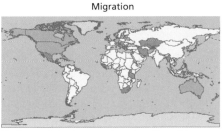

Red countries have net emigration, blue countries have net immigration. Yellow countries have little or no change.

Urban population by percentage

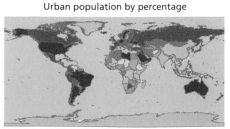

Darker shades of purple show countries where a higher percentage of the population lives in cities.

Greenhouse gas emissions

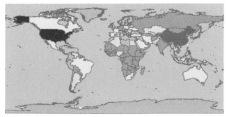

Greenhouse gas emissions are lowest in green countries, higher in yellow and orange countries, and highest in red countries.

Features have spatial relationships

Besides asking questions about the information in attribute tables, you can also ask questions about the spatial relationships among features—for example, which ones are nearest others, which ones cross others, and which ones contain others. The GIS uses the coordinates of features to compare their locations.

Which cities are within 50 kilometers of a river?

Which countries have a river that crosses their border?

Which countries share a border with China?

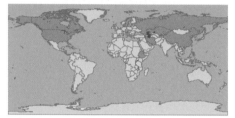

Which countries contain a lake completely within their borders?

New features can be created from areas of overlap

Questions about attributes and spatial relationships identify existing features that do or do not have certain qualities. To solve some geographic problems, however, a GIS must create new features. Suppose you want to find suitable places for growing amaranth, a nutritious grain originally grown by the Aztecs in Central America. You know that in Mexico amaranth is grown in areas of moderate elevation (1,000 to 1,500 meters) that have an average yearly rainfall of 500 to 800 millimeters and loam or sandy-loam soil. You also know that the plant requires a fairly long growing season, at least 120 days without frost.

You have layers of elevation, rainfall, growing season, and soil type for North and South America.

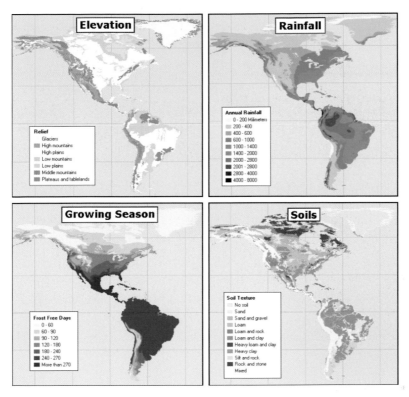

To find places that meet the specified conditions, the GIS looks for areas of overlap among features in the different layers. Wherever there is overlap between four features with the right attributes—the right elevation, the right amount of rainfall, the right growing season, and the right kind of soil—a new feature is created. The new feature's boundary is the area of overlap, which is different from the boundaries of each of the four features it was created from.

The result of the analysis is a new layer that shows where amaranth can be grown.

New layer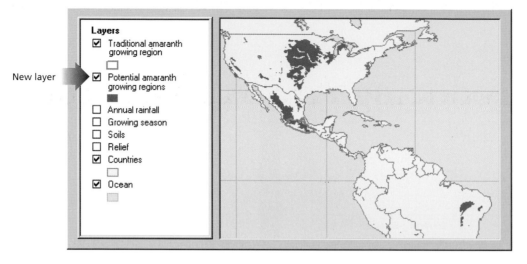

You now have some idea of what a GIS is and what it can do. In the next chapter, you'll learn a little about ArcGIS Desktop, the newest GIS software from ESRI.

Introducing ArcGIS Desktop

ESRI® ArcGIS Desktop consists of ArcView, ArcEditor, and ArcInfo. These three software products look and work the same—they differ only in how much they can do. ArcEditor does more than ArcView, and ArcInfo does more than ArcEditor. This book teaches ArcView, but everything you learn applies to all three products. All ArcGIS Desktop products can share the same maps and data.

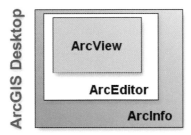

With ArcView, you can make maps, query data, analyze spatial relationships, and edit feature shapes and attributes. With ArcEditor, you can also create and edit certain spatial data formats that can be displayed in ArcView but not edited.

ArcInfo has more tools than ArcView or ArcEditor for analyzing certain kinds of spatial data. ArcInfo also comes with ArcInfo Workstation, a separate system that has been a GIS standard for many years and is still widely used.

This book includes a copy of ArcView 8 that is good for 180 days. To do the exercises, you can use this copy or any licensed copy of ArcView 8.x, ArcEditor 8.x, or ArcInfo 8.x.

Each version of ArcGIS Desktop includes the same three applications—ArcMap™, ArcCatalog™, and ArcToolbox™.

The ArcMap, ArcCatalog, and ArcToolbox applications

In ArcMap, you make maps from layers of spatial data, choose colors and symbols, query attributes, analyze spatial relationships, and design map layouts. The ArcMap interface contains a list (or table of contents) of the layers in the map, a display area for viewing the map, and menus and tools for working with the map.

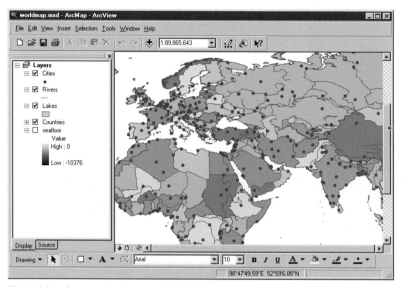

The table of contents shows you the four layers that make up this map.

In ArcCatalog, you browse spatial data contained on your computer's hard disk, on a network, or on the Internet. You can search for spatial data, preview it, and add it to ArcMap. ArcCatalog also has tools for creating and viewing metadata (information about spatial data, such as who created it and when, its intended use, its accuracy, and so forth).

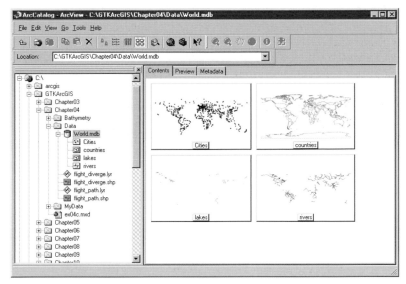

On the left, geographic data is organized in a tree structure. On the right, you can see thumbnail graphics of data or click the Preview and Metadata tabs to find out more about the data.

In ArcToolbox, you can use tools to convert spatial data from one format to another and to change the map projection of data. With the ArcInfo version of ArcGIS Desktop, many analysis tools are also included.

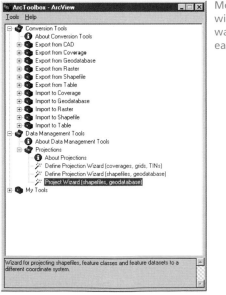

Most tools have a wizard interface that walks you through each step of a task.

Extending ArcGIS Desktop

You can extend the capabilities of ArcView, ArcEditor, or ArcInfo with a number of products. Three of these (ArcGIS Spatial Analyst, ArcGIS 3D Analyst™, and ArcGIS Geostatistical Analyst) are on the software CD that comes with this book. The book does not teach you how to use them, but you may want to explore them on your own. Like ArcView, the extensions are good for 180 days.

With ArcGIS Spatial Analyst, you can create raster (cell-based) surfaces, query them, and do overlay analysis on them. You can also derive new surfaces from other raster or vector layers. For example, you can derive a slope surface from an elevation surface or a population density surface from population points.

With ArcGIS 3D Analyst, you can visualize and analyze vector and raster data in three dimensions. You can "fly through" terrain and examine it from any angle. You can determine which areas on a surface are visible from given points and whether a line of sight exists from one point to another.

With ArcGIS Geostatistical Analyst, you can create continuous surfaces from a small number of sample points by predicting the values at unsampled locations.

ArcGIS StreetMap™ contains street data for the entire United States. You can use it to create street maps and to find nearly any U.S. street address.

ArcPress™ for ArcGIS improves map printing speed and renders high-quality maps without requiring additional memory or hardware.

The MrSID™ Encoder for ArcGIS compresses large images (such as satellite images and aerial photographs) and displays them without losing accuracy.

The ArcGIS System

ArcGIS Desktop is part of a larger system, the ArcGIS System, which includes ArcSDE™ (Spatial Database Engine™) and ArcIMS® (Internet Map Server).

ArcSDE lets you work with geographic data stored in a relational database management system such as Oracle®, Microsoft® SQL Server™, IBM® DB2®, or Informix®. ArcSDE manages the exchange of information between ArcGIS and the relational database, enabling many users to share and edit centrally stored geographic data at the same time.

ArcIMS delivers GIS over the Internet. You can build Web sites that provide maps, data, and GIS applications (such as those that give driving directions or find the nearest automated teller machine). ArcIMS Web sites bring GIS to people who don't have GIS software and may include tools for zooming, querying, symbolizing, and analyzing maps. ArcIMS can also send maps and data over the Internet directly to ArcGIS Desktop products.

In the next chapter, you'll start working with ArcGIS Desktop by exploring the ArcMap application.

Exploring ArcMap

Displaying map data
Navigating a map
Looking at feature attributes

ArcMap is an application for displaying maps and investigating them, for analyzing maps to answer geographic questions and producing maps that make analysis persuasive. The ArcMap application window consists of a map display for viewing spatial data, a table of contents for listing the layers shown in the display, and a variety of toolbars for working with the data.

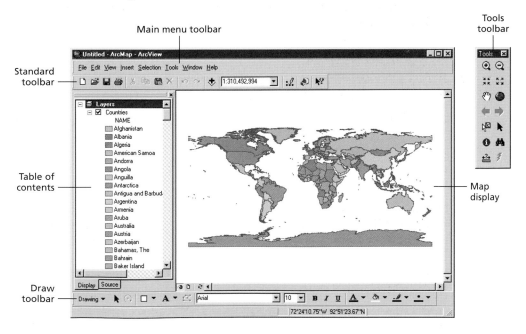

You can change the way ArcMap looks to suit your preferences and the kind of work you do. Toolbars can be hidden or shown. New commands can be added to them. They can be docked at different places in the application window or can float independently of it.

To dock a floating toolbar, drag it to the interface. To undock it, click the vertical gray bar at its left edge and drag it away from the interface. To hide or show a toolbar, click the View menu, point to Toolbars, and check or uncheck the toolbar name.

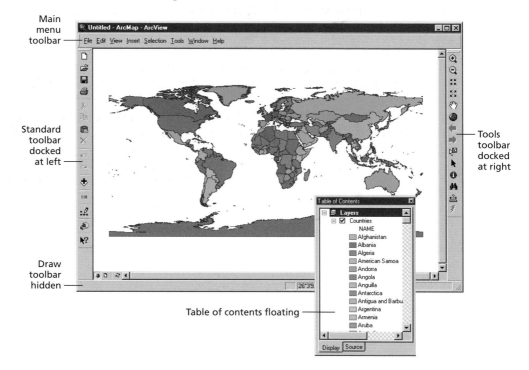

This book assumes that you are working with the default interface. The exercise graphics reflect this, with one exception—toolbars are always shown horizontally.

Changes you make to the interface are applied to subsequent ArcMap sessions, so if you dock a toolbar in one session, it will be docked the next time you start ArcMap, and if you resize the application window, it will keep the new size in the next session. Changes like this will not significantly affect the exercises, but may give you slightly different results for such operations as labeling that are influenced by the size of the map display.

For more information about customizing the interface, click the Contents tab in ArcGIS Desktop Help and navigate to *Customizing ArcMap and ArcCatalog*.

Displaying map data

In this exercise, you'll learn how to display data in ArcMap. You'll learn how to navigate maps and get information about map features.

You will be able to do the exercises only if you have installed the 180-day trial version of ArcView 8 that comes with this book, or if you have a licensed version of ArcView 8.x, ArcEditor 8.x, or ArcInfo 8.x software on your computer.

Exercise 3a

You work for an aviation history foundation that is researching the last flight of Amelia Earhart. In 1937, Earhart was near the end of a flight around the world when her plane disappeared over the Pacific Ocean. The United States government spent over four million dollars searching for Earhart and her navigator, Fred Noonan. The foundation believes Earhart may have crashed on Nikumaroro, one of several tiny islands that make up the country of Kiribati, and would like to mount an expedition to look for the wreckage. You have been asked to manage a GIS project that will help organize data and acquaint potential sponsors with the foundation's plans.

1 Start ArcMap by double-clicking the ArcMap icon on your computer desktop. (Alternatively, click the Start button on the Windows® taskbar, point to Programs, point to ArcGIS, and click ArcMap.)

When ArcMap opens, you see the ArcMap dialog on top of the application window. The Tools toolbar floats to the side.

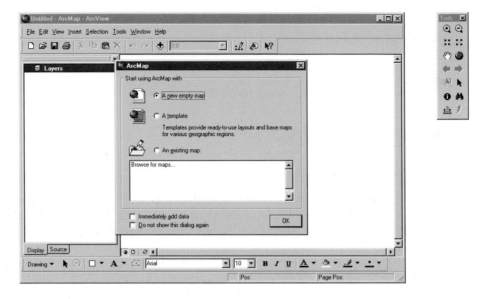

2 In the ArcMap dialog, click the option to start using ArcMap with an existing map. In the scrolling box at the bottom of the dialog, the phrase "Browse for maps..." is highlighted. Click OK.

3 In the Open dialog, navigate to **C:\GTKArcGIS\Chapter03** (or to the folder where you installed the GTKArcGIS data). Click **ex03a.mxd**, as shown in the following graphic, and click Open.

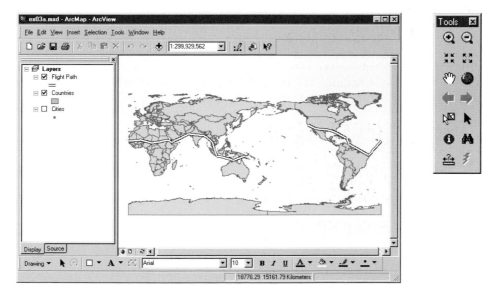

The map document opens. The map looks different from many world maps because it is centered on the South Pacific area where Amelia Earhart vanished, rather than on the prime meridian (which runs through Greenwich, England).

The map shows the countries of the world, the oceans, and Earhart's flight path before she disappeared. Each of these categories of geographic information (countries, ocean, flight path) is called a *layer*.

The table of contents lists the names of the layers in the map. It shows the color or symbol used to draw each layer and tells you, by a check mark, whether or not the layer is visible. The Flight Path and Countries layers are currently visible. The Cities layer is not.

4 In the table of contents, click on the check box next to the Countries layer to turn it off.

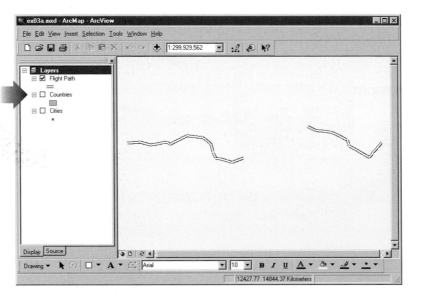

The countries disappear on the map.

5 In the table of contents, click on the Countries check box to turn it back on. Click the check box next to the Cities layer to turn it on as well.

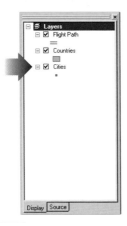

The Cities layer is checked but you still can't see the cities. This is because data is displayed on the map in the order of the layers in the table of contents. The Cities layer is at the bottom, covered by the countries.

6 In the table of contents, click on the Cities layer name to highlight it. Click and drag the layer to the top of the table of contents, then release the mouse button. As you drag the layer, a horizontal black bar indicates its position.

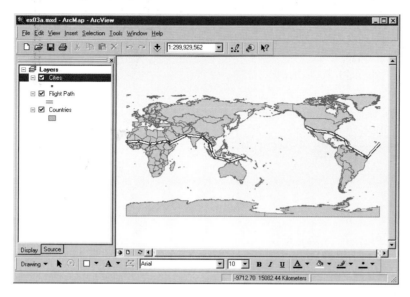

Now you can see the cities on the map. Each of them is a stop on Earhart's route. You'll change the layer name to make this clear.

7 In the table of contents, right-click on the Cities layer name. A context menu opens. Many ArcMap operations are started from context menus.

8 On the context menu, click Properties to open the Layer Properties dialog. Click the General tab.

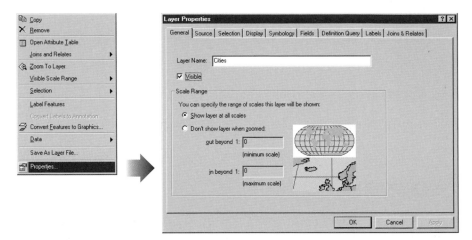

The Layer Properties dialog has several tabs for setting layer properties, most of which you'll use in the course of this book.

9 In the Layer Name text box, highlight the name "Cities" and type **Cities Earhart Visited** in its place. Make sure that the dialog matches the following graphic, then click OK.

The layer is renamed in the table of contents.

You will now track the progress of Earhart's round-the-world flight, which began on the west coast of the United States. She chose an equatorial route so as to circle the globe at its full circumference and flew east to minimize the effects of storms and headwinds.

10 On the Tools toolbar, click the Zoom In tool. (Move the mouse pointer over it to see its name.) Your toolbar may be oriented vertically. You can change its orientation if you like by dragging one of its corners.

11 Move the mouse pointer over the map. The cursor changes to a magnifying glass. Drag a box around the United States, approximately as shown in the following graphic. (If you make a mistake, click either the Full Extent or Go Back To Previous Extent buttons and try again.)

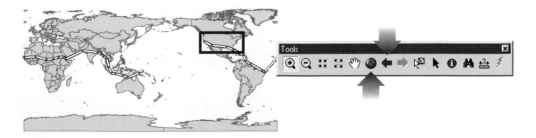

The display zooms in on the United States.

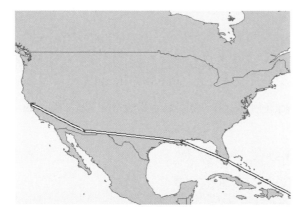

Zooming in or out changes the display scale, which is shown on the Standard tool-bar. When the map showed the whole world, the scale was about 1:300,000,000. This means that map features are displayed at one three hundred millionths of their actual size. The scale should now be about 1:50,000,000. (Scale is also affected by the size of the ArcMap application window.)

Although the cities are not labeled, you can find out their names and get other information about them with ArcMap tools.

12 On the Tools toolbar, click the Select Elements tool.

13 Move the cursor over the westernmost city on the display. The city name displays as a map tip.

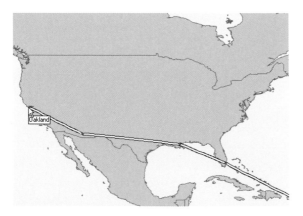

Map tips are a layer property. They can be turned on or off on the Display tab of the Layer Properties dialog. You can see map tips no matter which tool is selected.

14 Move the cursor over the other three cities on the display. They are Tucson, New Orleans, and Miami. You may also be able to see San Juan, Puerto Rico.

To make the names visible at all times, you can label the cities.

15 In the table of contents, right-click on the Cities Earhart Visited layer and click Label Features.

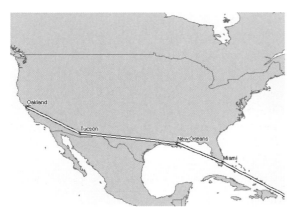

The name of each city appears next to the map feature. From Miami, Earhart flew southeast to Puerto Rico and then to South America.

16 On the Tools toolbar, click the Pan tool.

17 Move the mouse pointer over the map. The cursor changes to a hand. Click and drag the display up and to the left until Miami is in the upper left corner of the window. Release the mouse button.

You can get information about any of the cities Earhart visited with the Identify tool.

18 On the Tools toolbar, click the Identify tool.

19 On the map, click on the city of Natal. You must click exactly on the city or you will identify something else, either a segment of the flight path or the country of Brazil. If this happens, close the Identify Results dialog and try again.

The Identify Results dialog opens.

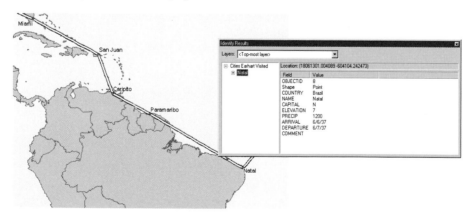

The Identify Results dialog shows you the country and city name, and various facts about Natal, such as its elevation (meters), its average annual precipitation (millimeters), and the dates Earhart and Noonan arrived and departed.

20 Close the Identify Results dialog. On the Tools toolbar, click the Full Extent button.

The map zooms to its original extent.

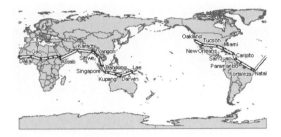

In the next exercise, you will follow the rest of Earhart's journey to the point where she and Noonan disappeared.

21 If you want to save your work, click the File menu and click Save As. Navigate to **C:\GTKArcGIS\Chapter03\MyData**. Rename the file **my_ex03a.mxd** and click Save.

22 If you are continuing with the next exercise, leave ArcMap open. Otherwise, click the File menu and click Exit. Click No if prompted to save your changes.

Navigating a map

In this exercise, you'll continue to work with ArcMap's navigational tools. You will also learn how to create spatial bookmarks, which save a specific view of a map.

Exercise 3b

Earhart and Noonan crossed the Atlantic at night. When they saw the west coast of Africa, they realized they were north of their intended destination—the city of Dakar in Senegal. They landed at the first airstrip they saw, in the Senegalese city of St. Louis, and from there made the short flight to Dakar. They proceeded to fly across Africa and Asia, making their last stop in Lae, Papua New Guinea. They intended to go on to tiny Howland Island in the South Pacific, then to Hawaii and back to California.

1 Start ArcMap. In the ArcMap dialog, click the option to use an existing map. In the list of maps, double-click Browse for maps. (If ArcMap is already running, click the File menu and click Open.) Navigate to **C:\GTKArcGIS\Chapter03**. Click **ex03b.mxd** and click Open.

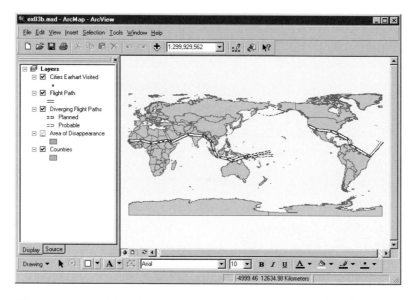

The map resembles the one in the previous exercise but has two additional layers. The Diverging Flight Paths layer contains two line features. One represents the course Earhart and Noonan planned to take. The other represents the course the foundation believes they actually followed.

The Area of Disappearance layer is shown in the table of contents with a grayed-out check mark. This means that its visibility depends on the map's display scale. This layer includes hundreds of Pacific islands too small to be represented on a general world map. When you zoom in to look at the end of Earhart's flight, this layer will become visible.

2 On the Tools toolbar, click the Zoom In tool.

3 On the map, drag a rectangle that includes the northern half of Africa and reaches to India, as shown in the following graphic.

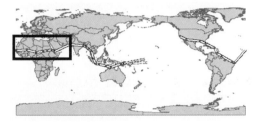

The display zooms in on the African stretch of the route. If your display doesn't show the west coast of Africa, use the Pan tool to adjust it.

At this scale, the city labels appear. The display of labels, like that of map features, can be made scale-dependent in the Layer Properties dialog. In this map, labels appear only when the scale is larger than 1:100,000,000. (The larger the scale, the nearer features are to their actual size.)

4 On the Tools toolbar, click the Pan tool.

5 Drag the display to the left to follow the flight path.

From Assab (in what is now Eritrea) on the east coast of Africa, Earhart flew to Karachi (now in Pakistan). She then headed south, flying over southeast Asia to Indonesia.

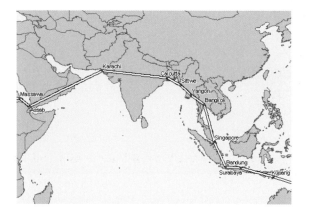

6 Continue panning along the route.

From Darwin, Australia, Earhart flew to her last known stop in Lae, Papua New Guinea. At this point, the path the foundation believes she followed diverges from the planned flight path.

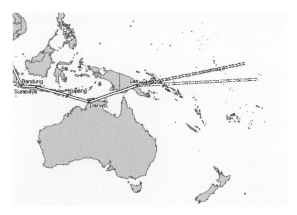

In the table of contents, the check mark by the Area of Disappearance layer is no longer grayed-out. (The layer displays at scales larger than 1:100,000,000.) The features in this layer are small islands. Until you zoom in very close, you see mostly outlines.

7 In the table of contents, right-click on the Area of Disappearance layer and click Zoom To Layer.

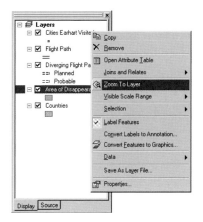

You can see a number of tiny islands in the display, but it looks as if both flight paths stop in the middle of the ocean.

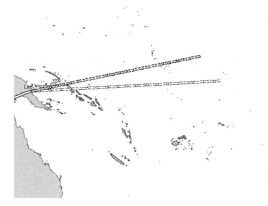

8 Click the Window menu and click Magnifier. A magnification window opens on top of the display.

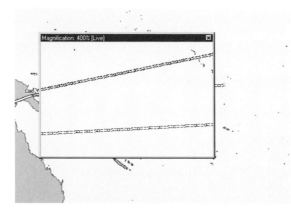

When you move the magnification window over the map, the area seen through the window is magnified four times.

9 Drag the magnification window to the right. As you drag it, it displays a crosshair to show you the point on which it's centered. Place the crosshair on the end of the probable flight path and release the mouse.

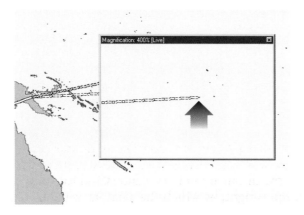

If your eyes are good, you can discern the tiny island of Nikumaroro at the end of the probable flight path. If not, you will soon get a better look.

10 Close the magnification window. On the Tools toolbar, click the Zoom In tool.

11 On the map, drag a rectangle that includes the ends of both the planned and probable flight paths.

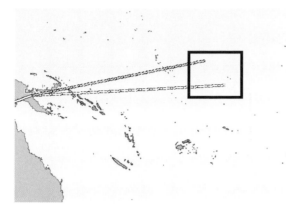

The display zooms in.

Even at this scale, it's hard to see land. Earhart and Noonan disappeared somewhere in this watery expanse. You will set a bookmark to save this map extent. You'll return to it later to measure the distance from Howland Island to Nikumaroro— the distance, if the foundation is right, by which the aviators were off course.

12 Click the View menu, point to Bookmarks, and click Create.

The Spatial Bookmark dialog opens.

13 Replace the existing text with **End of Flight**, as shown in the following graphic, then click OK.

Now you'll zoom in for a close look at the islands at the ends of the two flight paths. You'll use bookmarks that have already been created.

14 Click the View menu, point to Bookmarks, and click Howland Island.

The display zooms in on Howland Island at the end of the planned flight path. Earhart intended to refuel here before going on to Hawaii.

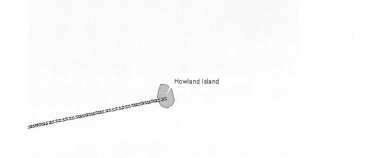

15 Click the View menu, point to Bookmarks, and click Nikumaroro Island. The display zooms in on Nikumaroro Island.

Clothing and empty food tins found on the west bank of the island suggest that Earhart and Noonan may have crashed nearby. In addition, Earhart said, in her last message to the U.S. Coast Guard cutter *Ithaca*, "We are in line of position 158 degrees - 337 degrees . . ." The line she mentioned is a sun line, used in celestial navigation, that runs directly through both Howland Island and Nikumaroro.

If, indeed, Earhart crashed on or near Nikumaroro, she and Noonan were far off course.

16 Click the View menu, point to Bookmarks, and click End of Flight. The display zooms to the extent you bookmarked.

17 On the Tools toolbar, click the Measure tool.

18 Move the mouse pointer over the display. The cursor is a ruler with a small crosshair. Place the crosshair at the end of the planned flight path and click to begin a line. Move the cursor to the end of the probable flight path and double click to end the line.

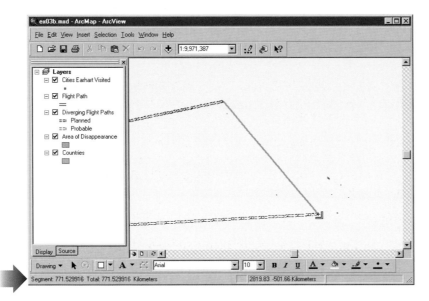

The length of the line is displayed in the ArcMap status bar at the bottom of the application. If the probable path is the actual one, Earhart and Noonan were off course by about 770 kilometers. Poor maps, cloud cover, the scarcity of landmarks, and the sheer length of the planned flight from Lae all may have contributed.

19 If you want to save your work, click the File menu and click Save As. Navigate C:\GTKArcGIS\Chapter03\MyData. Rename the file **my_ex03b.mxd** and click Sa

20 If you are continuing with the next exercise, leave ArcMap open. Otherwise, click the File menu and click Exit. Click No if prompted to save your changes.

Looking at feature attributes

In a GIS, a feature on a map may be associated with a great deal of information—more than can be displayed at any given time. This information is stored in an attribute table. A layer's attribute table contains a row (or record) for every feature in the layer and a column (or field) for every attribute or category of information.

When you clicked on the city of Natal to identify it at the end of exercise 3a, the information you saw in the Identify Results dialog was the information stored in the layer attribute table.

In this exercise, you will look at the attribute tables for two map layers. You will learn how to change a table's appearance and how to get statistical information from it.

Exercise 3c

The long transatlantic flight from Brazil to Senegal put Earhart north of her intended destination. The flight from Lae to Howland Island would have been even longer. You will look at the lengths of the various stages of the flight.

1 Start ArcMap. In the ArcMap dialog, click the option to use an existing map. In the list of maps, double-click Browse for maps. (If ArcMap is already running, click the File menu and click Open.) Navigate to **C:\GTKArcGIS\Chapter03**. Click **ex03c.mxd** and click Open.

You see the familiar map of the world and of Earhart's flight.

Now you will open the attribute table for the Cities Earhart Visited layer.

2 In the table of contents, right-click on the Cities Earhart Visited layer and click Open Attribute Table.

OBJECTID	Shape*	COUNTRY	NAME	CAPITAL	ELEVATION	PRECIP	ARRIVAL	DE
1	Point	USA	Tucson	N	1045	300	5/21/37	5/2
2	Point	USA	New Orleans	N	0	1700	5/22/37	5/2
3	Point	USA	Miami	N	24	1700	5/23/37	6/1
4	Point	Puerto Rico	San Juan	Y	36	1700	6/1/37	6/2
5	Point	Venezuela	Caripito	N	126	1700	6/2/37	6/3
6	Point	Suriname	Paramaribo	Y	11	2400	6/3/37	6/4
7	Point	Brazil	Fortaleza	N	15	1200	6/4/37	6/6
8	Point	Brazil	Natal	N	7	1200	6/6/37	6/7
9	Point	Senegal	Saint Louis	N	21	500	6/8/37	6/8
10	Point	Senegal	Dakar	Y	25	800	6/8/37	6/9
11	Point	Mali	Gao	N	240	300	6/9/37	6/1
12	Point	Chad	N'djamena	Y	352	800	6/10/37	6/1
13	Point	Sudan	Al Fashir	N	812	300	6/11/37	6/1
14	Point	Sudan	Khartoum	Y	525	150	6/13/37	6/1
15	Point	Eritrea	Massawa	N	47	300	6/13/37	6/1

Record: 1 | Show: All Selected | Records (0 out of 28 Selected.) | Options ▾

3 Scroll down through the table. There are twenty-eight records, one for each city. Scroll across the table to look at the attributes.

There are ten attributes, or fields. The OBJECTID field contains a unique identification number for every record. The Shape field describes the feature geometry. Among the other attributes are the name of each city, the dates Earhart arrived and departed, and comments on any unusual activity.

The intersection of a record and a field is a cell. A cell contains an attribute value. For example, the attribute value of the NAME field for the first record is "Tucson."

You'll narrow the display width of the field so you can see more attributes without having to scroll.

4 Scroll back all the way to the left. Place the mouse pointer on the vertical black bar between the NAME and CAPITAL fields. The cursor changes to a two-headed arrow.

OBJECTID	Shape*	COUNTRY	NAME	CAPITAL	ELEVATION	PRECIP	ARRIVAL	DE
15	Point	Eritrea	Massawa	N	47	300	6/13/37	6/1
16	Point	Eritrea	Assab	N	58	150	6/14/37	6/1
17	Point	Pakistan	Karachi	N	49	150	6/15/37	6/1
18	Point	India	Calcutta	N	6	1700	6/17/37	6/1
19	Point	Myanmar	Sittwe	N	33	4800	6/18/37	6/1
20	Point	Myanmar	Yangon	N	14	2400	6/19/37	6/2
21	Point	Thailand	Bangkok	Y	3	1200	6/20/37	6/2
22	Point	Singapore	Singapore		1	2400	6/20/37	6/2
23	Point	Indonesia	Bandung	N	970	2400	6/21/37	6/2
24	Point	Indonesia	Surabaya	N	34	1700	6/24/37	6/2
25	Point	Indonesia	Kupang	N	126	1200	6/27/37	6/2
26	Point	Australia	Darwin	N	23	1200	6/28/37	6/2
27	Point	Papua New Guinea	Lae	N	56	4800	6/29/37	7/2
28	Point	USA	Oakland	N	45	500	<Null>	5/2

Record: 1 | Show: All Selected | Records (0 out of 28 Selected.) | Options ▾

5 Drag the cursor to the left. As you drag, the original field width is marked by a vertical red line and the new width by a vertical black line. Release the mouse button somewhere before you start cutting off city names.

	OBJECTID	Shape*	COUNTRY	NAME	CAPITAL	ELEVATION	PRECIP	ARRIVAL	DEPARTUR	
▶	1	Point	USA	Tucson	N	1045	300	5/21/37	5/22/37	
	2	Point	USA	New Orleans	N	0	1700	5/22/37	5/23/37	
	3	Point	USA	Miami	N	24	1700	5/23/37	6/1/37	Mecha
	4	Point	Puerto Rico	San Juan	Y	36	1700	6/1/37	6/2/37	
	5	Point	Venezuela	Caripito	N	126	1700	6/2/37	6/3/37	
	6	Point	Suriname	Paramaribo	Y	11	2400	6/3/37	6/4/37	
	7	Point	Brazil	Fortaleza	N	15	1200	6/4/37	6/6/37	Mecha
	8	Point	Brazil	Natal	N	7	1200	6/6/37	6/7/37	
	9	Point	Senegal	Saint Louis	N	21	500	6/8/37	6/8/37	Uninter
	10	Point	Senegal	Dakar	Y	25	800	6/8/37	6/9/37	
	11	Point	Mali	Gao	N	240	300	6/9/37	6/10/37	
	12	Point	Chad	N'djamena	Y	352	800	6/10/37	6/11/37	
	13	Point	Sudan	Al Fashir	N	812	300	6/11/37	6/13/37	
	14	Point	Sudan	Khartoum	Y	525	150	6/13/37	6/13/37	Two-ho
	15	Point	Eritrea	Massawa	N	47	300	6/13/37	6/14/37	

Attributes of Cities Earhart Visited
Record: 1   Show: All Selected   Records (0 out of 28 Selected.)   Options ▾

If the display does not refresh properly, you can minimize or close the table and reopen it.

The last letter of the DEPARTURE field name is cut off. You'll widen this field.

6 Scroll to the right side of the table. Place the mouse pointer on the vertical black bar between the DEPARTURE and COMMENT fields. Drag the cursor slightly to the right to see the entire field name.

	NAME	CAPITAL	ELEVATION	PRECIP	ARRIVAL	DEPARTURE	COMMENT	
▶	Tucson	N	1045	300	5/21/37	5/22/37		
	New Orleans	N	0	1700	5/22/37	5/23/37		
	Miami	N	24	1700	5/23/37	6/1/37	Mechanical/Prep work	
	San Juan	Y	36	1700	6/1/37	6/2/37		
	Caripito	N	126	1700	6/2/37	6/3/37		
	Paramaribo	Y	11	2400	6/3/37	6/4/37		
	Fortaleza	N	15	1200	6/4/37	6/6/37	Mechanical work/tuneup	
	Natal	N	7	1200	6/6/37	6/7/37		
	Saint Louis	N	21	500	6/8/37	6/8/37	Unintended destination - navigational error	
	Dakar	Y	25	800	6/8/37	6/9/37		
	Gao	N	240	300	6/9/37	6/10/37		
	N'djamena	Y	352	800	6/10/37	6/11/37		
	Al Fashir	N	812	300	6/11/37	6/13/37		
	Khartoum	Y	525	150	6/13/37	6/13/37	Two-hour stop in Khartoum	
	Massawa	N	47	300	6/13/37	6/14/37		

Attributes of Cities Earhart Visited
Record: 1   Show: All Selected   Records (0 out of 28 Selected.)   Options ▾

The elevation and precipitation fields could contribute to a study of the weather Earhart faced. The CAPITAL field is probably not useful for any analysis connected with the flight. You will hide this field.

7 Place the mouse pointer on the vertical black bar between the CAPITAL and ELEVATION fields. Click and drag the cursor to the right-hand border of the NAME field and release the mouse button. The CAPITAL field is hidden.

COUNTRY	NAME	ELEVATION	PRECIP	ARRIVAL	DEPARTURE	COMMENT
USA	Tucson	1045	300	5/21/37	5/22/37	
USA	New Orleans	0	1700	5/22/37	5/23/37	
USA	Miami	24	1700	5/23/37	6/1/37	Mechanical/Prep work
Puerto Rico	San Juan	36	1700	6/1/37	6/2/37	
Venezuela	Caripito	126	1700	6/2/37	6/3/37	
Suriname	Paramaribo	11	2400	6/3/37	6/4/37	
Brazil	Fortaleza	15	1200	6/4/37	6/6/37	Mechanical work/tuneup
Brazil	Natal	7	1200	6/6/37	6/7/37	
Senegal	Saint Louis	21	500	6/8/37	6/8/37	Unintended destination - navigational error
Senegal	Dakar	25	800	6/8/37	6/9/37	
Mali	Gao	240	300	6/9/37	6/10/37	
Chad	N'djamena	352	800	6/10/37	6/11/37	
Sudan	Al Fashir	812	300	6/11/37	6/13/37	
Sudan	Khartoum	525	150	6/13/37	6/13/37	Two-hour stop in Khartoum
Eritrea	Massawa	47	300	6/13/37	6/14/37	

Record: 1 — Show: All Selected Records (0 out of 28 Selected.) Options

If you wanted to restore the hidden field, you would double-click on the border between the NAME and ELEVATION field names.

You can rearrange the order of fields as well. It would be more natural to have the city name appear before the country name.

8 Scroll to the left. Click on the column heading of the NAME field. The field is highlighted.

OBJECTID	Shape*	COUNTRY	NAME	ELEVATION	PRECIP	ARRIVAL	DEPARTURE	C
1	Point	USA	Tucson	1045	300	5/21/37	5/22/37	
2	Point	USA	New Orleans	0	1700	5/22/37	5/23/37	
3	Point	USA	Miami	24	1700	5/23/37	6/1/37	Mechanical/Prep w
4	Point	Puerto Rico	San Juan	36	1700	6/1/37	6/2/37	
5	Point	Venezuela	Caripito	126	1700	6/2/37	6/3/37	
6	Point	Suriname	Paramaribo	11	2400	6/3/37	6/4/37	
7	Point	Brazil	Fortaleza	15	1200	6/4/37	6/6/37	Mechanical work/t
8	Point	Brazil	Natal	7	1200	6/6/37	6/7/37	
9	Point	Senegal	Saint Louis	21	500	6/8/37	6/8/37	Unintended destina
10	Point	Senegal	Dakar	25	800	6/8/37	6/9/37	
11	Point	Mali	Gao	240	300	6/9/37	6/10/37	
12	Point	Chad	N'djamena	352	800	6/10/37	6/11/37	
13	Point	Sudan	Al Fashir	812	300	6/11/37	6/13/37	
14	Point	Sudan	Khartoum	525	150	6/13/37	6/13/37	Two-hour stop in K
15	Point	Eritrea	Massawa	47	300	6/13/37	6/14/37	

Record: 0 — Show: All Selected Records (0 out of 28 Selected.) Options

Drag the column heading to the left. The cursor becomes a pointer with a small rectangle, showing that a field is being moved. When the vertical red line is between the Shape and COUNTRY fields, as shown in the following graphic, release the mouse button.

OBJECTID	Shape*	COUNTRY	NAME	ELEVATION	PRECIP	ARRIVAL	DEPARTURE	C
1	Point	USA	Tucson	1045	300	5/21/37	5/22/37	
2	Point	USA	New Orleans	0	1700	5/22/37	5/23/37	
3	Point	USA	Miami	24	1700	5/23/37	6/1/37	Mechanical/Prep v
4	Point	Puerto Rico	San Juan	36	1700	6/1/37	6/2/37	
5	Point	Venezuela	Caripito	126	1700	6/2/37	6/3/37	
6	Point	Suriname	Paramaribo	11	2400	6/3/37	6/4/37	
7	Point	Brazil	Fortaleza	15	1200	6/4/37	6/6/37	Mechanical work/t
8	Point	Brazil	Natal	7	1200	6/6/37	6/7/37	
9	Point	Senegal	Saint Louis	21	500	6/8/37	6/8/37	Unintended destina
10	Point	Senegal	Dakar	25	800	6/8/37	6/9/37	
11	Point	Mali	Gao	240	300	6/9/37	6/10/37	
12	Point	Chad	N'djamena	352	800	6/10/37	6/11/37	
13	Point	Sudan	Al Fashir	812	300	6/11/37	6/13/37	
14	Point	Sudan	Khartoum	525	150	6/13/37	6/13/37	Two-hour stop in K
15	Point	Eritrea	Massawa	47	300	6/13/37	6/14/37	

Record: 0   Show: All Selected   Records (0 out of 28 Selected.)   Options ▾

The field names are rearranged.

OBJECTID	Shape*	NAME	COUNTRY	ELEVATION	PRECIP	ARRIVAL	DEPARTURE	C
1	Point	Tucson	USA	1045	300	5/21/37	5/22/37	
2	Point	New Orleans	USA	0	1700	5/22/37	5/23/37	
3	Point	Miami	USA	24	1700	5/23/37	6/1/37	Mechanical/Prep v
4	Point	San Juan	Puerto Rico	36	1700	6/1/37	6/2/37	
5	Point	Caripito	Venezuela	126	1700	6/2/37	6/3/37	
6	Point	Paramaribo	Suriname	11	2400	6/3/37	6/4/37	
7	Point	Fortaleza	Brazil	15	1200	6/4/37	6/6/37	Mechanical work/t
8	Point	Natal	Brazil	7	1200	6/6/37	6/7/37	
9	Point	Saint Louis	Senegal	21	500	6/8/37	6/8/37	Unintended destina
10	Point	Dakar	Senegal	25	800	6/8/37	6/9/37	
11	Point	Gao	Mali	240	300	6/9/37	6/10/37	
12	Point	N'djamena	Chad	352	800	6/10/37	6/11/37	
13	Point	Al Fashir	Sudan	812	300	6/11/37	6/13/37	
14	Point	Khartoum	Sudan	525	150	6/13/37	6/13/37	Two-hour stop in K
15	Point	Massawa	Eritrea	47	300	6/13/37	6/14/37	

Record: 0   Show: All Selected   Records (0 out of 28 Selected.)   Options ▾

Records, as well as fields, can be highlighted. When a record is highlighted in a table, its corresponding feature is highlighted on the map. A highlighted record or feature is said to be selected.

10 Click the gray tab at the left edge of the first record in the table. The record is selected.

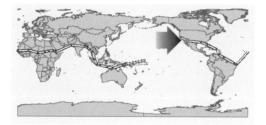

	OBJECTID	Shape*	NAME	COUNTRY	ELEVATION	PRECIP	ARRIVAL	DEPARTURE	C
	1	Point	Tucson	USA	1045	300	5/21/37	5/22/37	
	2	Point	New Orleans	USA	0	1700	5/22/37	5/23/37	
	3	Point	Miami	USA	24	1700	5/23/37	6/1/37	Mechanical/Prep w
	4	Point	San Juan	Puerto Rico	36	1700	6/1/37	6/2/37	
	5	Point	Caripito	Venezuela	126	1700	6/2/37	6/3/37	
	6	Point	Paramaribo	Suriname	11	2400	6/3/37	6/4/37	
	7	Point	Fortaleza	Brazil	15	1200	6/4/37	6/6/37	Mechanical work/t
	8	Point	Natal	Brazil	7	1200	6/6/37	6/7/37	
	9	Point	Saint Louis	Senegal	21	500	6/8/37	6/8/37	Unintended destina
	10	Point	Dakar	Senegal	25	800	6/8/37	6/9/37	
	11	Point	Gao	Mali	240	300	6/9/37	6/10/37	
	12	Point	N'djamena	Chad	352	800	6/10/37	6/11/37	
	13	Point	Al Fashir	Sudan	812	300	6/11/37	6/13/37	
	14	Point	Khartoum	Sudan	525	150	6/13/37	6/13/37	Two-hour stop in K
	15	Point	Massawa	Eritrea	47	300	6/13/37	6/14/37	

Record: |◄ ◄ [0] ► ►| Show: All Selected Records (1 out of 28 Selected.)   Options ▼

11 Move the attribute table away from the map display. Tucson is highlighted on the map.

12 At the bottom of the attribute table, click the Options menu and click Clear Selection.

🔍 Find & Replace...
🔲 Select By Attributes...
🗐 Select All
▤ Clear Selection
↔ Switch Selection
   Add Field...
   Related Tables ►
▣ Create Graph...
   Add Table to Layout
⟳ Reload Cache
   Export...
   Appearance...

The record is unselected in the table and the feature is unselected on the map.

13 Close the table. In the table of contents, right-click on the Flight Path layer and click Open Attribute Table.

	FID	Shape*	LENGTH	FROM_CITY	TO_CITY
▶	0	Polyline	1414.502	Oakland	Tucson
	1	Polyline	2323.93	Tucson	New Orleans
	2	Polyline	1186.745	New Orleans	Miami
	3	Polyline	1783.788	Miami	San Juan
	4	Polyline	974.294	San Juan	Caripito
	5	Polyline	1004.282	Caripito	Paramaribo
	6	Polyline	2132.179	Paramaribo	Fortaleza
	7	Polyline	423.762	Fortaleza	Natal
	8	Polyline	3184.838	Natal	St. Louis
	9	Polyline	180.017	St. Louis	Dakar
	10	Polyline	1947.841	Dakar	Gao
	11	Polyline	1738.11	Gao	N'djamena
	12	Polyline	1151.221	N'djamena	Al Fashir
	13	Polyline	800.72	Al Fashir	Khartoum
	14	Polyline	793.462	Khartoum	Massawa
	15	Polyline	469.813	Massawa	Assab

Record: ◄◄ ◄ 1 ► ►◄ Show: All Selected Records (0 out of 27 Selected.) Options ▼

The table contains a record for each stage of Earhart's flight. The attributes include the starting city (FROM_CITY), the destination city (TO_CITY), and the flight length (LENGTH) in kilometers.

The flight from Lae to Howland Island would have been 4,120 kilometers. The cumulative effect of small navigation errors over this distance might plausibly account for Earhart and Noonan's going well off course. You'll sort the LENGTH field to compare the distances of the flight segments they completed.

14 Right-click on the LENGTH field name and click Sort Descending.

The records are ordered by length of flight segment from longest to shortest.

	FID	Shape*	LENGTH	FROM_CITY	TO_CITY
	8	Polyline	3184.838	Natal	St. Louis
	16	Polyline	3009.786	Assab	Karachi
	17	Polyline	2380.498	Karachi	Calcutta
	1	Polyline	2323.93	Tucson	New Orleans
	6	Polyline	2132.179	Paramaribo	Fortaleza
	10	Polyline	1947.841	Dakar	Gao
	26	Polyline	1908.391	Darwin	Lae
	3	Polyline	1783.788	Miami	San Juan
	11	Polyline	1738.11	Gao	N'djamena
	21	Polyline	1431.381	Bangkok	Singapore
	0	Polyline	1414.502	Oakland	Tucson
	24	Polyline	1248.818	Surabaya	Kupang
	2	Polyline	1186.745	New Orleans	Miami
	12	Polyline	1151.221	N'djamena	Al Fashir
	22	Polyline	1006.791	Singapore	Bandung
	5	Polyline	1004.282	Caripito	Paramaribo

Record: ◄◄ ◄ 0 ► ►◄ Show: All Selected Records (0 out of 27 Selected.) Options ▼

The longest completed leg of the flight, 3,184 kilometers, was over water from Natal, Brazil, to St. Louis, Senegal. This was also a flight that had significant navigational error. (The aviators were about 175 kilometers off course from their intended destination, Dakar.)

Sorting a field is useful for seeing high and low values, but ArcMap can give you more detailed information.

15 Right-click on the LENGTH field and click Statistics. The Statistics of flight_path dialog opens.

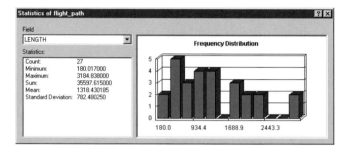

The Statistics box displays the number of records in the table (27) and the minimum, maximum, sum, mean, and standard deviation values. The average flight length, for example, was 1,318 kilometers.

The Frequency Distribution chart represents the distribution of values graphically. You can see that most of the flights were under 1,500 kilometers and that only two were over 2,500 kilometers.

16 Close the Statistics dialog. Close the Attributes of Flight Path table.

In the next chapter, you will see how the data for the Earhart project is managed in ArcCatalog.

17 If you want to save your work, click the File menu and click Save As. Navigate to **C:\GTKArcGIS\Chapter03\MyData**. Rename the file **my_ex03c.mxd** and click Save.

18 Click the File menu and click Exit. Click No if prompted to save your changes.

Exploring ArcCatalog

Browsing map data
Searching for map data
Adding data to ArcMap

ArcCatalog is an application for managing geographic data. You can copy, move, and delete data; search for data; look at data before deciding whether to add it to a map; and create new data. The ArcCatalog application window includes the catalog display for looking at spatial data, the catalog tree for browsing data, and several toolbars.

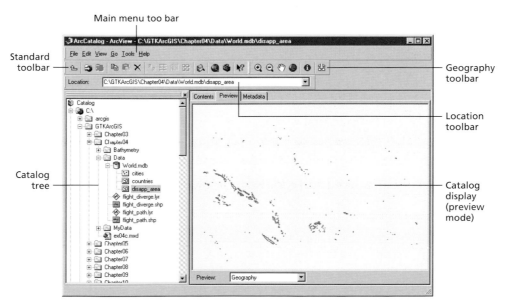

The ArcCatalog interface can be customized in the same ways as ArcMap. In this chapter, for example, the Geography toolbar is placed next to the Standard toolbar. In your application, it may be beneath it.

Spatial data comes in many different formats, including geodatabases, coverages, shapefiles, CAD files, rasters, and TINs. Each format is identified by its own icon in ArcCatalog. The shapefile icon, for example, is a green rectangle. Different patterns on the green rectangle distinguish point, line, and polygon shapefiles.

In this book, you'll use geodatabase, shapefile, and raster data. You'll also use layer files, which are not spatial data sets, but rather instructions for displaying spatial data sets with certain colors, symbol markers, line widths, and so on. Layer files, too, have their own ArcCatalog icon. You'll learn more about layer files and spatial data formats throughout this book.

Browsing map data

ArcCatalog gives you more information about spatial data than you can get from Windows Explorer or other file browsers. It can show you which folders contain spatial data and what kinds of spatial data they contain. It lets you preview features and attributes of data before you add the data to a map. It lets you examine and edit metadata, which is information about your data, such as when and how it was created.

Exercise 4a

As the GIS manager of the aviation history foundation's Earhart project, you need to be familiar with its spatial data. You'll use ArcCatalog to look at this data and get information about it.

The exercise instructions assume you have installed the data for *Getting to Know ArcGIS Desktop* to the default directory (**C:\GTKArcGIS**). If you have installed the data elsewhere, you'll need to substitute the correct paths.

1 On your computer desktop, double-click the ArcCatalog shortcut icon. (Or, click the Start button on the Windows taskbar, point to Programs, point to ArcGIS, and click ArcCatalog.)

The ArcCatalog application window opens. The catalog tree lists the data and services that ArcCatalog is connected to. By default, there is a connection to each local drive on your computer. Your application will look different from the following graphic depending on the drives you have.

You can also connect to subdirectories, network drives, relational databases, Internet servers, and other services.

Once you connect to a folder, you can access the data it contains. By default, ArcCatalog does not show file name extensions, but in this exercise it will be helpful to see them.

2 Click the Tools menu and click Options. In the Options dialog, click the General tab.

The Options dialog lets you specify the types of data ArcCatalog displays and the information it shows about them (file name, file size, date modified, and so on). You can distinguish folders containing spatial data from those that don't, and make many other customizations to the way data is displayed.

3 Uncheck Hide file extensions, as shown in the following graphic, then click OK.

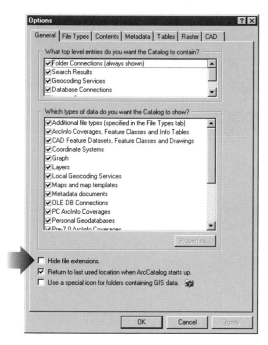

To access the spatial data in the GTKArcGIS folder more quickly, you'll create a connection to it.

4 On the Standard toolbar, click the Connect To Folder button.

The Connect to Folder dialog opens. Your dialog may look different depending on your local and network drives.

5 In the Connect to Folder dialog, click the plus sign (+) next to the (C:) drive to view its contents. Click on the GTKArcGIS folder, as shown in the following graphic, then click OK.

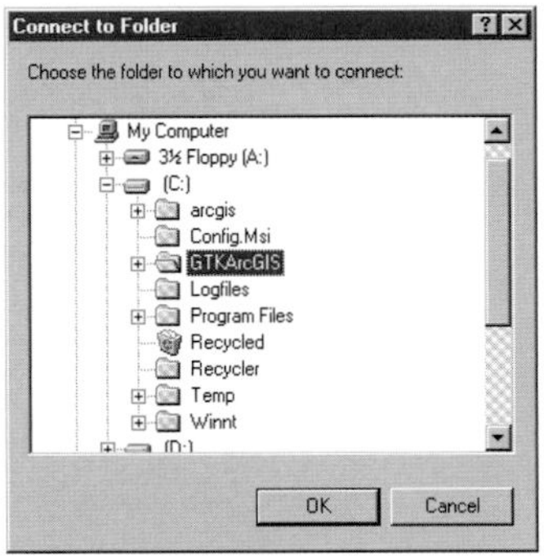

A connection is made to **C:\GTKArcGIS**.

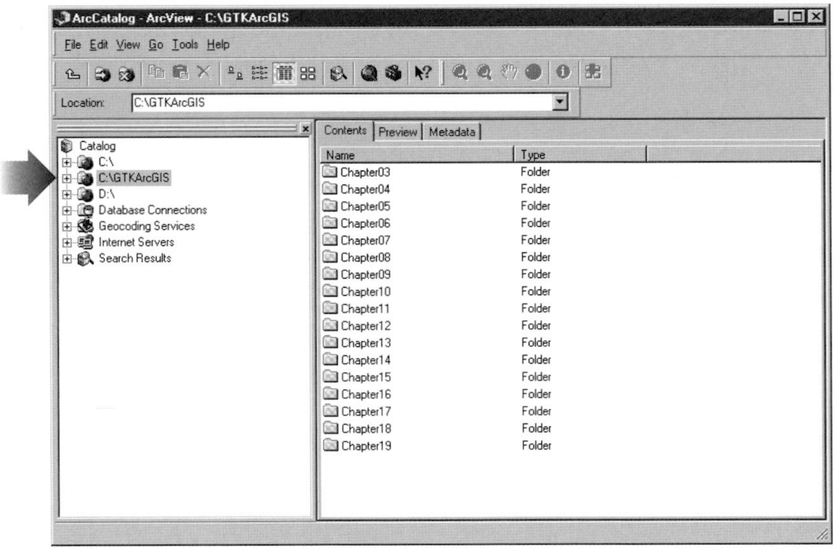

6 In the catalog tree, click the plus sign next to C:\GTKArcGIS. Click the plus sign next to the Chapter04 folder. It contains three folders, Bathymetry, Data, and MyData, and one map document, ex04c.mxd.

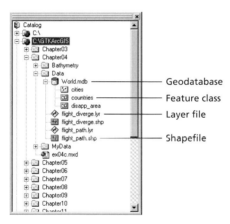

7 Click the plus sign next to the Data folder. It contains a geodatabase (World.mdb), two shapefiles, and two layer files. Click the plus sign next to World.mdb.

The geodatabase contains three feature classes. A feature class is a group of points, lines, or polygons representing geographic objects of the same kind. The cities feature class contains point features, the other two contain polygon features. This data was used to make the map of Earhart's flight in the previous chapter.

exercise 4a

8 On the Standard toolbar, make sure the Details button is selected.

9 In the catalog tree, click on **World.mdb**. In the catalog display, make sure the Contents tab is active.

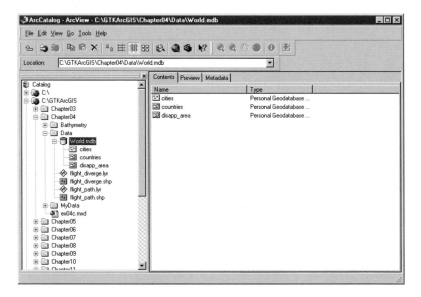

Four adjacent buttons on the Standard toolbar change how files look on the Contents tab. The Large Icons button displays large icons horizontally. The List button displays small icons vertically. The Details button is like the List button except that it also shows the file type—in this case, geodatabase feature classes. The Thumbnails button allows you to create small images of spatial data sets. Whenever a folder or a geodatabase is highlighted in the catalog tree, these four buttons are enabled.

10 On the Standard toolbar, click the Thumbnails button.

The display changes to show thumbnail images for each file. At the moment, the thumbnails are simply larger versions of the icons. A thumbnail that shows an image of a data set can help you decide quickly if you want to use the data or not. You'll create a thumbnail for the countries feature class.

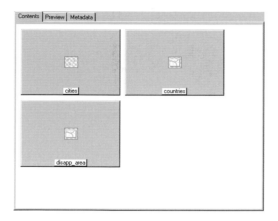

11 In the catalog tree, click on the **countries** feature class in the World geodatabase. In the catalog display, click the Preview tab. The geographic data for countries displays in pale yellow.

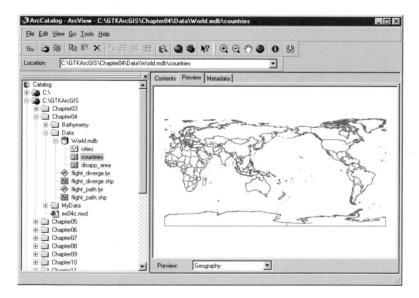

12 On the Geography toolbar, click the Create Thumbnail button.

An image of the data shown on the Preview tab is saved as a thumbnail graphic.

13 In the catalog display, click the Contents tab to see the thumbnail.

A thumbnail graphic may not be enough. The preview tab and the tools on the Geography toolbar let you further investigate a data set before deciding if you want to use it in a map.

14 In the catalog display, click the Preview tab again. On the Geography toolbar, click the Zoom In tool.

15 Drag a box around the area north of Australia, as shown in the following graphic. The exact size doesn't matter.

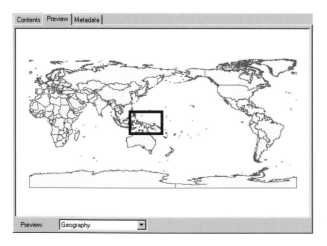

16 On the Geography toolbar, click the Identify tool.

17 Click on a feature to identify it. If you don't see it flash green, move the Identify Results window away from the display and click the feature again.

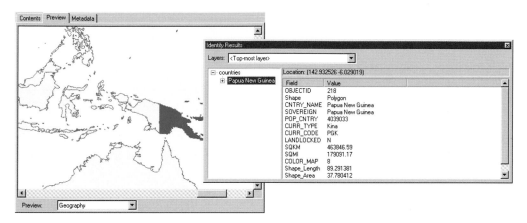

18 Close the Identify Results window. On the Geography toolbar, click the Full Extent button to zoom to the full extent of the data.

You can preview the attributes of a data set as well as its geography.

19 At the bottom of the catalog display, click the Preview drop-down list and click Table. The display shows you the attribute table of the countries feature class.

20 Scroll through the table to see the attributes. When you're finished, click the Preview drop-down list and click Geography.

The third tab in the catalog display is the Metadata tab. Metadata provides technical information about a data set, such as its coordinate system, its spatial extent, and descriptions of its attributes. It also provides descriptive information about when and how the data was created and what its appropriate uses are.

Technical metadata is maintained by ArcCatalog; descriptive information must be maintained by the people who use and manage the data. ArcCatalog doesn't require you to maintain metadata, but you should.

21 In the catalog display, click the Metadata tab. You see the name of the countries feature class, the thumbnail you created, and three blue tabs. The Description tab is highlighted.

22 Scroll down. Clickable green headings give a description of the data and other general information. Scroll up to the top.

23 Click the Spatial tab and scroll down for information about the coordinate system and spatial boundaries of the data. Scroll back to the top.

24 Click the Attributes tab and scroll down. Click on a green heading to learn more about the attribute.

For more information about metadata, click the Contents tab in ArcGIS Desktop Help and navigate to *ArcCatalog > Working with metadata*.

25 In the catalog display, click the Contents tab. In the catalog tree, click on **World.mdb**. On the Standard toolbar, click the Details button.

The display changes to show the contents of the World geodatabase. This is the starting place for the next exercise.

26 If you are continuing with the next exercise, leave ArcCatalog open. Otherwise, click the File menu and click Exit.

Changes that you make to files in ArcCatalog, unlike those you make to a map document, are saved when you make them. Therefore, you are not prompted to save changes.

Searching for map data

With ArcCatalog, you can search for geographic data sets on disk or across a network. You can search for data by name or file type, by geographic location, by creation date, or by other properties contained in the metadata.

Exercise 4b

In this exercise, you will search ArcCatalog for other data sources that may be useful to the Earhart project. You will also preview more data sets.

1 If necessary, start ArcCatalog.

If ArcCatalog is open from the previous exercise, you are connected to the **C:\GTKArcGIS** folder, as shown in the following graphic.

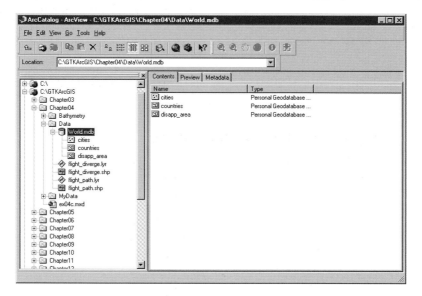

If you started a new ArcCatalog session, you are connected to the **C:** folder and your catalog tree looks slightly different. In this exercise, it doesn't matter.

2 On the Standard toolbar, click the Search button.

The Search dialog opens with the Name & location tab active.

The tabs on the Search dialog give you different ways to search for data. On the Name & location tab, you search by file name or type. On the Geography tab, you search by geographic location. On the Date tab, you search by the date files were last accessed or by other dates in the metadata. On the Advanced tab, you search for keywords or other metadata text.

First, you will restrict your search to the contents of the Chapter04 folder.

3 Click the Browse button next to the Look in text box.

The Browse for location to start search dialog opens.

4 In the Browse dialog, navigate to **C:\GTKArcGIS**. Click on the **Chapter04** folder, as shown in the following graphic, then click Add.

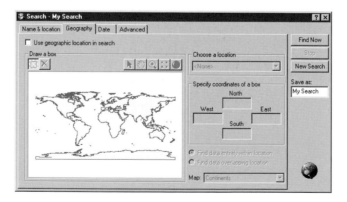

The search is now limited to the contents of the Chapter04 folder.

5 On the Search dialog, click the Geography tab.

You will concentrate your search for data on the area where Earhart disappeared. Geographical searches use latitude and longitude coordinates to find data; specifically, they check the bounding coordinates stored in a data set's spatial metadata to see if these lie within the latitude–longitude values of the search area. If they do, the data set is returned in the search results.

6 On the Geography tab, check Use geographic location in search.

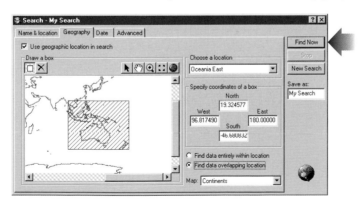

You can search for data by drawing a box on the map, by choosing a part of the world, or by entering latitude and longitude coordinates.

7 Click the Choose a location drop-down arrow and click Oceania East.

This is the part of the world where Earhart disappeared. The map zooms in and a shaded rectangle covers the search area.

8 Near the bottom of the dialog, click the Find data overlapping location option. ArcCatalog will find any spatial data that falls at least partly within the rectangle. Make sure that the dialog matches the following graphic, then click Find Now.

When all data sets have been found, the ArcCatalog status bar at the bottom of the application window displays the message, "Catalog search finished."

9 Close the Search dialog.

My Search is added under Search Results in the catalog tree. The display lists short-cuts to the data sets that were found. You have already seen most of them, but there is a raster data set called seafloor.tif that you haven't seen before.

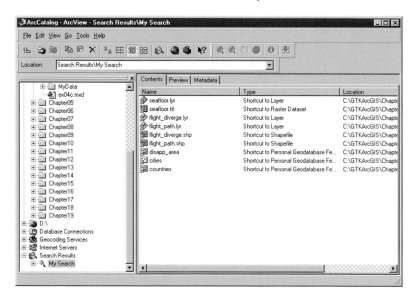

10 In the catalog display, right-click on seafloor.tif and click Go To Target.

The catalog tree opens to the location of the data.

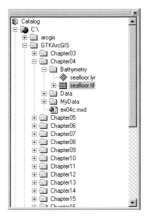

The seafloor raster data set is in the Bathymetry folder under Chapter04, along with a layer file called seafloor.lyr.

11 In the catalog tree, make sure the seafloor raster (the one with the square bumpy icon) is highlighted. In the catalog display, click the Preview tab.

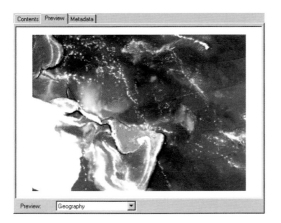

You see a raster data set of seafloor elevation in East Oceania. The data may be useful in a map of the area where Earhart disappeared. For example, you could zoom in on Nikumaroro Island and find out how deep the water around it is. This information might affect operations to find and recover plane wreckage. The black-and-white image, however, is not easy to interpret as seafloor elevation. The seafloor layer file displays the elevation data in shades of blue.

12 In the catalog tree, click on **seafloor.lyr** (the one with the diamond-shaped bumpy icon).

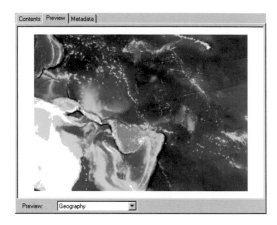

In the layer file, the depth of the water is indicated by the shade of blue; darker is deeper. White areas are land.

13 On the Geography toolbar, click the Identify tool.

14 Click on a few locations to identify elevation values (described as pixel values in the Identify Results window). The values are in meters. If you click on a spot of land, you should get the value No Data.

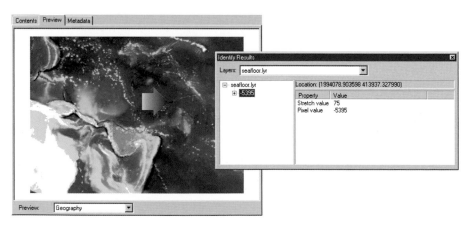

15 Close the Identify Results window. In the catalog tree, click the minus sign next to the Bathymetry folder to collapse it. Click the plus sign next to the Data folder to expand it.

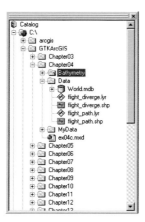

Besides the World geodatabase, the folder contains shapefiles and layer files for the Earhart flight paths.

16 Make sure the Preview tab is active in the display. Click on the flight_diverge shapefile (the one with the green icon) to preview it. Next, click on the flight_diverge layer file (the yellow icon) and preview it.

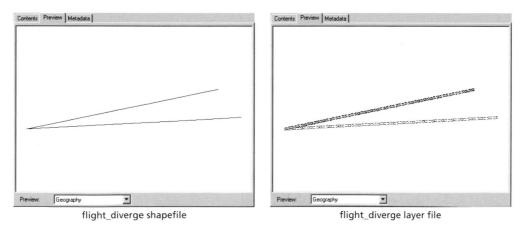

flight_diverge shapefile   flight_diverge layer file

The shapefile displays as two blue lines. The layer file shows the thick dotted lines that you saw in the previous chapter.

Layer files allow you to store symbology information—the colors, shapes, and sizes that you choose for features—so you never have to recreate it. Every layer file is associated with and depends on a spatial data file. The flight_diverge layer file won't display in ArcMap unless the flight_diverge shapefile is accessible on disk.

In the next exercise, you will add data and layer files from ArcCatalog to ArcMap.

17 If you are continuing with the next exercise, leave ArcCatalog open. Otherwise, click the File menu and click Exit.

Adding data to ArcMap

One way to add data to ArcMap is to drag it from ArcCatalog. Once it's there, you can look at it, as you did in the previous chapter, as a map display and table of contents. This is called data view. You can also look at it as if it were on a page that you send to a printer. This is called layout view.

In layout view, you see map layers organized in one or more rectangles on a larger background rectangle. The smaller rectangles are called data frames and the background is called the virtual page.

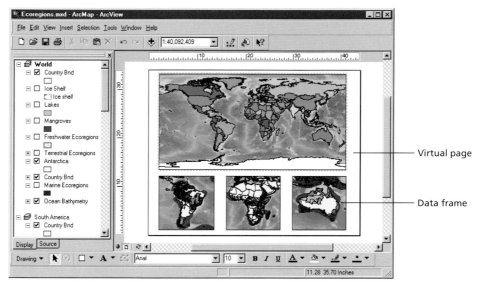

A map document in layout view. The map has four data frames, each marked with a yellow icon in the table of contents.

In data view, by contrast, you see just one data frame at a time.

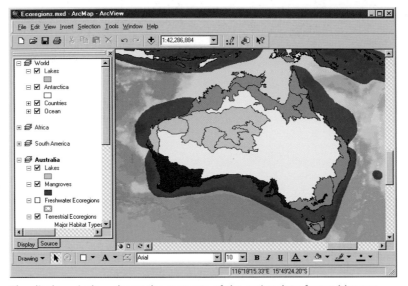

The display window shows the contents of the active data frame (the one boldfaced in the table of contents).

Exercise 4c

The aviation history foundation hopes to raise money for an expedition to look for the wreckage of Earhart's plane. Part of your job is to create maps to interest potential investors. In chapter 19, you'll learn in detail about creating maps for presentation. For now, you'll learn how to add data to ArcMap from ArcCatalog and how to work with data frames in ArcMap.

1 If necessary, start ArcCatalog.

If ArcCatalog is open from the previous exercise, you are connected to **C:\GTKArcGIS\Chapter04\Data\flight_diverge.lyr**, as shown in the following graphic. If you started a new ArcCatalog session, navigate to this location now and click the Preview tab if necessary.

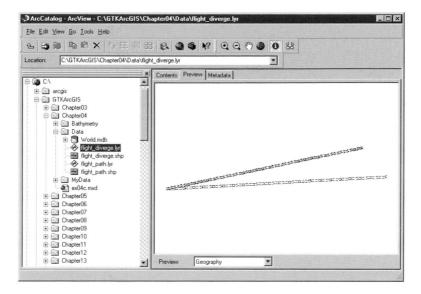

2 On the Standard toolbar, click the Launch ArcMap button.

3 In the ArcMap dialog, click the option to start using ArcMap with an existing map, as shown in the following graphic, and click OK.

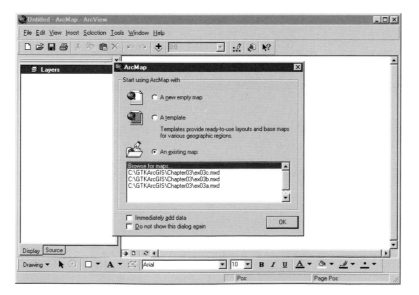

Adding data to ArcMap

4 In the Open file browser, navigate to **C:\GTKArcGIS\Chapter04**. Click on the file **ex04c.mxd** to highlight it and click Open.

You see the familiar map of Amelia Earhart's flight. The map has one data frame, called Earhart Flight Path, that contains three layers. You will add a layer for the diverging flight paths.

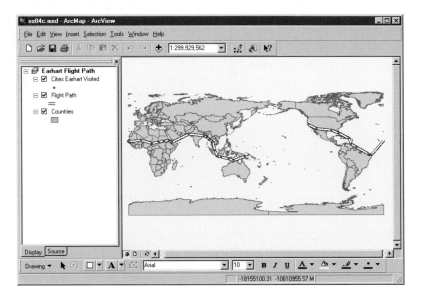

5 Position the ArcCatalog and ArcMap application windows so that you can see both the catalog tree and the ArcMap display window.

6 In the catalog tree, click on the flight_diverge layer file (yellow icon). Drag the file anywhere over the ArcMap display window and release the mouse button. Make ArcMap the active application by clicking on its title bar.

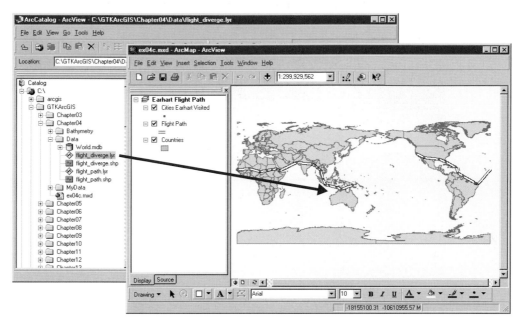

The layer file is added to ArcMap.

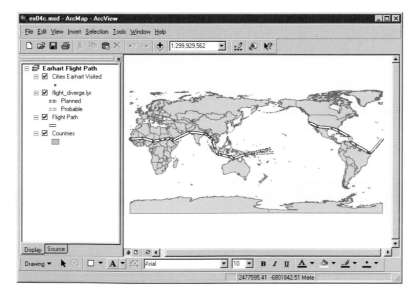

You'll rename the layer file.

7 In the table of contents, right-click on flight_diverge.lyr and click Properties.

8 In the Layer Properties dialog, click the General tab. Replace the layer name with **Diverging Flight Paths**, as shown in the following graphic, then click OK.

The layer name is changed in the table of contents.

Now you will add a second data frame to the map to show a close-up of the area where Earhart disappeared.

9 In ArcMap, click the View menu and click Layout View.

You see the map as if on a piece of paper. A new toolbar, the Layout toolbar, opens. The Earhart Flight Path data frame occupies the top half of the virtual page.

CHAPTER 4 • EXPLORING ARCCATALOG

10 Click the Insert menu and click Data Frame.

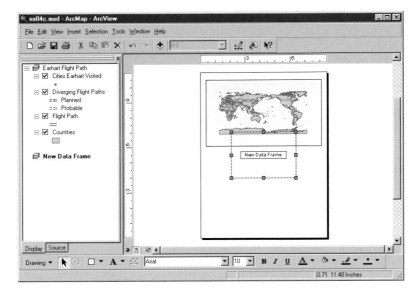

A data frame is added to the layout and its name, New Data Frame, appears in the table of contents. The name is boldfaced, indicating that it is the *active* data frame—the one that layers will be added to.

11 In the layout window, move the mouse pointer over the new data frame. The cursor changes to a four-headed arrow. Drag the frame beneath the Earhart Flight Path frame so the two don't overlap.

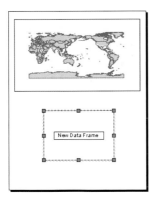

You'll switch back to data view to add layers to the new data frame. (You could do this in layout view as well.)

12 Click the Data View button in the lower left corner of the layout window. This button and the Layout View button next to it can be used instead of the View menu to switch between views.

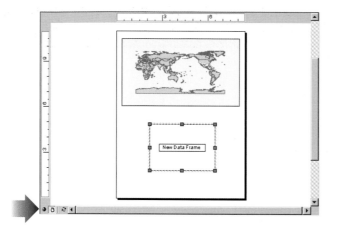

The display window is empty because the active data frame (New Data Frame) contains no layers.

13 Make ArcCatalog the active application by clicking on its title bar. In the catalog tree, click the plus sign next to the World geodatabase and click on **disapp_area**. Drag the feature class to the ArcMap display window and release the mouse button.

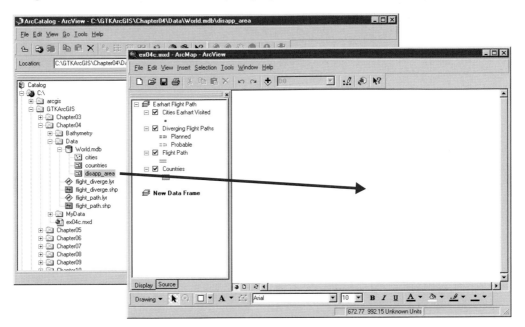

14 Make ArcMap the active application. The feature class is added as a layer to the new data frame.

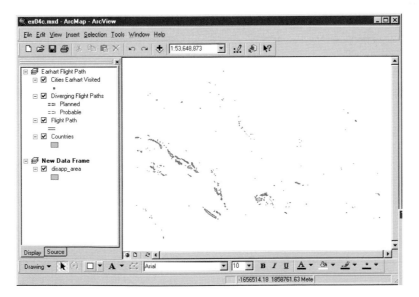

ArcMap assigns a random color to the disapp_area layer, so your color may be different.

15 Make ArcCatalog the active application. In the catalog tree, click the plus sign by the Bathymetry folder and click on the seafloor layer file. Drag the layer file to ArcMap and make ArcMap the active application.

The seafloor.lyr layer displays underneath the disapp_area layer.

Now you will copy the Diverging Flight Paths layer from the Earhart Flight Path data frame to the new data frame.

16 In the ArcMap table of contents, right-click on the Diverging Flight Paths layer in the Earhart Flight Path data frame. On the context menu, click Copy.

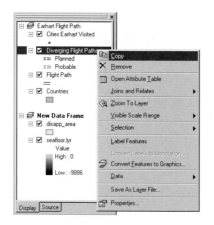

17 In the table of contents, right-click on New Data Frame. On the context menu, click Paste Layer.

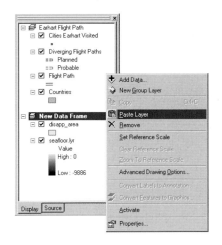

The Diverging Flight Paths layer is pasted into the new data frame and displays on the map.

18 Click the Layout View button in the lower left corner of the layout window.

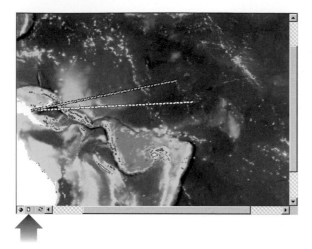

The data frame displays the data you've added to it.

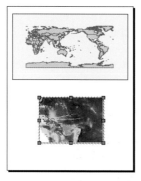

Now you'll change the color of the disapp_area layer to make it contrast with the blue of the seafloor layer.

19 Click the Data View button to switch back to data view. In the table of contents, right-click on the polygon symbol for the disapp_area layer. A color palette opens.

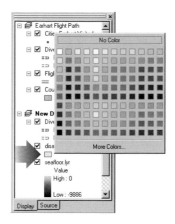

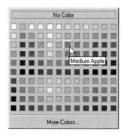

20 Move the mouse pointer over the color palette. Each color square is identified by name. Click Medium Apple.

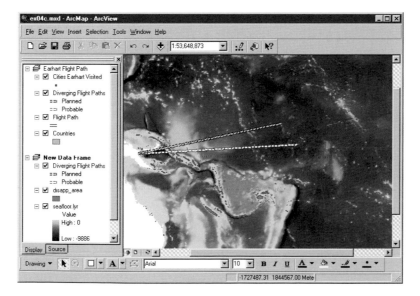

The color of the layer is updated in the table of contents and in the map features.

Finally, you will rename the data frame.

21 In the table of contents, right-click on New Data Frame. On the context menu, click Properties. The Data Frame Properties dialog opens. Click the General tab.

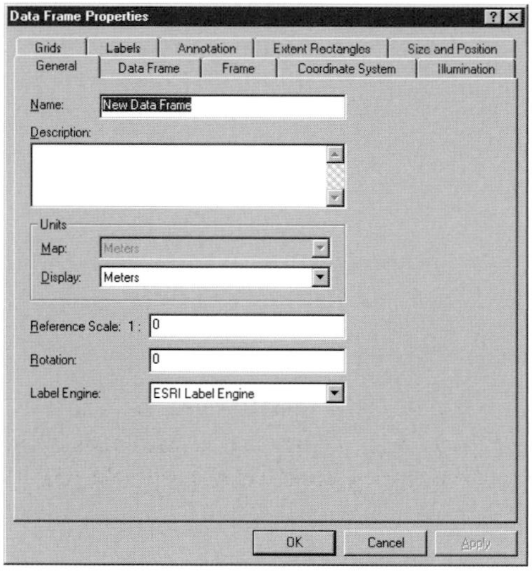

22 In the Name box, New Data Frame is highlighted. Type **Area of Disappearance** in its place, as shown in the following graphic, then click OK.

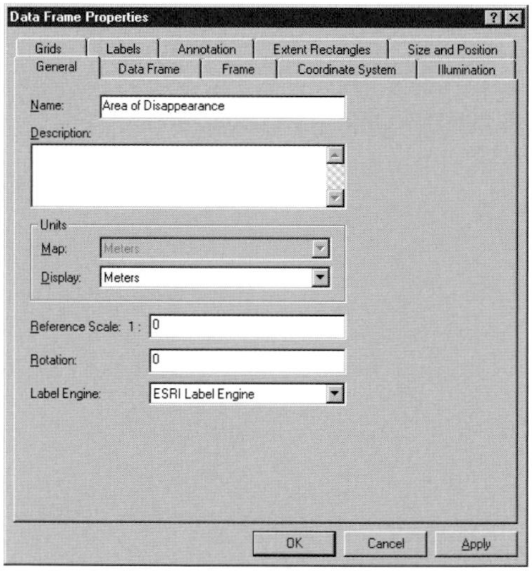

The new name is displayed in the table of contents.

You know how to preview data in ArcCatalog and look at its metadata. You can use ArcCatalog to search for geographic data on disk. And you know how to add layers from ArcCatalog to ArcMap. You'll have no trouble managing the data for the Earhart project.

23 Make ArcCatalog the active application. Click the File menu and click Exit.

24 Close the Layout toolbar. If you are continuing to the next chapter, leave ArcMap open. Otherwise, click the File menu and click Exit. Click No when prompted to save changes.

Symbolizing features and rasters

Changing symbology
Symbolizing features by categorical attributes
Using styles and creating layer files
Symbolizing rasters

Symbolizing features means assigning them colors, markers, sizes, widths, angles, patterns, transparency, and other properties by which they can be recognized on a map. Often, symbols mimic nature: a lake polygon is blue and fire hydrants are marked by icons that look like fire hydrants. Sometimes the relationship is less straightforward. On a street map, varying line thicknesses may show whether a street is a local road, an arterial, or a highway without implying that the widths on the map are proportional to the widths of the actual streets. Symbology may also be purely conventional. Cities, for example, are often symbolized as dots, though cities are seldom round.

By varying symbol properties, you convey information about features.

Left: fill patterns and colors differentiate intermittent lakes, perennial lakes, and salt pans.
Center: line thickness, color, and solidity show railways and main, secondary, and local roads.
Right: unique icons mark major and minor cities.

Symbology is also influenced by scale. A city may be a dot on one map and a polygon on another.

Scale 1:13,000,000

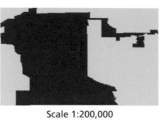

Scale 1:200,000

Left: Redlands, California, represented as a point.
Right: Redlands, California, represented as a polygon.

ArcGIS has thousands of symbols for common map features. Symbols are organized by style (Environmental, Transportation, Weather, and so on) to make it easy to locate the ones you need. You can also create your own symbols.

When a data set is added to ArcMap, all its features have the same symbology. To assign new symbology, you use information from a field in the layer attribute table.

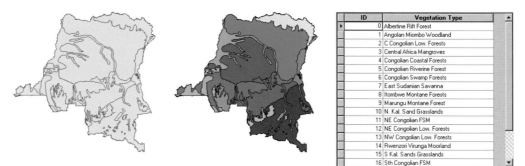

Ecoregions in the Democratic Republic of the Congo. Left: all features have the same symbology. Center: each feature has a different fill color. Right: the Vegetation Type values used to supply the fill colors.

You can save a layer's symbology by making a layer (.lyr) file. When you add a layer file to a map, the features are already symbolized the way you want.

Symbolizing raster layers is similar to symbolizing feature layers, but with fewer options. The only property that can be controlled is the color of the cells that comprise the raster.

Changing symbology

Data sets added to ArcMap have default symbology. Points are displayed with small circles, for instance, and polygons have outlines. The colors for points, lines, and polygons are randomly chosen.

In this exercise, you'll change the default symbology for a polygon layer of countries and a point layer of cities. You'll also change the background color of the data frame.

Exercise 5a

You are a graphic designer donating your time to create a poster about Africa for Geography Awareness Week. Sponsored by the National Geographic Society, Geography Awareness Week is held every November and includes GIS Day among its many events and programs.

The Africa Atlas poster will consist of nine maps displaying cities, countries, rivers, wildlife, topography (surface relief), population, and natural resources. It will be distributed to elementary schools around the country.

The completed poster, measuring 44 by 34 inches, will look like the one in the following graphic. In this exercise, you will create the first of the nine maps, depicting major cities.

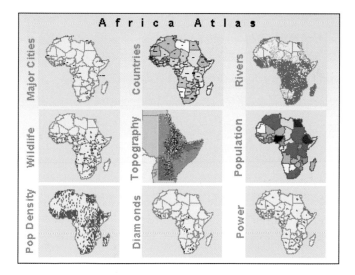

When you finish chapter 6, you can send your poster to a plotter, if you have access to one. Alternatively, you can send a letter-size version of the poster to a desktop printer.

1. Start ArcMap. In the ArcMap dialog, click the option to use an existing map. In the list of existing maps, double-click Browse for maps. (If ArcMap is already running, click the File menu and click Open.) Navigate to **C:\GTKArcGIS\Chapter05**. Click **ex05a.mxd** and click Open.

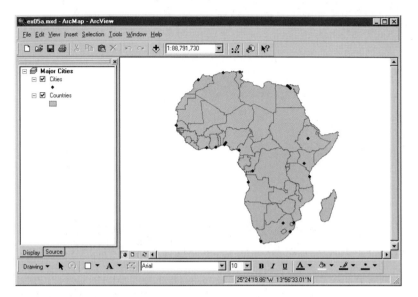

The table of contents has a data frame called Major Cities that includes a Cities layer and a Countries layer. Countries are symbolized in pale purple, cities as dark gray points. Each city has a population of one million or more.

You'll change the symbology for both the countries and the cities.

2 In the table of contents, right-click the symbol for the Countries layer to open the color palette. In the palette, click Sahara Sand.

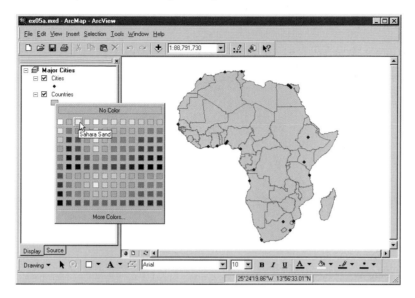

The countries are redrawn in the new color. Polygon features are composed of two symbols, a fill and an outline. To change the color or width of the outline, you open the Symbol Selector.

3 In the table of contents, click the symbol for the Countries layer. The Symbol Selector dialog opens.

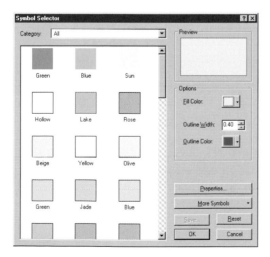

The scrolling box on the left contains predefined symbols. The Options frame on the right allows you to pick colors and set outline widths.

4 In the Options frame, click the Outline Color square to open the color palette. In the color palette, click **Gray 40%**. Click OK at the bottom of the Symbol Selector dialog.

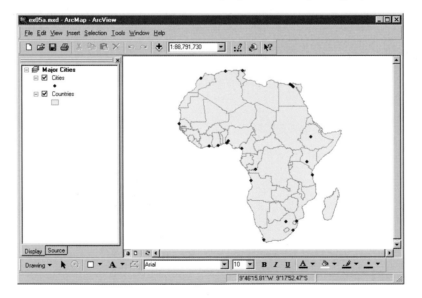

The cities stand out more distinctly against the lighter gray outlines of the countries.

Now, you'll change the symbology for the cities. You'll make them larger, change their color, and label them.

5 In the table of contents, click the point symbol for the Cities layer. The Symbol Selector dialog opens. In the scrolling box of predefined point symbols, click Circle 2. In the Options frame, click the Size down arrow to change the symbol size to **10** points.

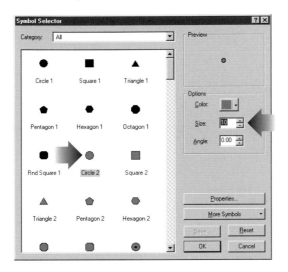

6 Click the Color square to open the color palette. In the color palette, click Ginger Pink. Click OK in the Symbol Selector dialog.

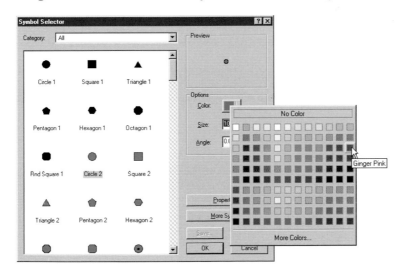

On the map, the cities display with the new symbol.

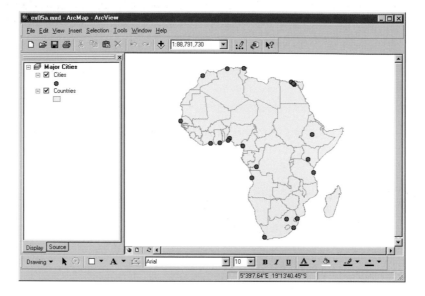

7 In the table of contents, right-click the Cities layer name (not the symbol) and click Label Features.

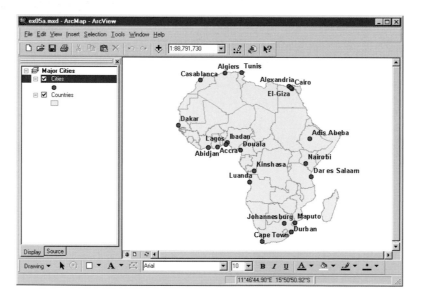

The cities are labeled with their names. Depending on the size of your ArcMap window, and the scale, your labels may be positioned differently from those in the graphic. In chapter 7, you'll learn how to change the size, color, and font of labels.

Next, you'll change the background color of the data frame.

8 In the table of contents, right-click on the Major Cities data frame, and click Properties. The Data Frame Properties dialog opens. Click the Frame tab (not the Data Frame tab).

9 On the Frame tab, click the Background drop-down arrow and click Lt Blue. When the background color is applied, as shown in the following graphic, click OK in the Data Frame Properties dialog.

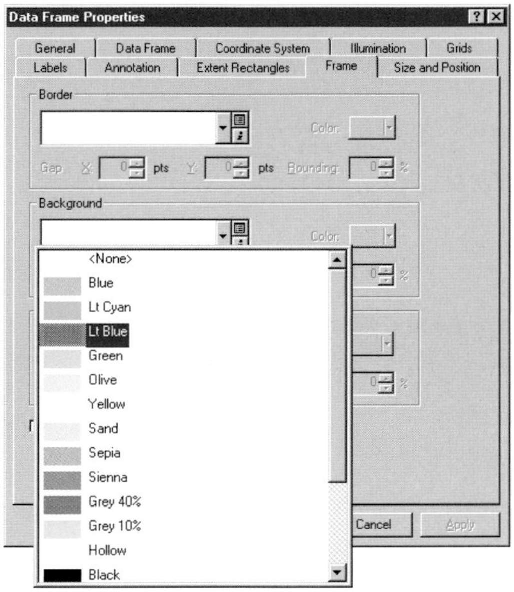

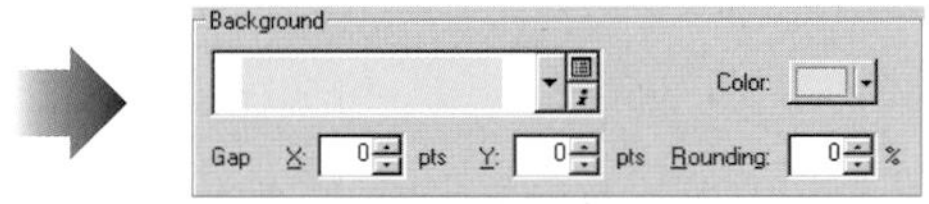

The color is applied to the data frame.

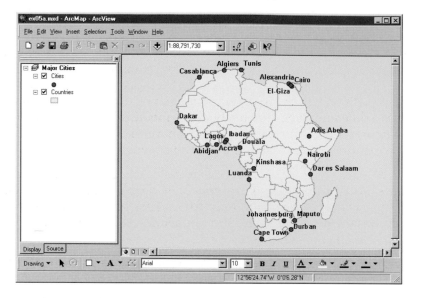

You have finished the major cities map. In the next exercise, you'll make a map in which each country has unique symbology. You'll also symbolize the rivers of Africa.

10 If you want to save your work, click the File menu and click Save As. Navigate to **C:\GTKArcGIS\Chapter05\MyData**. Rename the file **my_ex05a.mxd** and click Save.

11 If you are continuing with the next exercise, leave ArcMap open. Otherwise, click the File menu and click Exit. Click No if prompted to save your changes.

Symbolizing features by categorical attributes

In the last exercise, each city had the same marker symbol and all countries were drawn in the same color. You can make symbology more informative by assigning a different symbol to each unique value, or to distinct ranges of values, in the layer attribute table. For example, you might symbolize a polygon layer of countries according to their names. Every feature would have a unique color because every country has a different name. You might also symbolize countries by their political systems. Features with the same system would have the same color: republics might be blue, constitutional monarchies purple, and communist states red.

Attributes that are names or descriptions are called categorical attributes (or qualitative or descriptive attributes). They are usually text, but they may be numbers if the numbers are codes standing for descriptions. Attributes that are measurements or counts of features are called quantitative attributes. A country's area in square kilometers is a measurement. Its population is a count.

In this exercise, you'll symbolize features by categorical attributes. You'll work with quantitative attributes in chapter 6.

Exercise 5b

You are continuing your work on the Africa Atlas poster. You'll symbolize countries by name, so that each has a unique color. Then you'll symbolize African rivers. To give each river a unique color would be confusing—there are too many of them. Instead, you'll symbolize them by an attribute that identifies them as perennial or intermittent.

1 Start ArcMap. In the ArcMap dialog, click the option to use an existing map. In the list of existing maps, double-click Browse for maps. (If ArcMap is already running, click the File menu and click Open.) Navigate to **C:\GTKArcGIS\Chapter05**. Click **ex05b.mxd** and click Open.

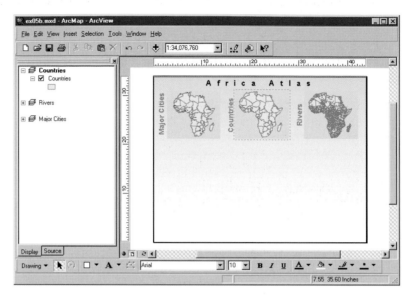

The map opens in layout view. You see the Major Cities data frame you symbolized in the last exercise and two new ones: Countries and Rivers. The Countries data frame has a dashed line around it because it is active.

2 Click the View menu and click Data View.

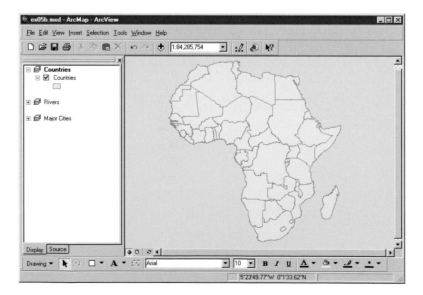

The Countries data frame is active and contains one layer, also called Countries. All features in the layer are symbolized with the same color. To give each feature its own color, you'll open the Layer Properties dialog.

3 Right-click the Countries layer and click Properties. The Layer Properties dialog opens. Click the Symbology tab.

The Show box on the left side of the dialog lists different methods for symbolizing features. Some methods have more than one option. By default, Features is selected. It has only one option—Single symbol.

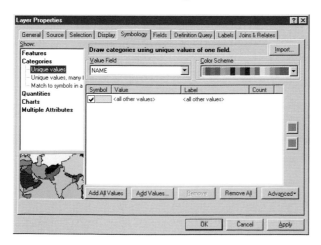

Since you want to symbolize each country with its own color, you need an attribute with a unique value for each feature—the country name is an obvious choice.

4 In the Show box, click Categories.

The Unique values option of the Categories method is highlighted and the dialog changes. The Value Field drop-down list contains the fields in the attribute table that can be used to symbolize the countries. The Color Scheme drop-down list contains different color patterns that can be applied. (The scheme displayed in your dialog may be different.) The large window in the middle of the dialog shows which features in the layer are being symbolized. You can symbolize all features or just some of them.

5 Make sure the Value Field drop-down list is set to NAME. At the bottom of the dialog, click Add All Values.

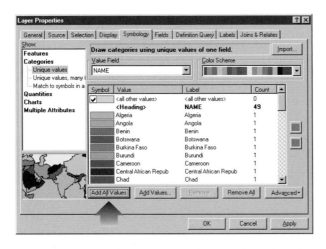

Each feature in the Countries layer is listed in the Value column and has a symbol from the color scheme assigned to it. The Label column displays the feature name as it will appear in the table of contents. It will be the same as the value unless you change it.

The Count column tells you the number of features being symbolized and the number of features that have each value. In this case, the count is one for each value because each country's name is unique.

You will change the color scheme.

6 In the Color Scheme drop-down list, right-click on the colors (not on the drop-down arrow). On the context menu, click Graphic View to uncheck it. The image of the color scheme is replaced by its name. Again, yours may be different.

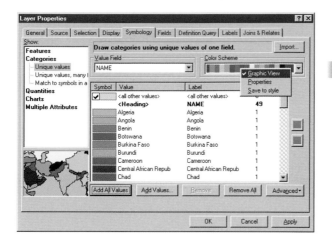 

7 Click the Color Scheme drop-down arrow and scroll down until you see Pastels. Click to select it. The features are assigned symbols from the new color scheme.

8 In the Symbol column, click the check box next to <all other values> to uncheck it. The <all other values> symbol is used when you want to assign unique symbology to some features in a layer and want the rest to be identical. That isn't the case here. Make sure your dialog matches the following graphic, then click OK.

In the map, the countries are symbolized in pastels. (The association between shades and countries may be different on your map.) The table of contents shows the name of each country and its symbol.

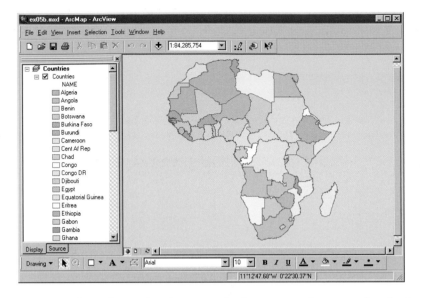

After a color scheme has been applied, you can change individual colors. For example, you could right-click on the symbol for Algeria in the table of contents and change it to Mars Red or Steel Blue.

The countries are distinguished by unique symbols, but the symbols don't make it easy to identify countries. (How quickly can you find Malawi?) You will label the countries with their names.

9 In the table of contents, right-click on the Countries layer and click Label Features.

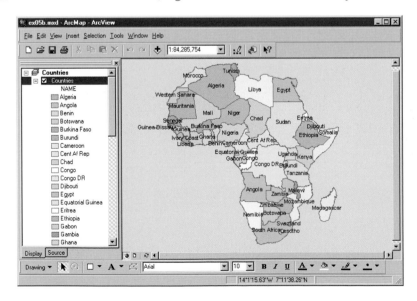

As with the cities, your country labels may look different depending on the size of your ArcMap window. Your country map is finished. Your last task in this exercise is to create a map of African rivers.

10 In the table of contents, click the minus signs next to the Countries layer and the Countries data frame.

11 Right-click on the Rivers data frame and click Activate. Click the plus sign next to the data frame. The data frame contains a Rivers layer and a Countries layer.

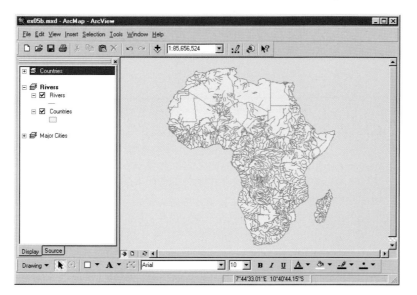

Before you symbolize the rivers, you'll look at the attribute table to see what information is available.

12 Right-click the Rivers layer and click Open Attribute Table.

FID	Shape	NAME	TYPE	STATUS	NAVIG
0	Polyline	Medjerda	perennial	secondary	nonnavigable
1	Polyline	Medjerda	perennial	secondary	nonnavigable
2	Polyline	Medjerda	perennial	secondary	nonnavigable
3	Polyline	Mellegue	perennial	secondary	nonnavigable
4	Polyline	Siliana	perennial	secondary	nonnavigable
5	Polyline	Cheliff	perennial	secondary	nonnavigable
6	Polyline	Sebisseb	intermittent	secondary	nonnavigable
7	Polyline	Nahr-Ouassel	perennial	secondary	nonnavigable
8	Polyline	Moulouya	perennial	main	nonnavigable
9	Polyline	Oued Ouerrha	perennial	secondary	nonnavigable
10	Polyline	Oued Sebou	perennial	secondary	nonnavigable
11	Polyline	Hammam	perennial	secondary	nonnavigable
12	Polyline	Oued Sebou	perennial	secondary	nonnavigable
13	Polyline	Oued el Mitta	intermittent	secondary	nonnavigable
14	Polyline	Tafna	perennial	secondary	nonnavigable
15	Polyline	Oued el Arab	intermittent	secondary	nonnavigable

Record: |◄| ◄| 1 |►| ►| Show: All Selected Records (0 out of 1621 Selected.) Options ▼

The attributes include the river name, its type (perennial or intermittent), its status (main or secondary), and its navigability. You'll symbolize rivers by type.

13 Close the table. In the table of contents, double-click on the Rivers layer to open the Layer Properties dialog. (Double-clicking is a shortcut for right-clicking and choosing Properties.) On the Layer Properties dialog, click the Symbology tab.

14 In the Show box, click Categories and make sure the Unique values option is highlighted. Click the Value Field drop-down arrow and click TYPE. Click Add All Values.

There are two values in the TYPE field: intermittent and perennial. At the moment, they are symbolized with pastels (assuming this is the last color scheme you used). You'll change the symbology.

ADDING VALUES

You may want to focus on some features in a layer and deemphasize or ignore others. The Add Values button (next to Add All Values) lets you select particular attribute values and assign symbology to features that have them. Other features are assigned a single symbol—the one designated for <all other values>. If the <all other values> check box is unchecked, these features are not displayed at all.

15 In the Symbol column, double-click the line symbol next to the intermittent value to open the Symbol Selector.

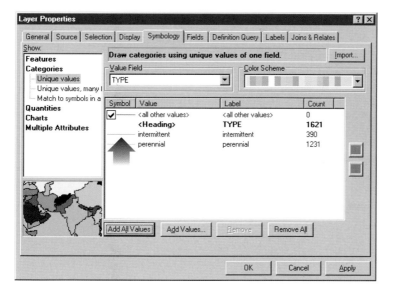

16 In the Symbol Selector, scroll down two thirds of the way until you see the Stream, Intermittent symbol. Click the symbol as shown in the following graphic, then click OK in the Symbol Selector.

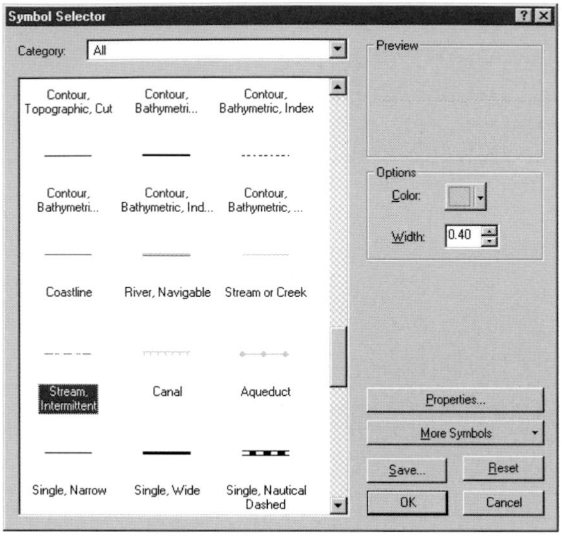

17 In the Symbol column of the Layer Properties dialog, double-click the symbol next to the perennial value. The Symbol Selector opens again. Click the River symbol as shown in the following graphic, then click OK.

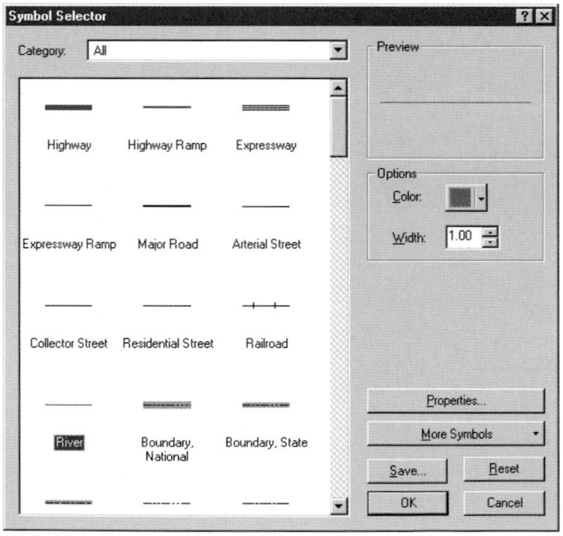

18 In the Symbol column of the Layer Properties dialog, click the check box next to <all other values> to uncheck it. Make sure that your dialog matches the following graphic, then click OK.

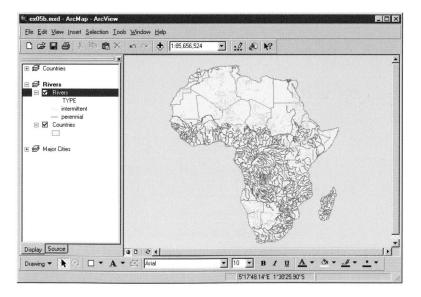

In the map, the rivers are displayed with the new symbology.

The map shows that central Africa is a dense network of perennial rivers while the northern and southwestern parts of the continent have few rivers that run year-round.

You'll check your progress on the Africa Atlas poster.

19 Click the View menu and click Layout View.

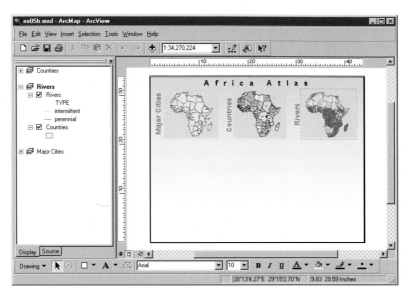

Your layout has three data frames, showing major cities, countries, and rivers.

In the next exercise, you'll symbolize wildlife habitat.

20 If you want to save your work, click the File menu and click Save As. Navigate to **C:\GTKArcGIS\Chapter05\MyData**. Rename the file **my_ex05b.mxd** and click Save.

21 If you are continuing with the next exercise, leave ArcMap open. Otherwise, click the File menu and click Exit. Click No if prompted to save your changes.

Using styles and creating layer files

In the previous exercises, you worked with point, line, and polygon symbols in the Symbol Selector dialog, colors on the color palette, color schemes in the Layer Properties dialog, and background colors in the Data Frame Properties dialog.

All these symbols and colors belong to the ESRI style. A style is a collection of pre-defined symbols, colors, and other map elements such as labels, north arrows, scale bars, and borders. ArcGIS has over twenty styles, and you can make new ones by combining elements from existing styles and creating your own symbols.

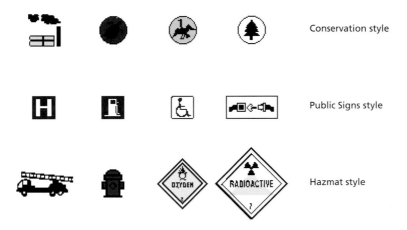

Conservation style

Public Signs style

Hazmat style

For information on creating and modifying styles, click the Contents tab in ArcGIS Desktop Help and navigate to *ArcMap > Working with styles and symbols*.

Having invested time in symbolizing a layer, you may want to save it as a layer file (a file with a .lyr extension). As you saw in chapter 4, layer files store symbology information for a data set.

Exercise 5c

In this exercise, you'll use symbols from the Conservation style to create a map that shows where elephants, giraffes, and zebras are found. Then you'll save the symbolized layer as a layer file.

1 Start ArcMap. In the ArcMap dialog, click the option to use an existing map. In the list of maps, double-click Browse for maps. (If ArcMap is already running, click the File menu and click Open.) Navigate to **C:\GTKArcGIS\Chapter05**. Click **ex05c.mxd** and click Open.

The map opens in layout view. You see the three data frames you've already symbolized and a fourth called Wildlife.

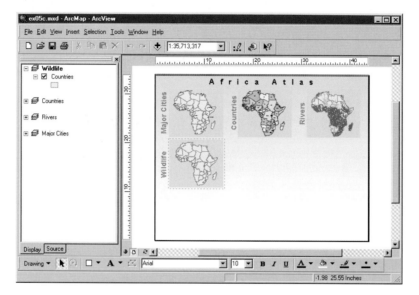

2 Click the View menu and click Data View.

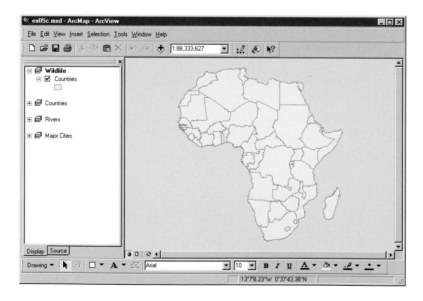

The active data frame contains a layer of countries. You'll add a layer of animal locations. In chapter 4, you added layers to ArcMap by dragging them from ArcCatalog. When ArcCatalog isn't open, you can use the Add Data button.

3 On the Standard toolbar, click the Add Data button.

4 In the Add Data dialog, navigate to **C:\GTKArcGIS\Chapter05\Data**. Click on Animals.shp. Make sure that your dialog matches the following graphic, then click Add.

A point layer called Animals is added to the map. It displays with the default point symbol in a randomly chosen color.

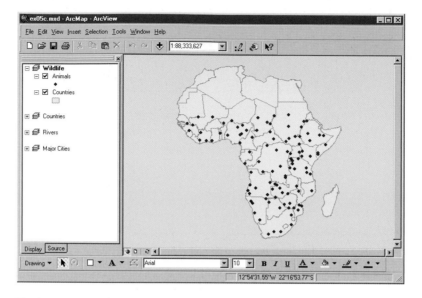

Each point in the Animals layer represents a significant population of elephants, giraffes, or zebras in the area around the point. Because the points have the same symbol, you can't tell which animal is which. You'll first symbolize the layer using an attribute of animal names, then you'll apply symbols for each type of animal.

5 Double-click on the Animals layer. On the Layer Properties dialog, click the Symbology tab. In the Show box, click Categories. Make sure the Unique Values option is highlighted.

The Value Field is already set to ANIMALNAME. Disregard the color scheme. You won't use it when you pick the animal symbols.

6 Click Add All Values. Values for elephants, giraffes, and zebras are added to the dialog. In the Symbol column, click the check box next to <all other values> to uncheck it. Make sure your dialog matches the following graphic, then click OK.

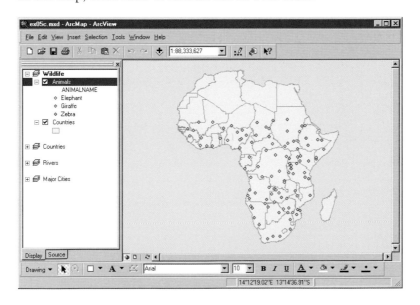

In the map, each kind of animal has its own color.

The map would be easier to read if the point symbols looked like the animals they represent.

7 In the table of contents, click on the point symbol next to Elephant. The Symbol Selector opens. If you scroll through the list of symbols, you'll find there's nothing that looks like an elephant.

8 Click More Symbols to display the list of styles.

When a style is loaded, it has a check mark beside it. By default, only the ESRI style and your personal style are loaded. (Your personal style is empty unless you've added symbols to it.)

9 Click the Conservation style to load it.

Symbols from the Conservation style are added below the ESRI symbols in the Symbol Selector. You can load as many styles in a map document as you want. The more you add, however, the longer it will take to scroll through the Symbol Selector.

10 Scroll to the bottom of the symbol box and click the Elephant symbol. In the Options frame, change the Size to **14** points. Click the Color square and click Delft Blue on the color palette. (The color palette now shows additional colors that belong to the Conservation style.) Click OK on the Symbol Selector dialog.

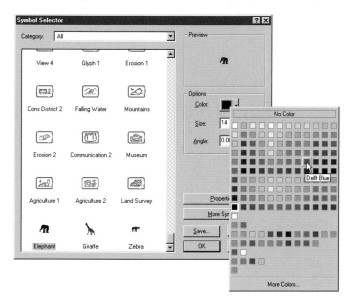

The elephant symbols are added to the map.

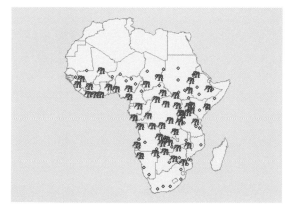

11 In the table of contents, click on the point symbol next to Giraffe. In the Symbol Selector, scroll to the bottom of the symbol box and click the Giraffe symbol.

12 In the Options frame, change the Size to **22**. Click the Color square and click Raw Umber on the color palette. Make sure your dialog matches the following graphic, then click OK in the Symbol Selector dialog to add the giraffe symbols to the map.

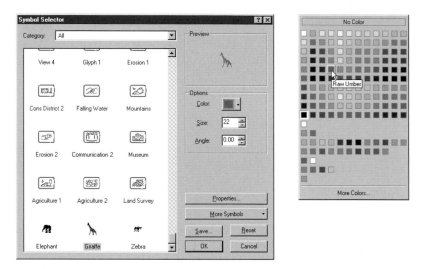

13 In the table of contents, click the Zebra symbol. In the Symbol Selector, scroll to the bottom of the symbol box and click the Zebra symbol. You'll leave its color black and its size 18 points. Click OK in the Symbol Selector dialog.

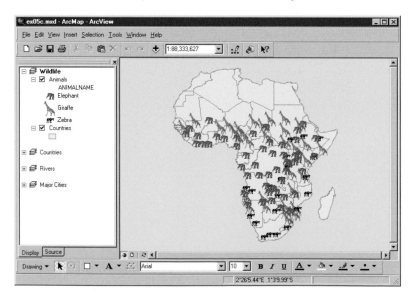

To use this Animals layer in another map—or send it to a colleague—without having to recreate the symbology, you can save it as a layer file.

14 In the table of contents, right-click on the Animals layer and click Save As Layer File.

15 In the Save Layer dialog, navigate to **C:\GTKArcGIS\Chapter05\MyData**. Accept the default file name of Animals.lyr. Make sure that your dialog matches the following graphic, then click Save.

The Animals layer file can now be added to any map. Because it references the Animals.shp shapefile, the shapefile must also be accessible on disk or across a network. If you send the layer file to someone else, you must also send the data source it references.

You'll check your progress on the poster.

16 Click the View menu and click Layout View.

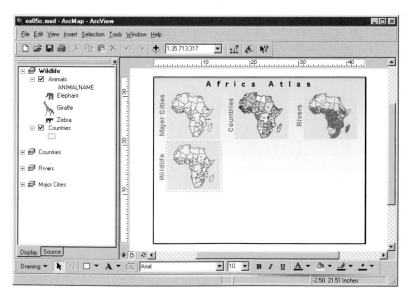

The poster is almost half finished. In the next exercise, you'll symbolize a raster data set of elevation.

17 If you want to save your work, click the File menu and click Save As. Navigate to **C:\GTKArcGIS\Chapter05\MyData**. Rename the file **my_ex05c.mxd** and click Save.

18 If you are continuing with the next exercise, leave ArcMap open. Otherwise, click the File menu and click Exit. Click No if prompted to save your changes.

Symbolizing rasters

In chapter 1, you learned that a raster is a matrix of identically sized square cells. Each cell in a raster stores a value, usually a quantity of something such as elevation, rainfall, or temperature, that has been measured at the location represented by the cell.

When you symbolize a raster, you assign colors to cell values or ranges of cell values. Raster values usually lie on a continuous scale, such as the scale of integers or real numbers, and are symbolized by color ramps.

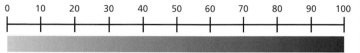

The shades of red in this color ramp become darker as the values increase from 0 to 100.

Rasters can represent many kinds of data and be symbolized with different color ramps.

From left to right: rasters of elevation, hillshade, and temperature for the same area. A hillshade raster shows an elevation surface in relief. It can be mathematically derived from an elevation raster by setting a certain angle and altitude of a light source.

Satellite images and aerial photographs are rasters in which the cell values are measurements of reflected light. Scanned maps are rasters in which the cell values are measurements made by the scanning device.

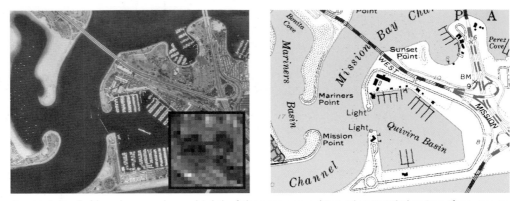

An air photo (left) and scanned map (right) of the area around San Diego's Mission Bay. If you zoom in close enough on any raster, its cell structure will be revealed, as shown by the inset in the red box.

You can display raster data in ArcGIS Desktop, but you cannot create it unless you have the ArcGIS Spatial Analyst extension. Raster data in many formats is available on the Internet and from commercial vendors.

Exercise 5d

The next map in your Africa Atlas poster will be a topographical map (one that shows elevation in relief) that includes both vector and raster data sets. Because the rasters take up a lot of disk space, your study area will be confined to the Greater Horn of Africa, which includes Somalia, Ethiopia, Eritrea, Djibouti, and parts of other countries.

1 Start ArcMap. In the ArcMap dialog, click the option to use an existing map. In the list of maps, double-click Browse for maps. (If ArcMap is already running, click the File menu and click Open.) Navigate to **C:\GTKArcGIS\Chapter05**. Click **ex05d.mxd** and click Open.

The map opens in layout view. You see the four data frames you've already symbolized and a fifth called Topography.

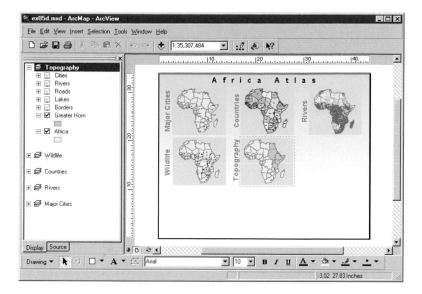

2 Click the View menu and click Data View.

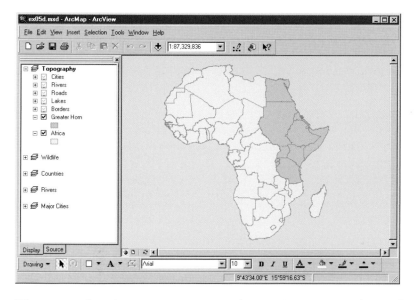

The active data frame contains seven layers. Countries in the study area are symbolized in orange. The Cities, Rivers, Roads, Lakes, and Borders layers are scale-dependent. You'll see them when you zoom in.

Now you'll add elevation and hillshade raster layers to the map.

3 On the Standard toolbar, click the Add Data button.

4 In the Add Data dialog, navigate to **C:\GTKArcGIS\Chapter05\Data**. Click on **afhorndem**. Hold down the Shift key and click on **afhornshd**. Make sure your dialog matches the following graphic, then click Add.

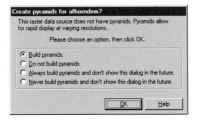

A message prompts you to create pyramids for afhorndem. By default, the option to build pyramids is selected.

5 Click OK to create pyramids for afhorndem.

When the process is finished, you're prompted to build pyramids for the other raster layer.

6 Click OK to create pyramids for afhornshd.

BUILDING PYRAMIDS

Pyramids are versions of a raster data set, varying from coarse to fine resolution, that are used to improve the drawing speed of raster layers as you zoom in or out. Coarse-resolution versions are used when you are zoomed at or near the full extent; finer-resolution versions are used as you zoom in. The coarseness of the resolution corresponds to the amount of detail you would expect to see at a given scale. You have to build pyramids only once for a raster data set. They are stored with the data as a file with extension .rrd. For more information, click the Contents tab in ArcGIS Desktop Help and navigate to *ArcMap > Working with rasters > Creating raster pyramids.*

The raster layers are added to the bottom of the table of contents. You'll rename them.

7 In the table of contents, double-click on the afhornshd layer. In the Layer Properties dialog, click the General tab. In the Layer Name text box, highlight the name afhornshd. Type **Hillshade** in its place.

8 Click OK.

9 In the table of contents, double-click on the afhorndem layer. In the Layer Properties dialog, click the General tab if necessary. Rename the layer **Elevation** and click OK.

To see the rasters, you need to change their position in the table of contents.

10 In the table of contents, click the Hillshade layer. Drag it above the Greater Horn layer. (As you drag, the current position of the layer is shown by a horizontal black bar.) Release the mouse button to drop the layer.

The Hillshade layer is repositioned in the table of contents and displays on the map.

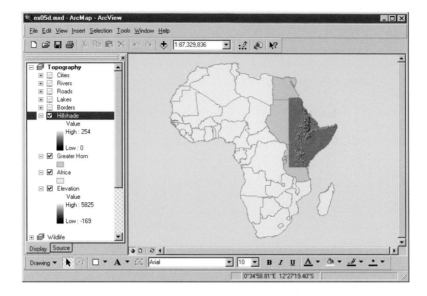

11 In the table of contents, drag the Elevation layer above the Hillshade layer.

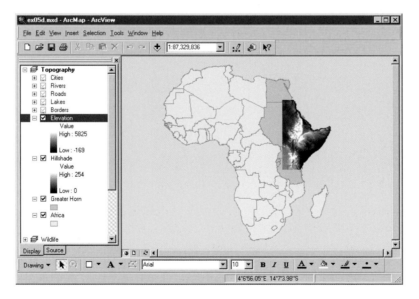

By default, rasters are drawn in shades of gray. You'll choose a different color ramp for the Elevation layer.

12 In the table of contents, right-click the Elevation layer and click Zoom to Layer. The map zooms in.

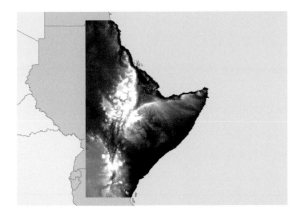

13 In the table of contents, double-click the Elevation layer. In the Layer Properties dialog, click the Symbology tab.

There are two symbology methods in the Show box: Stretched is the default. ArcMap makes subtle transitions along the selected color ramp, but doesn't give you precise information about which data values are associated with which shades of color. In the Classified method, color transitions are less subtle, but you can see exactly which value ranges correspond to which shades.

(If a raster layer has no more than 512 unique cell values, a Unique Values symbology method is available as well.)

14 In the Color Ramp drop-down list, right-click on the colors (not the drop-down arrow). On the context menu, click Graphic View to uncheck it. The color scheme is replaced by its name, Black to White.

15 Click the Color Ramp drop-down arrow. Scroll down to the Elevation #1 color ramp and click it. Right-click on the color ramp and click Graphic View to check it. Make sure the dialog matches the following graphic, then click OK in the Layer Properties dialog.

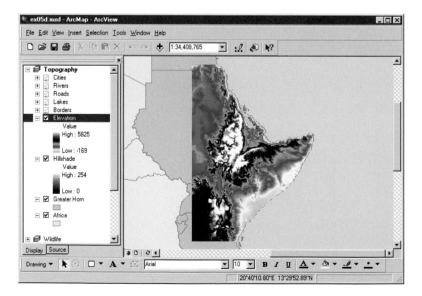

The Elevation #1 color ramp is applied to the layer. The colors grade from light blues at lower elevations through yellows, greens, oranges, and browns to gray and white at higher elevations.

To see surface relief you will make the Elevation layer partially transparent so that the Hillshade layer shows through.

16 Double-click the Elevation layer. In the Layer Properties dialog, click the Display tab. In the Transparent text box, highlight the default value of 0 and type **70**. The Elevation layer will be 70 percent transparent. Make sure your dialog matches the following graphic, then click OK.

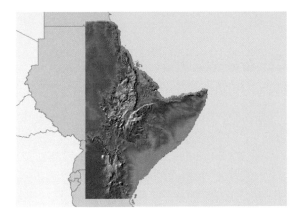

You now see both the elevation color ramp and the surface relief.

You'll zoom in to see the vector data displayed on top of the rasters.

17 Click the View menu, point to Bookmarks, and click Closeup 1. The map zooms in and the scale-dependent layers display.

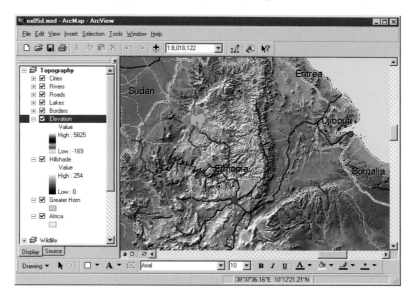

18 In the table of contents, right-click on the Elevation layer and click Zoom To Layer. The display zooms out to the Greater Horn.

You'll examine your progress on the Africa Atlas poster.

19 Click the View menu and click Layout View.

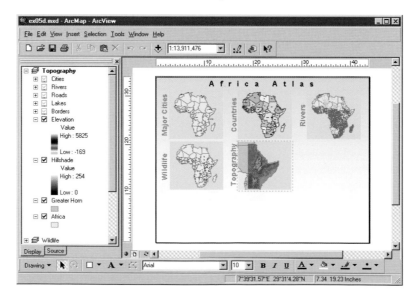

In the next chapter, you'll symbolize layers by quantitative attributes rather than categorical ones. You'll also learn how to classify data; that is, to adjust the value ranges to which symbols are applied. And you'll work with symbology methods that are used specifically with numeric data.

20 If you want to save your work, click the File menu and click Save As. Navigate to **C:\GTKArcGIS\Chapter05\MyData**. Rename the file **my_ex05d.mxd** and click Save.

21 If you are continuing to the next chapter, leave ArcMap open. Otherwise, click the File menu and click Exit. Click No when prompted to save your changes.

Classifying features and rasters

Classifying features by standard methods
Classifying features manually
Mapping density
Using graduated and chart symbols

With a few exceptions, like dates, feature attributes that are not categorical are quantitative—counted, measured, or estimated amounts of something. The population of a country, the length of a river, and the estimated size of an oil deposit are all quantitative attributes. Quantitative attributes are always numeric.

When you symbolize quantities, you want to see where attribute values lie in relation to one another on a continuous scale. Unless you are working with a very small range of values, the values must be divided into groups to make the symbology manageable. Dividing values into groups—or classes—requires that you choose both the number of classes and a method to determine where one class ends and another begins. Making these two decisions is called classifying data.

Because quantitative values are on a number scale (whether of integers, real numbers, or a specialized scale such as degrees Fahrenheit), the symbology applied to them is usually also scaled. ArcGIS has four ways to apply scaled symbology: by graduated color, graduated symbol, proportional symbol, and dot density.

Graduated color symbology, the most common, displays features as shades in a range of colors that changes gradually. The range is called a color ramp. If you symbolized the countries of Africa by population, each country would be drawn in a different shade of a color, such as blue, according to its population. Countries with large populations, like Nigeria, would be dark blue, while countries with small populations, like Djibouti, would be light blue. Graduated color symbology is most effective on polygon layers because subtle color differences are easier to detect on large features.

Graduated symbols represent features using different marker sizes. Normally used with point layers—to indicate, for instance, the population of a city—graduated symbols can also be used with lines or polygons. In the case of polygons, markers are drawn inside the features.

Proportional symbols vary in size proportionally to the value symbolized. For example, the marker for a city of 10,000,000 would be ten times larger than the marker for a city of 1,000,000 and one hundred times larger than the marker for a city of 100,000. Proportional symbols work best when the range of values for an attribute is not too wide.

Dot density, available for polygon layers only, represents quantities by a random pattern of dots. The greater the value, the more dots there are displayed within the feature boundary. Like proportional symbols, dot density maps convey quantities precisely because there is a fixed relationship between the number of dots and the attribute symbolized (for example, one dot equals 10,000 people). They can be misleading, however, because the random distribution of dots may be different from the actual distribution of values.

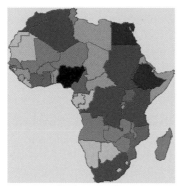

Graduated color

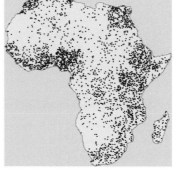

Dot density

Upper left, population by country: darker shades of red indicate larger populations.

Upper right, population density by country: dot clusters show densely populated countries.

Lower left, population for selected cities: each city falls into one of four population groups, and each group is assigned a different symbol size.

Lower right, population for selected cities: the size of the symbol is proportional to each city's population.

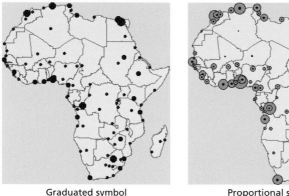

Graduated symbol

Proportional symbol

Classifying features by standard methods

ArcGIS has six classification methods: Natural Breaks (Jenks), Equal Interval, Defined Interval, Quantile, Standard Deviation, and Manual.

Natural Breaks is the default method. Developed by the cartographer George Jenks, it creates classes according to clusters and gaps in the data.

Equal Interval creates classes of equal value ranges. If the range of values is 1 to 100 and the number of classes is 4, this method will create classes from 1–25, 26–50, 51–75, and 76–100.

Defined Interval resembles Equal Interval except that the interval determines the number of classes rather than the other way around. If the range of values is 1 to 100, and you choose an interval of 10, this method will create 10 classes: 1–10, 11–20, 21–30, and so on.

Quantile creates classes containing equal numbers of features. If you choose 5 classes for a layer with 100 features, this method will create class breaks so that 20 features fall into each class. The value range varies from class to class.

Standard Deviation creates classes according to a specified number of standard deviations from the mean value.

With the Manual method, you can set whatever class breaks you like.

When you symbolize quantities, the maximum number of classes allowed by ArcGIS is 256.

Exercise 6a

In chapter 5, you created five maps for the Africa Atlas. You have four maps to complete. In this exercise, you'll make a population map and apply different classification methods and numbers of classes to it.

1 Start ArcMap. In the ArcMap dialog, click the option to use an existing map. In the list of existing maps, double-click Browse for maps. (If ArcMap is already running, click the File menu and click Open.) Navigate to **C:\GTKArcGIS\Chapter06**. Click **ex06a.mxd** and click Open.

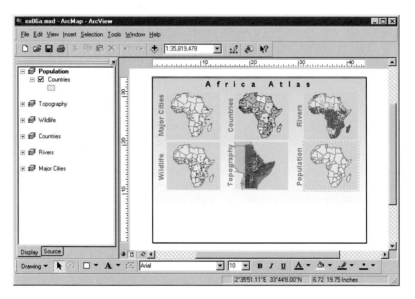

The map opens in layout view. You see five data frames you symbolized in chapter 5. The sixth data frame in the atlas is called Population. It has a dashed line around it because it is active. It is at the top of the table of contents.

CHAPTER 6 · CLASSIFYING FEATURES AND RASTERS

2 Click the View menu and click Data View.

3 In the table of contents, right-click the Countries layer (not the Countries data frame) and click Open Attribute Table.

FID	Shape*	NAME	KILOMETERS	POP1998	POP1994	POP2000	POP1980	Fl
0	Polygon	Algeria	2320972	27459230	24453010	30488943	18669010	
1	Polygon	Benin	116515	5175394	4593000	6487990	3464000	
2	Polygon	Botswana	580011	1446623	1217000	1700875	902000	
3	Polygon	Burkina Faso	273719	10164690	8776001	11814948	6962000	
4	Polygon	Burundi	27254	6011039	5299000	7374318	4114000	
5	Polygon	Cent Af Rep	621499	3149545	2951000	4007031	2320000	
6	Polygon	Chad	1168002	6308708	5537000	7296271	4477000	
7	Polygon	Congo	345430	2318276	2208000	3112338	1630000	
8	Polygon	Djibouti	21638	450751	409700	632718	300000	
9	Polygon	Egypt	982910	56133430	51390000	66851491	40792000	
10	Polygon	Eritrea	121941	3662271	3300000	4631792	2800400	
11	Polygon	Ethiopia	1132328	53142970	53400000	75512339	37717010	
12	Polygon	Gambia	10678	936026	848000	1187693	634000	
13	Polygon	Ghana	239981	16698090	14425000	20289781	10740000	
14	Polygon	Guinea	246077	6242007	5547000	7412033	4461000	
15	Polygon	Ivory Coast	322216	13498860	11713000	18533740	8194001	
16	Polygon	Kenya	584429	25835250	23277010	34492815	16632000	
17	Polygon	Lesotho	30352	1928269	1722000	2310857	1355000	
18	Polygon	Liberia	96296	2902441	2475000	3364289	1879000	

Record: 1   Show: All Selected   Records (0 out of 49 Selected.)   Options ▾

You'll use the POP2000 attribute because it has the most current data.

4 Right-click the POP2000 field name and click Sort Ascending. Scroll down through the table.

About half the countries have populations under ten million. Just a few have populations over forty million. Nigeria, with 161 million people, has more than double the population of Ethiopia.

5 Close the attribute table. In the table of contents, double-click the Countries layer name to open the Layer Properties dialog. Click the Symbology tab.

6 In the Show box, click Quantities.

The Graduated colors option of the Quantities method is highlighted and the dialog changes. The Value Field drop-down list shows the available attributes—numeric fields only.

7 Click the Value drop-down arrow and click POP2000.

By default, the values in the POP2000 field are grouped into five classes and the classification method is Natural Breaks.

8 If your color ramp is different from the one in the previous graphic, click the Color Ramp drop-down list and click the Yellow to Dark Red ramp. (To find it by name, right-click on the ramp and uncheck Graphic View.) Click OK in the Layer Properties dialog.

The symbology is applied to the map. The greater a country's population, the darker its color.

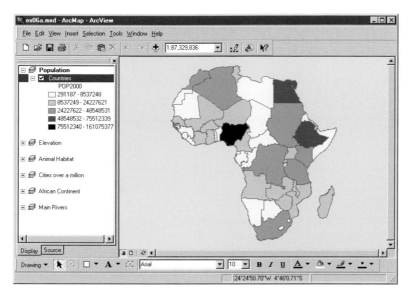

The number of features in each class is different. The class with the highest values has just one member: Nigeria. The next highest class has just two: Egypt and Ethiopia. The remaining 46 countries belong to the three lowest classes. This map shows that a few countries in Africa have much greater populations than the rest.

Your map has five classes but it might have more or fewer. It uses the Natural Breaks classification method, but could use one of the others.

9 In the table of contents, double-click the Countries layer to open the Layer Properties dialog. The Symbology tab is active.

10 Click the Classes drop-down arrow and click 3. The number of classes and their value ranges are adjusted. Click Apply and move the Layer Properties dialog away from the map display.

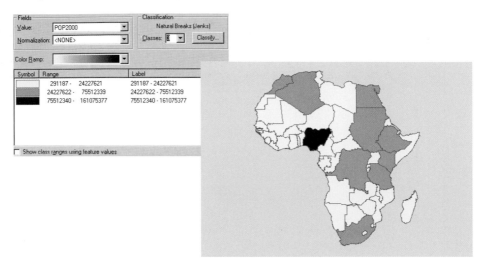

The map reflects the new classification. The highest population class still contains just a single country, but many countries that belonged to separate classes before are now grouped together. This map focuses attention on Nigeria as the most populous country on the continent.

11 On the Symbology tab, click Classify.

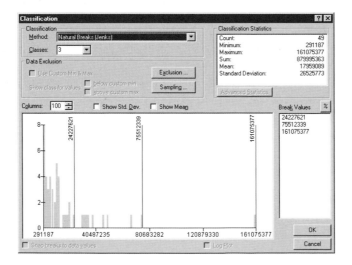

The Classification dialog displays the current classification method and the number of classes. You can also see statistics for the POP2000 field. The large window is a histogram, or frequency distribution chart.

UNDERSTANDING THE HISTOGRAM

The x-axis (horizontal) shows the range of values in the field. The y-axis (vertical) is a count of features. Vertical blue lines are class breaks (also shown in the Break Values box).

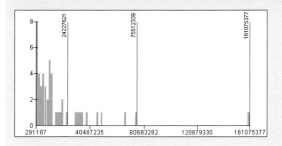

The gray columns represent percentages of the value range. The default number of gray columns is one hundred. In this case, the lowest value on the x-axis is 291,187 and the highest is 161,075,377. The value range is therefore 160,784,190, of which 1 percent (the amount represented by a single gray column) is 1,607,842.

The first gray column has a y-value of 8. This means that eight countries have populations under 1,899,029 (the start value of 291,187 plus 1,607,842). Another way to put it is that eight countries fall within the bottom 1 percent of the value range.

The second column has a y-value of 4. This means that four countries have populations over 1,899,029 but under 3,506,871 (1,899,029 plus 1,607,842). Cumulatively, twelve countries fall within the bottom 2 percent of the range.

The third column has a y-value of 3. Three countries have populations over 3,506,871 but under 5,114,713. Cumulatively, fifteen countries (of forty-nine total) fall within the bottom 3 percent of the range. The data is heavily skewed toward the low end.

A gray column isn't drawn if no features fall within the value range it would represent. The number of columns can be set to anything from ten to one hundred. With ten columns, for instance, each would represent 10 percent of the value range.

12 In the Columns box, highlight the default value of 100 and type **25**.

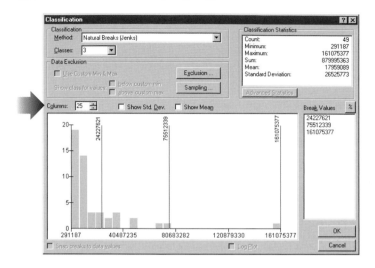

Now each gray column represents one twenty-fifth (or 4 percent) of the value range.

The histogram shows you where class breaks fall in relation to the data. The classification method is set to Natural Breaks (Jenks) where breaks reflect clusters in the data. For example, the population of Nigeria is more than twice that of any other country and is placed in a class by itself.

13 In the Classification frame, click the Method drop-down arrow and click Equal Interval. The class breaks are adjusted.

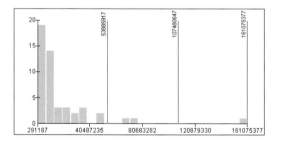

This method places breaks so that each class has the same range of values. In this case, almost all the values lie in the first class. Unlike Natural Breaks, it's possible with Equal Interval to have classes with no values in them. (You would see this if you increased the number of classes to four.)

14 Click the Method drop-down arrow and click Quantile.

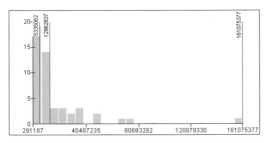

The Quantile method places breaks so that each class contains an approximately equal count of values. (In other words, each class includes about the same number of features.)

15 Click OK in the Classification dialog. The current classification settings are displayed on the Symbology tab. Click Apply and move the Layer Properties dialog away from the map display.

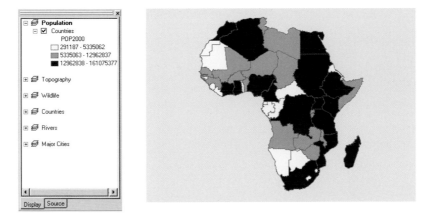

On the map, each population class includes a roughly equal number of countries. This map suggests—falsely—that countries with similar colors have similar population values. In fact, the value ranges for the three classes are very different.

For your final population map, you'll return to the Natural Breaks method.

16 On the Symbology tab, click Classify.

17 In the Classification dialog, click the Method drop-down arrow and click Natural Breaks (Jenks). Click the Classes drop-down arrow and click 7. Make sure your dialog matches the following graphic, then click OK.

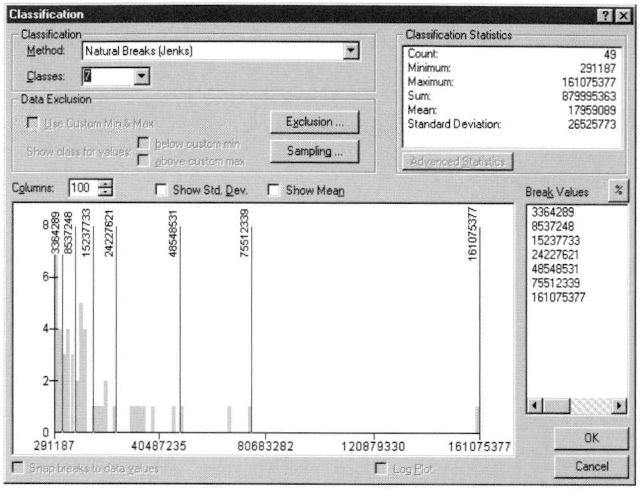

Before applying the changes to the map, you'll make the class labels easier to read by putting commas in.

18 On the lower portion of the Symbology tab, click the Label column heading and click Format Labels. The Number Format dialog opens.

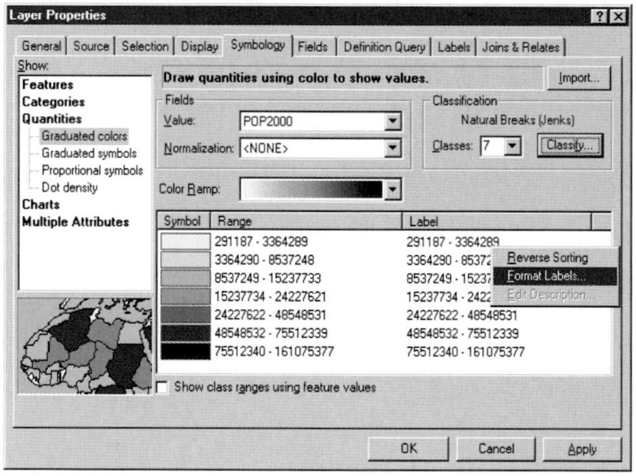

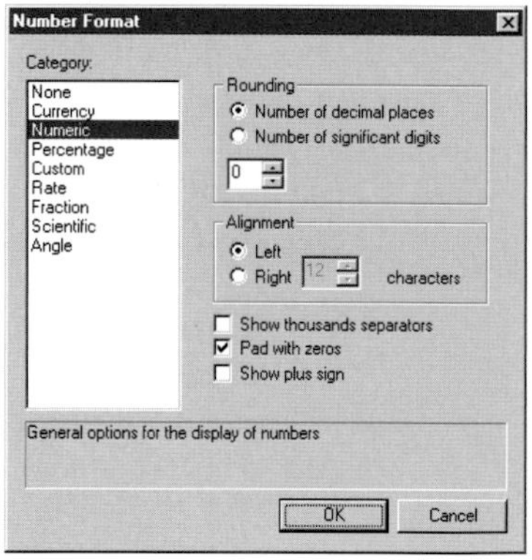

The Number Format dialog lets you adjust the formatting of numeric labels in many ways—you can control the number of decimal places displayed, insert commas to separate thousands, and change the alignment. You can also display numbers with special notation to indicate currency, percentages, and so on.

19 In the Number Format dialog, check the Show thousands separators check box. Click OK in the Number Format dialog.

20 At the bottom of the Symbology tab, click the check box to Show class ranges using feature values. Every class start and end now corresponds to a feature value. Make sure your Layer Properties dialog matches the following graphic, then click OK.

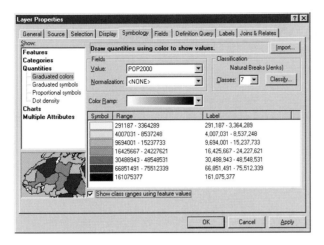

21 In the table of contents, scroll to the right, if necessary, to see the class ranges in their entirety.

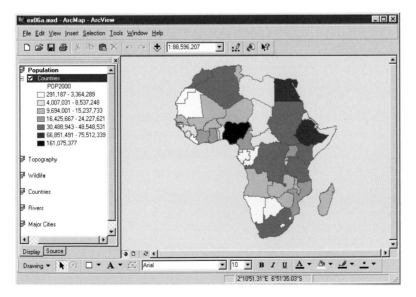

Countries are grouped with other countries that have similar populations. Nigeria remains in a class by itself. In the table of contents, the class breaks now indicate where there are gaps in the data. You can see, for instance, that there are no countries with populations between 49 and 66 million or between 76 and 161 million. The map is attractive and nicely represents an unevenly distributed data set.

You'll check your progress on the Africa Atlas poster.

22 Click the View menu and click Layout View.

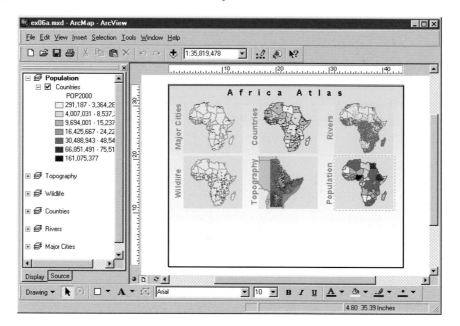

23 If you want to save your work, click the File menu and click Save As. Navigate to **C:\GTKArcGIS\Chapter06\MyData**. Rename the file **my_ex06a.mxd** and click Save.

24 If you are continuing with the next exercise, leave ArcMap open. Otherwise, click the File menu and click Exit. Click No if prompted to save your changes.

Classifying features manually

Manual classification is used to reveal significant groupings in data that standard classification methods miss. For example, a market researcher might want to distinguish census tracts in which the average household income is more than $100,000 a year or the 18 to 49 age group makes up a certain percentage of the population. To symbolize these values specifically, you would need to set class breaks manually.

Exercise 6b

In this exercise, you won't add a new map to the atlas. Instead, you'll make a refinement to the Topography map from chapter 5. You'll manually create a class to represent elevations below sea level.

1 Start ArcMap. In the ArcMap dialog, click the option to use an existing map. In the list of existing maps, double-click Browse for maps. (If ArcMap is already running, click the File menu and click Open.) Navigate to **C:\GTKArcGIS\Chapter06**. Click **ex06b.mxd** and click Open.

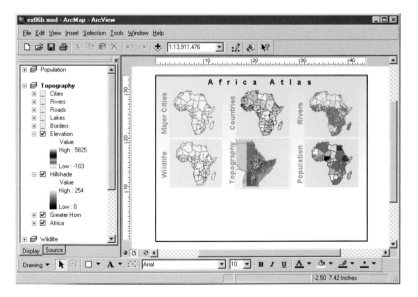

The map opens in layout view. You see the six data frames you've already symbolized.

2 Click the View menu and click Data View.

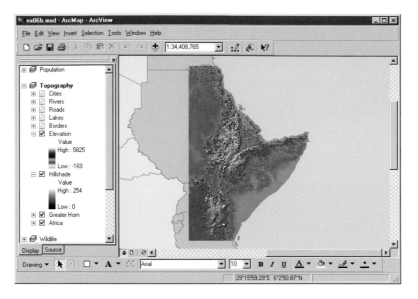

The Topography data frame is active. In the table of contents, you see that the elevation values range from a high of 5,825 to a low of −169 (in meters). You'll change the classification so that elevation values below sea level belong to their own class.

3 Click the View menu, point to Bookmarks, and click Elevation Area.

The map zooms in and the vector layers display. (The vector layers display at scales of 1:10,000,000 or larger. If you don't see them, zoom in.)

The area below sea level, outlined in yellow in the book (but not on your screen), lies along the northeastern border of Ethiopia and Eritrea.

4 In the table of contents, double-click the Elevation layer. In the Layer Properties dialog, click the Symbology tab.

To classify the values, you'll change the method to Classified.

5 In the Show box, click Classified.

By default, there are five classes and the classification method is Natural Breaks.

6 Click the Classes drop-down arrow and click 10. Right-click on the color ramp and uncheck Graphic View. Click the drop-down arrow, then scroll down and set the color ramp to Elevation #1.

The first class has a range of −169 to 287. You'll reset this break so that the class values range from −169 to 0.

7 Click Classify.

The histogram shows the distribution of values. The extreme high values belong to Mount Kilimanjaro.

8 In the Break Values box, click on the first value, 287, to highlight it. The blue line in the histogram corresponding to that value turns red. Type **0** and then click in the empty space at the bottom of the Break Values box.

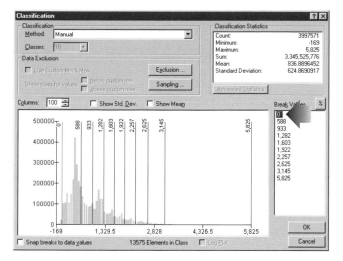

In the histogram, the class break moves to the left and is relabeled 0. In the Method drop-down list, the method automatically changes to Manual.

MANUAL CLASSIFICATION

Replacing values in the Break Values box is one way to adjust classes manually. You can also drag the blue class break lines in the histogram to new positions, right-click on a class break to delete it, or right-click in an empty part of the histogram to insert a new break.

To make sure that each class begins and ends with a value that exists in the attribute table, you can check Snap breaks to data values at the bottom of the Classification dialog. This usually results in gaps between classes, but more accurately describes the value distribution. For more information, click the Contents tab in ArcGIS Desktop Help and navigate to *ArcMap > Symbolizing your data > Setting a classification.*

9 Click OK in the Classification dialog. The Symbology tab is updated.

To make the areas below sea level show up better on the map, you'll symbolize them with a brighter color.

10 In the Symbol column, double-click on the light blue symbol assigned to the lowest elevation class. In the color palette, click Mars Red.

Finally, you'll format the labels. You don't need to show all those decimal places.

11 Click the Label column heading and click Format Labels. In the Rounding frame of the Number Format dialog, click the Number of decimal places option. Highlight the default value of 10 and type **0**. Make sure the Show thousands separators box is checked.

12 Click OK in the Number Format dialog. Make sure your Layer Properties dialog matches the following graphic, then click OK.

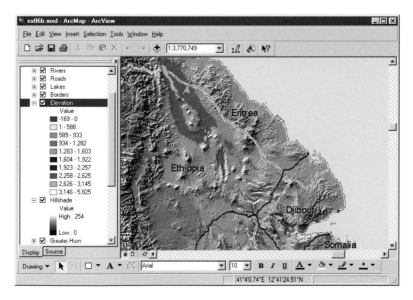

13 Click the View menu, point to Bookmarks, and click Below Sea Level. The area below sea level displays in red. (It isn't the bright red you may have expected, because the layer is 70 percent transparent.)

14 In the table of contents, right-click the Elevation layer and click Zoom To Layer.

The view zooms back to the scale that will be displayed on your poster. The areas below sea level are still visible.

You'll look at your Africa Atlas poster.

15 Click the View menu and click Layout View.

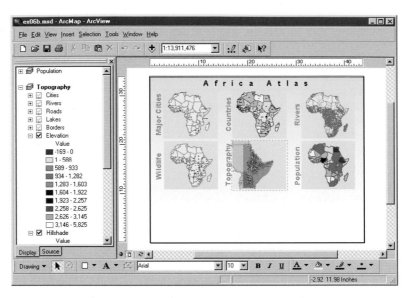

The poster is two-thirds finished. In the next exercise, you'll symbolize population density.

16 If you want to save your work, click the File menu and click Save As. Navigate to **C:\GTKArcGIS\Chapter06\MyData**. Rename the file **my_ex06b.mxd** and click Save.

17 If you are continuing with the next exercise, leave ArcMap open. Otherwise, click the File menu and click Exit. Click No if prompted to save your changes.

Mapping density

Nigeria has over 160,000,000 people. Rwanda has about 10,000,000. But which of the two is more densely populated? To answer that question, you would need to know the number of people per square unit of area. As long as you have both a population attribute and an area attribute, this is a straightforward operation—you simply divide population by area. Dividing one attribute by another to find the ratio between them is called *normalization*. It is commonly used to calculate density, but has other uses as well. For example, normalizing population by income gives income per capita.

Exercise 6c

In this exercise, you'll normalize population by area to make a population density map. You'll symbolize the map with graduated colors and by dot density.

1 Start ArcMap. In the ArcMap dialog, click the option to use an existing map. In the list of existing maps, double-click Browse for maps. (If ArcMap is already running, click the File menu and click Open.) Navigate to **C:\GTKArcGIS\Chapter06**. Click **ex06c.mxd** and click Open.

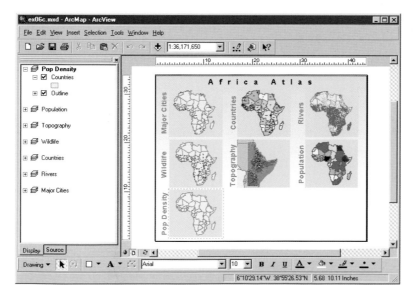

The seventh data frame in the Africa Atlas is called Pop Density.

2 Click the View menu and click Data View.

In the table of contents, the Population Density data frame is active.

3 In the table of contents, right-click the Countries layer (not the Countries data frame) and click Open Attribute Table.

The KILOMETERS attribute contains the size of each country in square kilometers. You'll divide the values in the POP2000 field by these values to obtain the population density of each country.

4 Close the table. Double-click the Countries layer to open the Layer Properties dialog. Click the Symbology tab.

5 In the Show box, click Quantities. The Graduated colors option is highlighted. In the Fields frame, click the Value drop-down arrow and click POP2000. Click the Normalization drop-down arrow and click KILOMETERS.

The values in the Range column now express population per square kilometer. In the Labels column, values are rounded, the default for normalized data.

6 If necessary, set the color ramp to Yellow to Dark Red. Click OK in the Layer Properties dialog.

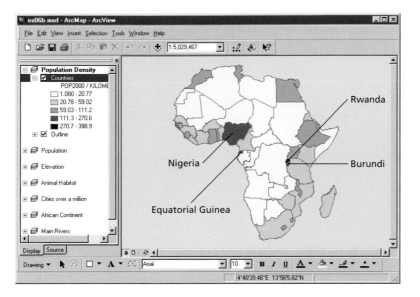

The class with the greatest population density again has a single member, but this time it's tiny Rwanda. The next highest class contains two other small countries, Burundi and Equatorial Guinea, along with Nigeria. Several countries with large populations turn out to have low population densities.

Graduated color maps are one way to represent density. Another way is with a dot density map.

7 Double-click the Countries layer to open the Layer Properties dialog. The Symbology tab is active.

8 In the Show box, click the Dot density option under Quantities.

On the left side of the Field Selection frame, numeric fields in the attribute table are listed in a box. You are symbolizing the POP2000 field.

9 Click POP2000 to highlight it. Click the right arrow symbol (>). The field is added to the box on the right side of the frame and a dot symbol is assigned to it. The color of your symbol may be different.

Next, you will set the symbol color for the dots. You will also turn the country outlines off to make the map easier to read.

10 In the symbol column, right-click the dot symbol. On the color palette, click **Gray 60%**.

11 In the Background frame, click the Line button.

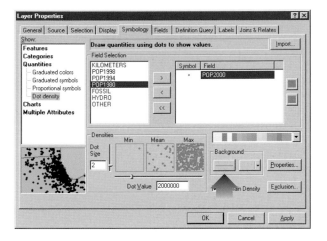

The Symbol Selector dialog opens.

12 In the Options frame of the Symbol Selector, click the Color square. On the color palette, click **No Color**. Click OK on the Symbol Selector dialog. This turns off the country outlines.

13 In the Densities frame of the Symbology tab, highlight the dot value (yours may be different from the one in the graphic) and type **750000**. The map will display one dot for every 750,000 people. Make sure the dialog matches the following graphic, then click OK.

The map shows, as you would expect, that the coastal countries of Africa are more densely populated than the interior.

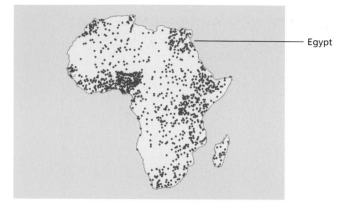

Egypt

Because the dot placement is random within each country, the arrangement of dots on your map won't match the graphic exactly. Dot density maps reveal meaningful overall patterns, but the random distribution of dots can be misleading if you focus on small areas. For example, the dots in Egypt are distributed throughout the country, when, in fact, almost all of Egypt's population lives along the Nile River.

CONTROLLING DOT PLACEMENT

Clicking Properties on the Symbology tab opens the Dot Density Symbol Properties dialog. By checking the Use Masking check box, you can specify either that dots be placed only within the mask area or that they be excluded from it. For example, you might use a lakes layer as a mask for a population density map to ensure that no dots were placed within lakes.

You'll check your progress on the Africa Atlas.

14 Click the View menu and click Layout View.

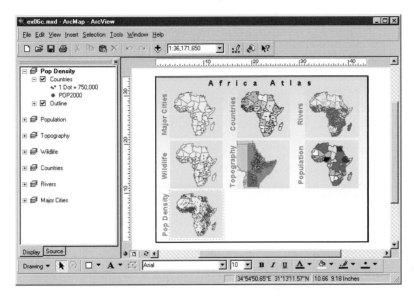

15 If you want to save your work, click the File menu and click Save As. Navigate to **C:\GTKArcGIS\Chapter06\MyData**. Rename the file **my_ex06c.mxd** and click Save.

16 If you are continuing with the next exercise, leave ArcMap open. Otherwise, click the File menu and click Exit. Click No if prompted to save your changes.

Using graduated and chart symbols

Graduated symbols use different marker sizes to represent features.

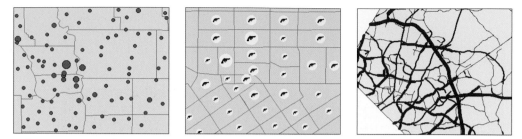

Left: a point layer of towns symbolized by population. Center: a polygon layer of neighborhoods symbolized by number of crimes. Right: a street layer symbolized by number of lanes per street.

Quantitative attributes are usually symbolized by one of the four Quantities options, but they can also be symbolized as Charts. This method allows you to symbolize several attributes at once by drawing pie, bar, or stacked bar charts on each feature in a layer.

Pie charts symbolize the percentages that various attributes contribute to a total. They might be used to show how much of a country's gross domestic product comes from agricultural production, industry, and services. They might show the percentages of a country's population that are 0 to 14 years old, 15 to 64, and 65 or older.

Bar charts compare attributes in cases where the values do not make up a whole. They might be used to compare a country's 1990 population to its 2000 population or income to spending.

Stacked bar charts represent the cumulative effect of attributes. For example, if you wanted to display the total number of personal communication devices in a country, you could symbolize the values for three different attributes—main-line telephones, cellular telephones, and computers with Internet access—as a stacked bar chart.

Exercise 6d

In this exercise you'll create the last two maps for the Africa Atlas. The first will use graduated symbols to show the size of diamond mines. The second will use pie charts to show the makeup of each country's electrical production.

1 Start ArcMap. In the ArcMap dialog, click the option to use an existing map. In the list of existing maps, double-click Browse for maps. (If ArcMap is already running, click the File menu and click Open.) Navigate to **C:\GTKArcGIS\Chapter06**. Click **ex06d.mxd** and click Open.

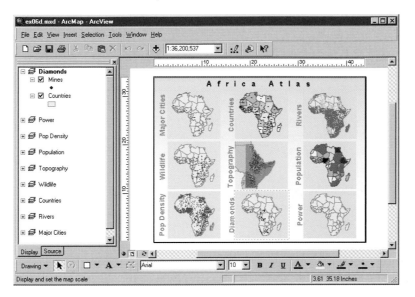

The last two data frames of the atlas will show the location of diamond mines and the sources of electric power.

2 Click the View menu and click Data View.

The points represent the locations of forty-eight diamond mines. Because all the point symbols are the same, you can't tell anything about the size of each mine.

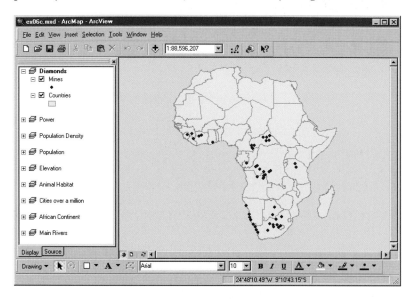

3 In the table of contents, right-click the Mines layer and click Open Attribute Table.

The layer attributes include the name of the mine, its size (small, medium, or large), and a SIZE_RANK field that translates the size values into numbers.

4 Close the table. In the table of contents, double-click the Mines layer to open the Layer Properties dialog. Click the Symbology tab.

CHAPTER 6 · CLASSIFYING FEATURES AND RASTERS

5 In the Show box, click Quantities, then click Graduated symbols.

6 In the Fields frame, click the Value drop-down arrow and click SIZE_RANK (the only numeric field in the table).

In the symbol column, three symbols appear. You'll change them to a symbol that looks more like a diamond.

exercise 6d

7 In the Template frame, click the point symbol to open the Symbol Selector.

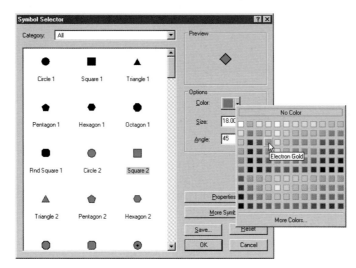

8 In the Symbol Selector, click the Square 2 symbol. In the Options frame, highlight the Angle value of 0.00 and type **45**. Click the Color square. On the color palette, click **Electron Gold**. Click OK in the Symbol Selector dialog.

The new symbols are applied on the Symbology tab.

You'll change the symbol sizes slightly.

9 In the Symbol Size from boxes, highlight 4 and change it to **6**. Highlight 18 and change it to **16**.

You'll also replace the numeric labels with descriptions.

10 In the Label column, click "1." An input box opens with the label highlighted in it. Type **Small** as the new label.

11 Press Enter to advance to the label "2" and replace it with **Medium**. Press Enter and replace the label "3" with **Large**. Click on some empty white space to close the last input box. Make sure the dialog matches the following graphic, then click OK.

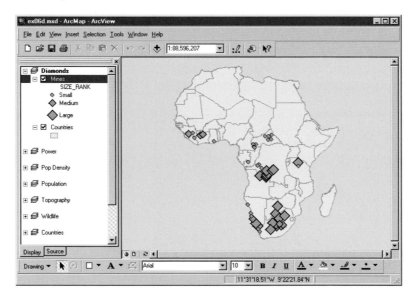

The map now shows the locations and sizes of diamond mines across the continent.

Now you'll use chart symbols to show the sources of electrical power in each country.

12 In the table of contents, click the minus sign by the Diamonds data frame. Right-click on the Power data frame and click Activate. Click the plus sign by the Power data frame.

13 Right-click the Countries layer and click Open Attribute Table. Scroll all the way to the right.

POP1994	POP2000	POP1980	FOSSIL	HYDRO	OTHER
24453010	30488943	18669010	99.77	0.23	0
4593000	6487990	3464000	100	0	0
1217000	1700875	902000	100	0	0
8776001	11814948	6962000	66.44	35.56	0
5299000	7374318	4114000	1.57	98.43	0
2951000	4007031	2320000	19.05	80.95	0
5537000	7296271	4477000	100	0	0
2208000	3112338	1630000	0.6	99.4	0
409700	632718	300000	100	0	0
51390000	66851491	40792000	78.72	21.28	0
3300000	4631792	2800400	100	0	0
53400000	75512339	37717010	7.35	89.34	3.31

Record: 1   Show: All Selected   Records (0 out of 49 Selected.)   Options

In addition to the name, size, and population attributes, three fields show what percentage of each country's electrical production comes from fossil fuels, hydro-electricity, and other means. You'll use pie charts to represent this data.

14 Close the table. Double-click the Countries layer to open the Layer Properties dialog. Click the Symbology tab.

15 In the Show box, click Charts. Make sure the Pie option is highlighted. The dialog changes to show the choices for pie charts. In the Field Selection frame, the box on the left shows all numeric attributes in the table.

Don't worry if your Background and Color Scheme settings are different.

16 In the box, click FOSSIL. Hold down the Shift key and click HYDRO and OTHER. When all three fields are selected, click the right arrow (>) to add them to the box on the right.

A symbol color is assigned to each attribute from the currently selected color scheme. You'll pick different colors.

17 In the Symbol column, right-click the FOSSIL symbol. In the color palette, click Mars Red. Right-click the HYDRO symbol and click Moorea Blue. Right-click the OTHER symbol and click Solar Yellow.

18 Click the Background color square to open the Symbol Selector.

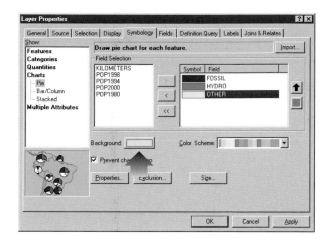

19 In the Options frame of the Symbol Selector, click the Fill Color square. On the color palette, click Sahara Sand. Click the Outline Color square. On the color palette, click Gray 40%. Make sure your dialog matches the following graphic, then click OK to return to the Layer Properties dialog.

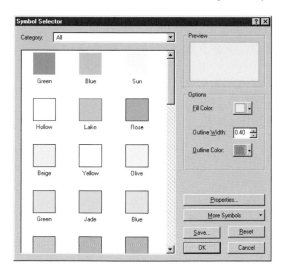

20 Near the bottom of the Symbology tab, click the Size button. The Pie Chart Size dialog opens. Highlight the default size of 32 points and type **16**.

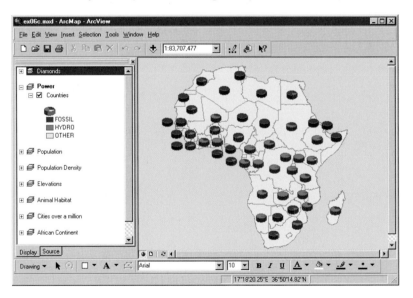

21 In the Pie Chart Size dialog, click OK. In the Layer Properties dialog, click Apply. Move the Layer Properties dialog away from the map.

Each country is displayed with a 3-D pie chart showing how much each energy source contributes to its production of electricity. On this map, the 3-D effect is a bit overwhelming.

22 Near the bottom of the Layer Properties dialog, click Properties to open the Chart Symbol Editor. In the 3-D frame, click the Display in 3-D check box to uncheck it. Make sure your dialog matches the following graphic, then click OK.

Removing the 3-D effect from the chart symbols will make them seem a little too large. (Click Apply if you want to check this.)

23 On the Symbology tab, click Size. In the Pie Chart Size dialog, highlight the current size of 16 points and type **12**. Click OK in the Pie Chart Size dialog and click OK in the Layer Properties dialog.

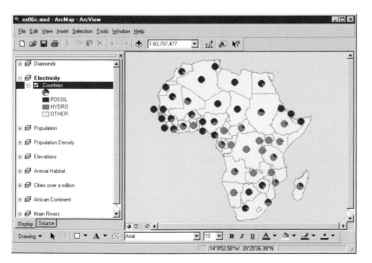

The map shows that in northern Africa (where oil is plentiful and water scarce) fossil fuels are the main source of electric power, while in central and southern Africa (where water is plentiful) power is generated chiefly by hydroelectricity.

It's time for a look at your finished poster.

24 Click the View menu and click Layout View.

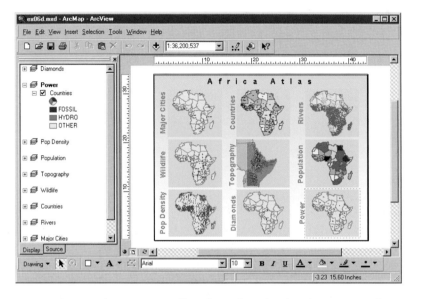

Your Africa Atlas poster will make a fine display for Geography Awareness Week. In the meantime, you can send it to a plotter or printer and hang it on your wall.

In the current map document, the map page size is set to E, 44 inches wide by 34 inches high. (You can confirm this by clicking the File menu and clicking Page Setup.) If you have access to a plotter, print this version. If not, you can make a letter-size version of the poster by printing the map document **letter_size.mxd** in the **C:\GTKArcGIS\Chapter06\Data** folder. Map elements in this document have been rescaled to fit a letter-size page. You'll find more information about printing maps in chapter 19.

25 If you want to save your work, click the File menu and click Save As. Navigate to **C:\GTKArcGIS\Chapter06\MyData**. Rename the file **my_ex06d.mxd** and click Save.

26 If you are continuing to the next chapter, leave ArcMap open. Otherwise, click the File menu and click Exit. Click No when prompted to save your changes.

Labeling features

Broadly speaking, a label is any text that names or describes a feature on a map, including proper names (Thailand, Trafalgar Square, Highway 30), generic names (Tundra, Hospital), descriptions (Residential, Hazardous), or numbers (7,000 placed on a mountain to indicate its elevation). In ArcMap, labels specifically represent values in a layer attribute table. You can add other bits of text to a map, but, strictly speaking, they are not labels. ArcMap has label styles for countries, cities, streets, and other common features. You can use these or choose your own fonts, sizes, and colors.

You can label all features in a layer at once and have ArcMap adjust the label placement as you work with the map. This is called dynamic labeling. You can set guidelines, but ArcMap chooses the exact label positions and changes them as you zoom, pan, or label additional layers. By default, ArcMap displays as many labels as it can without causing overlaps. Because overlaps are not allowed, labels that appear at one scale do not always appear at another. Dynamic labels cannot be selected or individually modified.

You can also label features one at a time in positions that you choose. This is called interactive labeling. The placement of interactive labels can be chosen by ArcMap or by you. Once placed, these labels can be selected, moved, and individually modified. ArcMap will not prevent overlaps or otherwise manage them.

Text added to a map behaves like an interactive label.

You can control the placement of dynamic labels by converting them to annotation. Annotation turns dynamic labels into text elements that can be individually moved and changed like interactive labels. Labels that have been converted to annotation can also be saved as a geodatabase feature class that is added to maps like any other data layer.

Using dynamic labels

Dynamic labels are easy to work with because they behave as a group. When you turn them on or off, change their symbols, or change the attribute value they express, these operations are applied to all labels in the layer. The drawback to dynamic labels is that ArcMap doesn't always put them just where you'd like. For this reason, they are usually converted to annotation in the late stages of map production.

In the following exercises, your map display will be redrawn many times as ArcMap adds and moves labels. If it fails to redraw as it should, click the Refresh View button at the bottom left corner of the map display.

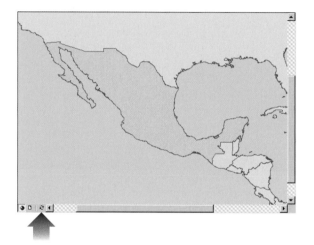

The positions ArcMap chooses for dynamic labels depend on many factors, including the size of your application window. Your results may be slightly different from those shown in the graphics.

Exercise 7a

You work for the Ministry of Tourism in Mexico and are making a map to promote travel in the southeastern states of Campeche, Chiapas, Quintana Roo, Tabasco, and Yucatán. The map will be published on the Internet, allowing map users worldwide to turn on various layers and navigate to different parts of the region, where beautiful beaches lie close to Mayan ruins. In this exercise, you'll label the five states and their major ruins. You'll also add text to the map.

1 Start ArcMap. In the ArcMap dialog, click the option to use an existing map. In the list of existing maps, double-click Browse for maps. (If ArcMap is already running, click the File menu and click Open.) Navigate to **C:\GTKArcGIS\Chapter07**. Click **ex07a.mxd** and click Open.

Mexico is shown in pink. The five states that will be on your tourist map are on the Yucatán peninsula in the southeast. You'll zoom in to them.

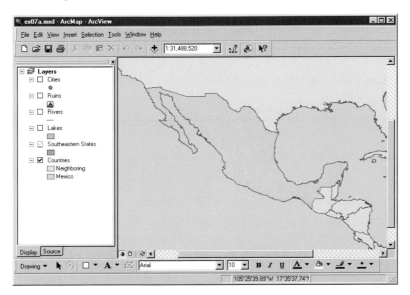

2 Click the View menu, point to Bookmarks, and click Southeastern States.

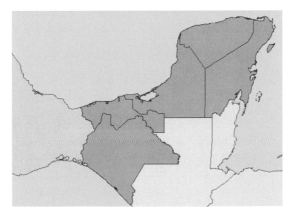

The Southeastern States layer displays only at scales larger than 1:20,000,000. You'll label the states in this layer dynamically.

3 In the table of contents, right-click the Southeastern States layer and click Label Features.

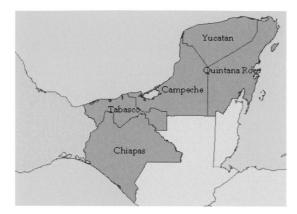

Each feature in the layer is labeled. ArcMap tries to put the labels in the center of each polygon. You'll change the font and color of the labels.

4 In the table of contents, right-click the Southeastern States layer and click Properties. On the Layer Properties dialog, click the Labels tab.

The Label Field drop-down list in the middle of the dialog shows you which field in the attribute table is being used for labels. Below this, the label symbology is previewed.

5 Click Symbol.

The Symbol Selector dialog opens.

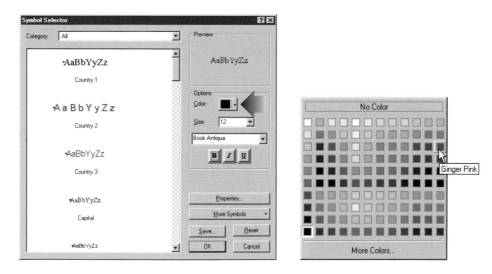

6 In the Options frame, click on the Color square. On the color palette, click Ginger Pink.

7 Click the drop-down arrow for setting the font. In the list of fonts, scroll up and click Arial.

8 In the Size drop-down list, click the default size of 12 and type **7** in its place.

9 Click the B (Boldface) button. Make sure that your dialog matches the following graphic, then click OK. Click OK in the Layer Properties dialog.

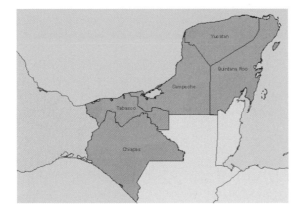

The new label properties are applied to the map.

Map readers would be better oriented if you labeled the Gulf of Mexico in the northwest part of the map. It so happens, however, that you don't have a layer of water bodies. The blue that represents water is simply the background color of the data frame. Since there is no Gulf of Mexico feature, there is nothing to label. Instead, you'll add text with the New Text tool.

10 On the Draw toolbar, click the New Text tool.

CHAPTER 7 • LABELING FEATURES

11 Move the mouse pointer over the map. The cursor changes to a crosshair with a "T." Click in the Gulf of Mexico to add a text box.

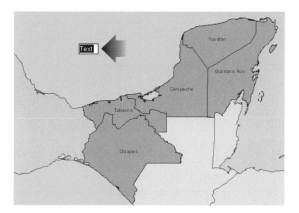

12 In the text box, type **Gulf of Mexico** and then press Enter.

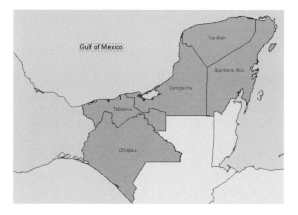

The text is drawn in Arial 10 point, as indicated on the Draw toolbar. The dashed blue line indicates that it's selected. You'll make the text larger.

13 Right-click on "Gulf of Mexico." On the context menu, click Properties. On the Properties dialog, click the Text tab and click Change Symbol.

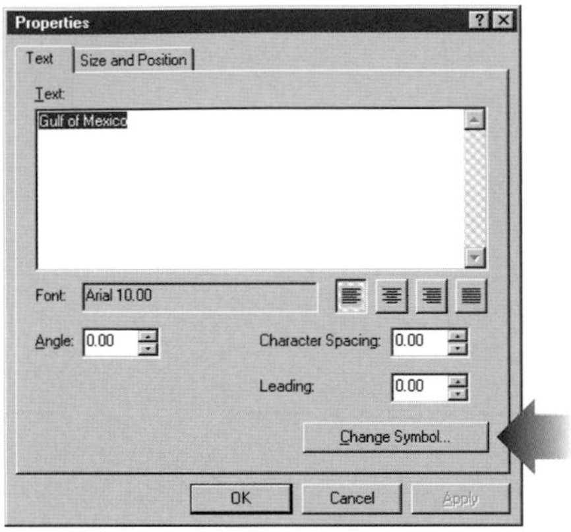

The Symbol Selector dialog opens.

14 In the Symbol Selector, scroll down until you see the predefined label style for Ocean, then click on it. Make sure that your dialog matches the following graphic, then click OK. Click OK again on the Properties dialog.

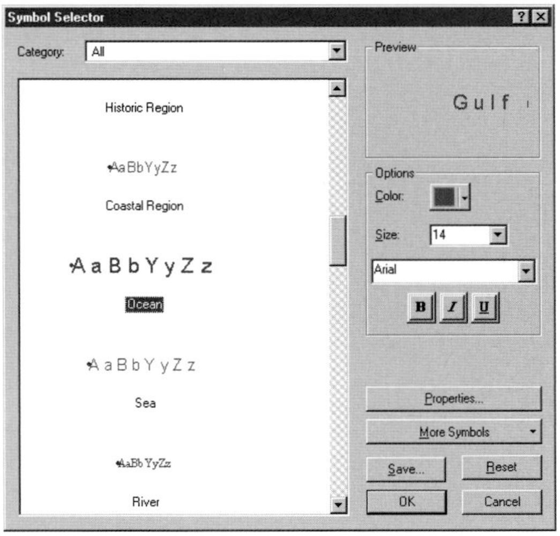

The new properties are applied to the text. Now that it's larger, the text may have to be moved.

15 Move the mouse pointer over the text. The cursor changes to a four-headed arrow. Drag the text so it matches the following graphic, then release the mouse button.

16 On the Tools toolbar, click the Select Elements tool. Click anywhere away from the selected text to unselect it.

Now you will display the locations of major Mayan ruins.

17 In the table of contents, turn on the Ruins layer.

These features have already been labeled to show when each ruin was built interesting, but less important for your map than the ruin's name. You will choose another field in the layer attribute table to use for labeling.

18 In the table of contents, right-click on the Ruins layer and click Properties. In the Layer Properties dialog, click the Labels tab. Click the Label Field drop-down arrow and click NAME. Make sure your dialog matches the following graphic, then click OK.

The ruins are now labeled with their names.

19 If you want to save your work, click the File menu and click Save As. Navigate to **C:\GTKArcGIS\Chapter07\MyData**. Rename the file **my_ex07a.mxd** and click Save.

20 If you are continuing with the next exercise, leave ArcMap open. Otherwise, click the File menu and click Exit. Click No if prompted to save your changes.

Setting rules for placing labels

ArcMap positions dynamic labels within guidelines that you set for it. Labels for points can occupy any of eight positions around the feature (above, below, above right, below right, and so on). You can prioritize these positions and prohibit particular ones. Labels for line features can be placed above, below, or on the features, and can be made to follow their curves. Labels for polygons don't have options—ArcMap places each label as close to the center of the polygon as it can.

Label priorities order the layers in a map by importance. If there isn't room to label two nearby features in different layers, only the feature in the layer with the higher priority will be labeled.

Exercise 7b

In this exercise, you will move the ruin labels and label rivers, which form a prominent part of the landscape. You'll also change the labeling priorities.

1 Start ArcMap. In the ArcMap dialog, click the option to use an existing map. In the list of existing maps, double-click Browse for maps. (If ArcMap is already running, click the File menu and click Open.) Navigate to **C:\GTKArcGIS\Chapter07**. Click **ex07b.mxd** and click Open.

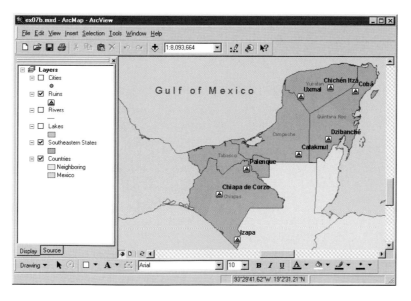

The map, zoomed in on the Yucatán region, looks as it did at the end of the last exercise. The ruin labels are not bad where they are, but might look better directly above the ruins.

2 In the table of contents, right-click the Ruins layer and click Properties. In the Layer Properties dialog, click the Labels tab.

3 Click Label Placement Options. In the Placement Properties dialog, click the Placement tab.

When labels are offset horizontally around points (the default), each possible position can be ranked. The graphic on the dialog shows the current setting. The feature is represented by the white square in the middle and the numbers in the surrounding squares rank each position—"1" is the most desirable and "3" the least. A "0" means that a label may not occupy that position. In the current setting, ArcMap places labels above and to the right of features as long as it can do so without overlapping other labels in any layer. All positions are allowed, although positions below and to the left of the feature are discouraged.

You want to center the labels above the features.

4 On the Placement Properties dialog, click Change Location to open the Initial point placement dialog.

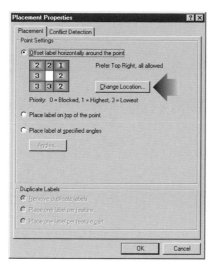 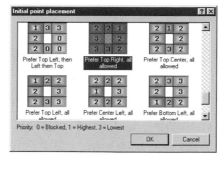

5 In the Initial point placement dialog, scroll up and click on the setting called Top Only, Prefer Center. Make sure that your dialog matches the following graphic, then click OK. Click OK on the Placement Properties dialog and click OK on the Layer Properties dialog.

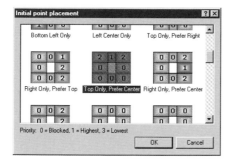

The ruin labels now appear directly above the features. If the map becomes crowded with other labels, the ruin labels will be shifted to the left or right of their current positions.

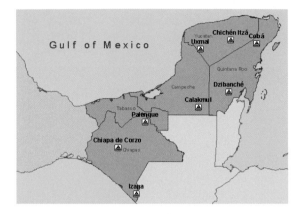

Now you'll turn on the Rivers and Lakes layers. When you do, ArcMap will move the Tabasco label to avoid overlapping a river.

6 In the table of contents, turn on the Rivers layer and the Lakes layer.

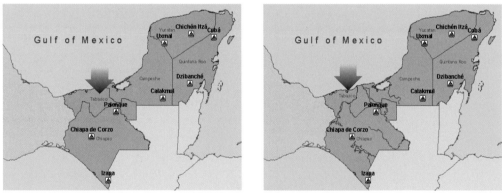

Before   After

7 In the table of contents, right-click on the Rivers layer and click Label Features.

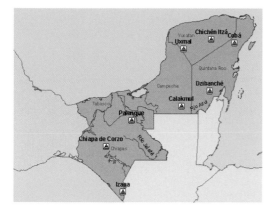

Only two rivers, Jalate and Azul, are labeled. Depending on the size of your ArcMap window, your results may be different. At this scale, more river labels can't be added without overlapping other labels.

To label more rivers, you'll change the label priority of the Rivers layer.

8 In the table of contents, right-click on the data frame name Layers and click Properties. The Data Frame Properties dialog opens. Click the Labels tab.

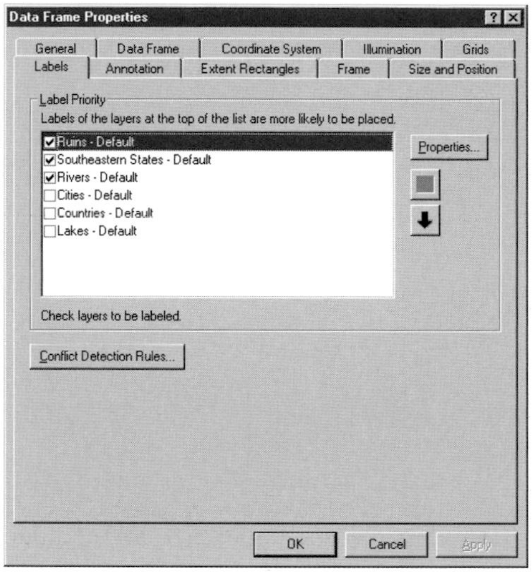

The Label Priority list shows all layers in the map. Layers with check marks are currently labeled. Layers are listed in order of labeling priority. You'll move the Rivers layer to the top.

9 In the Label Priority list, click on Rivers - Default. Click the up arrow twice to move the Rivers layer to the top of the list. Make sure your dialog matches the following graphic, then click OK.

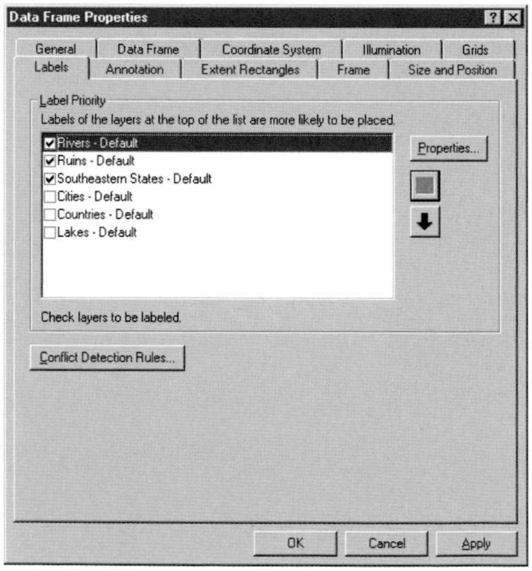

Moving the Rivers layer to the top of the list does not guarantee that all rivers will be labeled, but at least one more river, Mezcalapa, should be labeled.

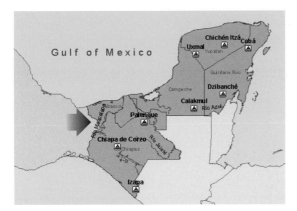

You'll make the river labels bold.

10 In the table of contents, right-click the Rivers layer and click Properties. On the Layer Properties dialog, click the Labels tab. Click Symbol.

11 In the Symbol Selector dialog, scroll down and click on the River label style. Click the B button to make the font bold. Make sure that your dialog matches the following graphic, then click OK. Click Apply on the Layer Properties dialog.

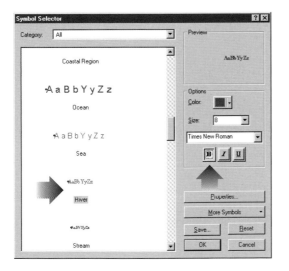

12 Move the Layer Properties dialog away from the map. The new properties are applied to the river labels.

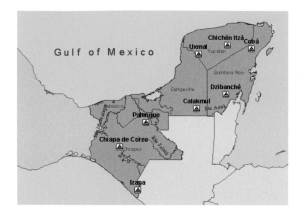

You'll make the labels follow the curves of the rivers.

13 On the Labels tab, click Label Placement Options.

14 In the Placement Properties dialog, click the Placement tab. On the Placement tab, click the check box to Produce labels that follow the curve of the line.

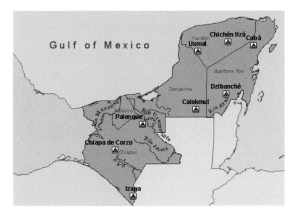

15 Click OK, then click OK on the Layer Properties dialog.

The river labels now follow the curves of the features. In addition, some rivers may be labeled that weren't labeled before and other labels may disappear.

At the present map scale, the river labels are starting to clutter the map. You'll make them scale-dependent so that you don't see them until you zoom in.

16 In the table of contents, right-click the Rivers layer and click Properties to open the Layer Properties dialog. Make sure the Labels tab is selected.

17 Click Scale Range to open the Scale Range dialog.

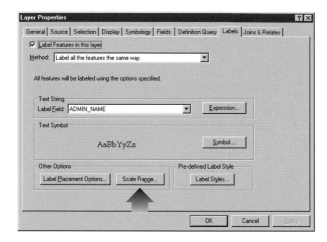

18 In the Scale Range dialog, click the Don't show labels when zoomed option. In the Out beyond 1 text box, type **3500000**. Make sure your dialog matches the following graphic, then click OK. Click OK in the Layer Properties dialog.

On the map, the river labels are no longer visible. They will be visible only at scales larger than 1:3,500,000. To see them, you'll zoom in to a bookmark.

19 Click the View menu, point to Bookmarks, and click Rivers.

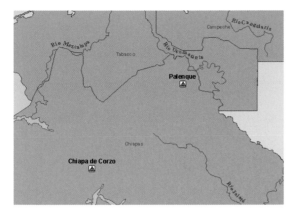

Now when tourists zoom in, they'll find the rivers labeled. When they zoom out, the river labels won't clutter the map.

20 If you want to save your work, click the File menu and click Save As. Navigate to **C:\GTKArcGIS\Chapter07\MyData**. Rename the file **my_ex07b.mxd** and click Save.

21 If you are continuing with the next exercise, leave ArcMap open. Otherwise, click the File menu and click Exit. Click No if prompted to save your changes.

Using interactive labels and creating annotation

Labeling interactively allows you to label only the features you want and to put labels exactly where you want them. Adding a label interactively is much like adding text—in fact, the Label tool is on the same drop-down tool palette as the text tools. The main difference is that labels come from values in an attribute table, whereas text is something you have to type.

You can combine the advantages of dynamic and interactive labeling by converting dynamic labels to annotation. Annotation is a set of text graphics that can be moved and symbolized individually, but that retains some group properties. For example, you can turn annotation for a layer on and off.

Annotation can also be saved as a feature class in a geodatabase. Suppose that you have carefully labeled a feature class of streets. Converting the labels to annotation and saving the annotation as a feature class will allow you to add the same labels to any map that contains the streets layer.

To move or resize labels in an annotation feature class, you start an editing session.

For more information about annotation, click the Contents tab in ArcGIS Desktop Help and navigate to *ArcMap > Labeling maps with text and graphics > About labeling*, and *ArcMap > Labeling maps with text and graphics > Organizing annotation into groups*, and *Working with geodatabases > Managing annotation*.

Exercise 7c

In this exercise, you'll label the city of Mérida, the regional capital. You'll also convert the labels for the Southeastern States layer to annotation.

1 Start ArcMap. In the ArcMap dialog, click the option to use an existing map. In the list of existing maps, double-click Browse for maps. (If ArcMap is already running, click the File menu and click Open.) Navigate to **C:\GTKArcGIS\Chapter07**. Click **ex07c.mxd** and click Open.

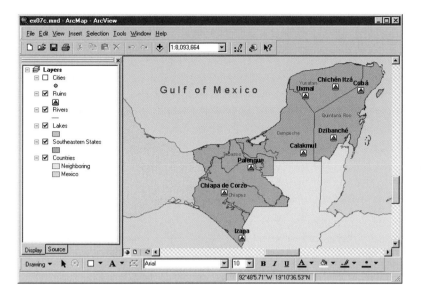

On the map, all layers except Cities are visible.

2 In the table of contents, turn on the Cities layer. The map shows major cities in the region.

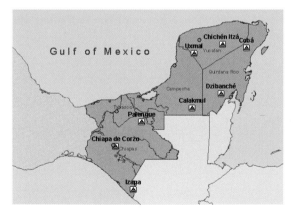

The northernmost city on the peninsula is Mérida. As the largest city in the region, and the one most tourists will fly into, it should have a label.

3 On the Draw toolbar, click the drop-down arrow by the New Text tool. On the palette of tools, click the Label tool.

The Labeling Options dialog opens.

The Placement frame has two options: you can let ArcMap choose the label position for you, or you can choose it yourself. You'll accept the default (Automatically find best placement) and adjust the position later.

4 Close the Labeling Options dialog. Locate the city of Mérida (map tips can help) and click to label it. If you miss and label the Yucatán region by mistake, press the Delete key, then click the Label tool and try again.

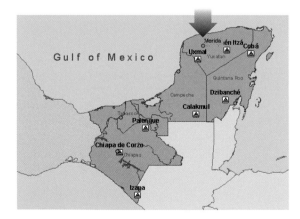

The label for Mérida obscures the label for the ruin of Chichén Itzá. You'll move it where it doesn't interfere with other labels.

5 On the Tools toolbar, click the Select Elements tool.

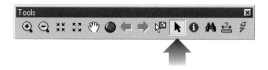

6 Move the mouse pointer over the Mérida label. The cursor changes to a four-headed arrow. Drag the label to a place just above and to the left of the point feature.

7 With the cursor over the Mérida label, right-click to open the context menu. On the context menu, point to Nudge and click Nudge Left. The label moves slightly to the left. Use the other Nudge options to put the label just where you want it.

The labels for Mérida and Chichén Itzá are both visible. (If you don't see both labels, you may need to enlarge your application window.)

8 Click somewhere away from the Mérida label to unselect it.

Some of the state labels are too close to cities or ruins. You'll convert them to annotation so that you can move them.

9 In the table of contents, right-click the Southeastern States layer and click Convert Labels to Annotation. The Convert Labels to Annotation dialog opens.

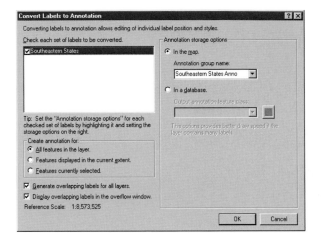

In the Annotation storage options frame, the option is set to store the annotation in the map rather than as a geodatabase feature class. This means that the labels will be converted to text graphics and saved in the map document. Other settings affect whether all or only some of the labels are converted and how overlapping labels are managed. You'll accept the defaults.

10 Click OK.

The labels are converted to annotation. In the process, their positions may change slightly and affect the display of other labels.

You'll move the labels for the states of Yucatán, Tabasco, and Chiapas to where they are less likely to be mistaken for the names of cities or ruins. Use the graphic following step 12 as a guide.

11 On the Tools toolbar, make sure the Select Elements tool is selected. Click on the Yucatán label and drag it to the southern part of the state.

12 Click on the Chiapas label and drag it slightly to the southeast. Click on the Tabasco label and drag it northwest across the river. Click somewhere away from the label to unselect it.

Your map is ready for review at the Ministry of Tourism. One benefit of maps published on the Internet is that users can turn layers on and off according to their interests. You may eventually want to add and label such layers as roads, minor ruins, resorts, and campgrounds.

13 If you want to save your work, click the File menu and click Save As. Navigate to **C:\GTKArcGIS\Chapter07\MyData**. Rename the file **my_ex07c.mxd** and click Save.

14 If you are continuing with the next chapter, leave ArcMap open. Otherwise, click the File menu and click Exit. Click No if prompted to save your changes.

Querying data

Identifying, selecting, finding, and hyperlinking features

Selecting features by attribute

Creating reports

A great strength of GIS is that it doesn't just show you where things are, it also tells you a lot about them. If you're curious about the road leading out of town, for example, you may be able to find out such things as its name, its length, its speed limit, and the number of lanes it has. If that road leads to a place like Carlisle, Pennsylvania, you might want to know the town's population (18,419), the median household income ($26,151), the median home value ($77,400), and many other things.

Much information about features can be conveyed by the way they are symbolized and labeled. But, for most features, it isn't possible to display everything that is known on a single map.

In ArcMap, there are several ways to retrieve unseen information about features. You can click on features to display their attributes. This is called identifying features. You can click on features to highlight them and look at their records in the layer attribute table. This is called selecting features interactively. You can write a query that automatically selects features meeting specific criteria (for example, three-bedroom houses with swimming pools). This is called selecting features by attributes. Or you can provide ArcMap with a piece of information, such as a name, and see which feature it belongs to. This is called finding features.

Attributes are not the only kind of information that can belong to a feature. Pictures, text documents, and Web pages can also be associated with features through hyperlinks. Clicking a hyperlinked feature opens a file on disk, points your Web browser to a URL, or runs a macro (a sequence of commands).

Identifying, selecting, finding, and hyperlinking features

The fastest way to get information about a single feature is to identify it. If you want to compare information about several features, the best way is to select the features on the map and look at their records in the layer attribute table. When you have a piece of information—a place name or address, for instance—but don't know which feature it belongs to, you can use the information to search the map for the feature.

Hyperlinks associate features with things that can't be stored as attribute values. A feature representing a government office, for example, could be linked to the office's Web page.

Exercise 8a

You are a real estate agent in Redlands, California. Many of your clients are new ESRI employees who have recently moved to the area. Your acquaintance with people in the industry helped you decide to use GIS in your own business.

Currently, you're working with a couple that has two children. They've asked to see properties in a neighborhood near the ESRI campus. They're looking for a three-bedroom house—preferably on a corner lot—and are willing to spend up to $175,000.

1 Start ArcMap. In the ArcMap dialog, click the option to use an existing map. In the list of existing maps, double-click Browse for maps. (If ArcMap is already running, click the File menu and click Open.) Navigate to **C:\GTKArcGIS\Chapter08**. Click **ex08a.mxd** and click Open.

The map shows local streets, land parcels in a neighborhood, and surrounding lots. The parcels are classified as either for sale or not for sale.

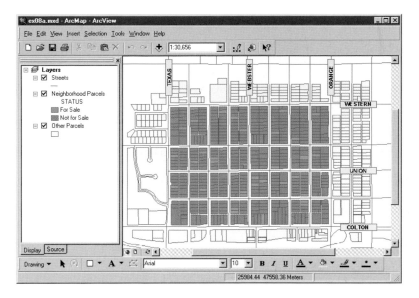

You will zoom in for a better look at the neighborhood and use the Identify tool to learn more about parcels that are for sale.

2 In the table of contents, right-click Neighborhood Parcels. On the context menu, click Zoom To Layer.

3 On the Tools toolbar, click the Identify tool.

4 On the map, click on one of the parcels for sale, such as the one in the following graphic. The Identify Results dialog opens.

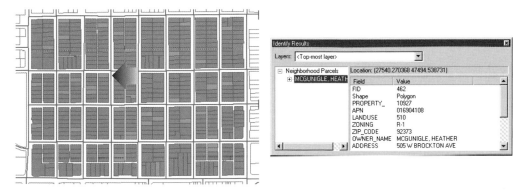

The scrolling box on the right side of the dialog displays the feature's attribute values. The box on the left tells you which layer is being identified (Neighborhood Parcels) and shows the value for the layer's primary display field (OWNER_NAME).

The Layers drop-down list at the top lets you pick the layer whose features you are identifying. By default, this is the topmost layer. (The topmost layer is the first one in the table of contents that contains a feature at the location you click.)

5 Click on a few more parcels for sale. The information in the Identify Results dialog changes.

Identifying features is the fastest way to get information about them, but it isn't convenient for comparing the attributes of several features. To do this, you'll select features on the map, then look at their records in the layer attribute table.

6 Close the Identify Results dialog. Click the Selection menu and click Set Selectable Layers.

By default, all layers are selectable. You want to select only features from the Neighborhood Parcels layer.

7 Uncheck the Streets and Other Parcels layers, as shown in the following graphic. Click Close.

8 Click the Selection menu and click Options.

In the Selection Options dialog, the selection tolerance is set to 3 pixels. Because you are working with small features that have many features adjacent to them, you'll reduce the tolerance. This ensures that when you click on a location, you won't select more than one feature at a time.

9 In the Selection tolerance box, replace the value of 3 with **0** as shown in the following graphic, then click OK.

10 Click the Selection menu, point to Interactive Selection Method, and click Add to Current Selection.

11 On the Tools toolbar, click the Select Features tool.

12 On the map, click on each of the eight corner parcels that are for sale. Each parcel you click on is added to the selection set. If you select a parcel by mistake, click the Selection menu, point to Interactive Selection Method, and click Remove From Current Selection. Then click on the selected parcel to unselect it. The ArcMap status bar shows how many parcels are selected.

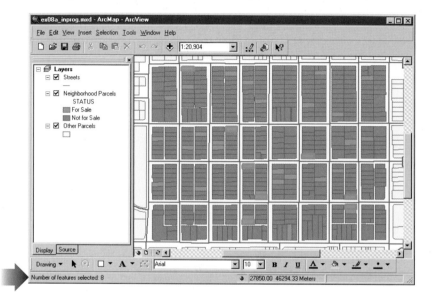

Selected parcels are outlined in cyan. In the attribute table for the layer, the records corresponding to the selected parcels are also highlighted.

13 Right-click Neighborhood Parcels and click Open Attribute Table. Scroll through the table until you see a highlighted record.

The records for selected parcels are highlighted but not grouped.

14 At the bottom of the attribute table, click Selected to show only the selected records.

15 Scroll through the table. You can now compare values like sales price or square footage for each house. Right-click on the SALE_PRICE field name. On the context menu, click Sort Descending.

Now the records are sorted in order from most expensive to least expensive. The first record shows a sales price of $166,500.

16 Click the gray tab to the left of the first record (the house at 901 Washington St.).

The record is highlighted in yellow as is the corresponding map feature. You may need to move the attribute table out of the way to see the highlighted feature.

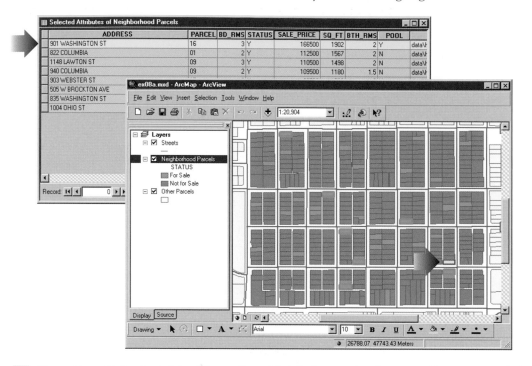

17 Close the attribute table. The yellow highlight on the feature disappears. Click the Selection menu and click Clear Selected Features.

CHANGING THE SELECTION COLOR FOR FEATURES AND RECORDS

The default selection colors can be changed. They can also be set independently for each layer in a map. For more information, click the Contents tab in ArcGIS Desktop Help and navigate to *ArcMap > Querying maps > Specifying how selected features highlight* and *ArcMap > Working with tables > Controlling a table's appearance*.

Attribute information is useful, but a photo conveys information that table attributes can't—such as whether a house is attractive to you. Pictures, documents, Web pages, and macros can be hyperlinked to features.

The attribute table of the Neighborhood Parcels layer has a field called IMAGE that contains paths to photographs of the three-bedroom corner houses that are for sale. You will tell ArcMap to hyperlink the features to the photos.

18 In the table of contents, double-click Neighborhood Parcels. In the Layer Properties dialog, click the Display tab.

19 Check Support Hyperlinks using field. Click the drop-down arrow and click IMAGE. By default, the hyperlink is to a document, rather than to a URL or macro. Make sure the dialog matches the following graphic, then click OK.

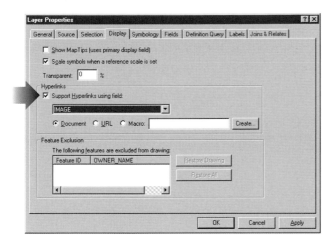

Now your clients can see photos of the properties before deciding whether to visit them.

20 On the Tools toolbar, click the Hyperlink tool.

On the map, hyperlinked features are outlined in blue.

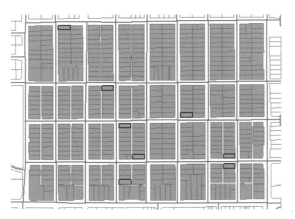

21 Click any hyperlinked feature to display a photo of the property. The photo opens in your default image-browsing software. After you look at it, close the application that opened it.

CREATING HYPERLINKS

There are two ways to create hyperlinks. One is to add document paths or URL addresses to a field in the layer attribute table. This is efficient if you are hyperlinking many features. The other way is to click on a feature and specify the document path or URL in a dialog. This is easier if you are just setting a few hyperlinks. It is also the only way that lets you hyperlink a feature to more than one object. For more information, click the Contents tab in ArcGIS Desktop Help and navigate to *ArcMap > Labeling maps with text and graphics > Map tips and hyperlinks.*

When you take your clients on a tour of the neighborhood, they see a house they like in spite of its not being on a corner. You jot down the address (831 Washington St.) so you can get more information back at the office. You'll use the Find tool to locate the house on the map and display its attributes.

22 On the Tools toolbar, click the Find tool to open the Find dialog.

23 In the Find dialog, click the Features tab. Type **831 Washington St** in the Find box. (Do not type a period after the "St" abbreviation.)

24 Click the In layers drop-down arrow and click Neighborhood Parcels. In the Search options, click In fields, then click the drop-down arrow and click ADDRESS. Make sure the dialog matches the following graphic, then click Find.

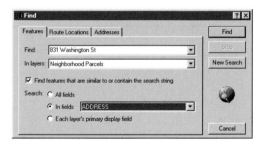

ArcMap searches the ADDRESS field of the Neighborhood Parcels attribute table for "831 Washington St" and displays the matching record.

Now that you've found the feature, you can locate it on the map and get its attributes.

25 Move the Find dialog away from the map but where you can still see it. Right-click on 831 WASHINGTON ST at the bottom of the dialog. On the context menu, click Identify feature(s).

The parcel flashes briefly in the lower right corner of the map and the Identify Results dialog opens. (If the Identify Results dialog covers the parcel, move it and repeat step 25.)

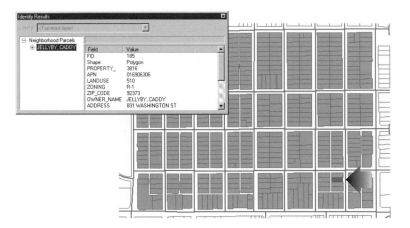

26 In the Identify Results dialog, scroll down to find the price and number of bedrooms. Scan the other attribute values. When you finish, close the Identify Results dialog and the Find dialog.

The house has three bedrooms, two-and-a-half bathrooms, and a swimming pool for an asking price of $159,900. It sounds great, and your clients are now willing to consider other houses that aren't on corners.

27 If you want to save your work, click the File menu and click Save As. Navigate to **C:\GTKArcGIS\Chapter08\MyData**. Rename the file **my_ex08a.mxd** and click Save.

28 If you are continuing with the next exercise, leave ArcMap open. Otherwise, click the File menu and click Exit. Click No if prompted to save your changes.

Selecting features by attribute

Interactive selection works when you can see what you're looking for on the map—corner lots, for instance. To select features according to qualities that you can't see on the map (such as having three bedrooms and a sale price under $175,000), you write a query.

A query selects features that meet specified conditions. The simplest query consists of an attribute (such as number of bedrooms), a value (such as three), and a relationship between them (such as "equal to"). Complex queries can be created by connecting simple queries with terms like "and" and "or."

Queries are not written in ordinary English but in Structured Query Language (SQL™). All you need to do, however, is open a dialog and click the attributes, values, and operators you want. ArcMap creates the query. There is also a Query Wizard that lets you write queries by choosing from drop-down lists.

Exercise 8b

Although your clients like the house at 831 Washington, they see no reason not to search a little further. You will help them select all three-bedroom houses in the neighborhood that have a sale price under $175,000.

1 Start ArcMap. In the ArcMap dialog, click the option to use an existing map. In the list of existing maps, double-click Browse for maps. (If ArcMap is already running, click the File menu and click Open.) Navigate to **C:\GTKArcGIS\Chapter08**. Click **ex08b.mxd** and click Open. Click No if you are prompted to save changes to an open document.

The map of neighborhood parcels displays.

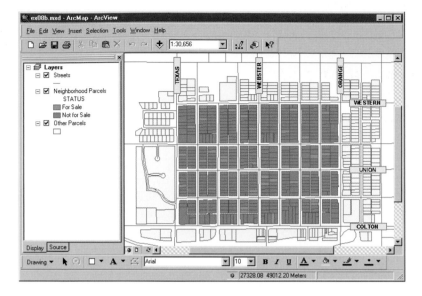

2 Click the Selection menu and click Select by Attributes. In the Select By Attributes dialog, click the Layer drop-down arrow and click Neighborhood Parcels.

The fields in the attribute table appear in the Fields scrolling box on the left of the dialog. When a field is highlighted, sample values display in the Unique values list on the right. (To see all values, click the Complete List button.) The buttons in the middle are used to choose operators and to connect queries.

The first condition you want to test is whether a house is for sale. Houses for sale have a STATUS of 'Y'.

3 In the Fields list, double-click "STATUS". Click the Equals (=) button. In the Unique sample values list, double-click 'Y'. The query is added to the expression box.

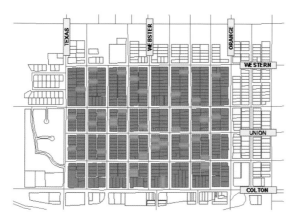

When you apply the query, ArcMap searches the attribute table for records that have 'Y' in the STATUS field. The corresponding features are selected on the map.

4 Click Apply and move the dialog out of the way. On the map, parcels that are for sale are selected.

You already knew which parcels were for sale from the layer symbology. You'll make the query more complex so that only three-bedroom houses for sale are selected.

5 In the Select By Attributes dialog, click the And button. In the Fields list, double-click "BD_RMS". Click the Equals (=) button. In the Unique sample values list, double-click 3. Your query should match the following graphic.

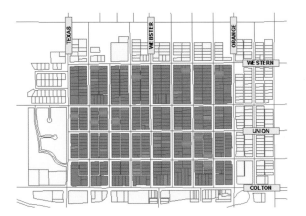

Records will be selected only if they have 'Y' in the STATUS field and 3 in the BD_RMS field.

6 Click Apply. On the map, fewer houses are selected because fewer satisfy both conditions.

You will add one more condition to the query.

7 In the Select By Attributes dialog, click the And button. In the Fields list, double-click "SALE_PRICE". Click the Less than (<) button. In the query box, press the space bar and type **175000**. Your query should match the following graphic.

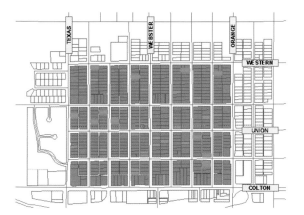

In the attribute table, only records with 'Y' in the STATUS field, 3 in the BD_RMS field, and a number less than 175000 in the SALE_PRICE field are selected.

8 Click Apply. On the map, one of the houses is unselected because its price was too high.

Eleven parcels are selected, including the house at 831 Washington and two corner lots from the original list. In the next exercise, you will make a report of the query results that your clients can take with them.

9 In the Select By Attributes dialog, click Clear to remove the query from the box. Click Close.

10 If you want to save your work, click the File menu and click Save As. Navigate to **C:\GTKArcGIS\Chapter08\MyData**. Rename the file **my_ex08b.mxd** and click Save.

11 If you are continuing with the next exercise, leave ArcMap open. Otherwise, click the File menu and click Exit. Click No if prompted to save your changes.

Creating reports

Reports let you organize, format, and print the information contained in an attribute table. ArcMap's built-in report generator, which you'll use in this exercise, allows you to create simple reports that can be added to a map layout as an alternative to adding a table. When you need to create more detailed reports that won't appear on a map, you can use Seagate® Crystal Reports™. This report-creation software comes with ArcGIS Desktop but is not automatically installed with ArcGIS.

Exercise 8c

In the last exercise, you selected eleven houses that met your clients' conditions. In this exercise, you will create a report they can take when they go to look at these houses.

1 Start ArcMap. In the ArcMap dialog, click the option to use an existing map. In the list of existing maps, double-click Browse for maps. (If ArcMap is running, click the File menu and click Open.) Navigate to **C:\GTKArcGIS\Chapter08**. Click **ex08c.mxd** to highlight it and click Open. Click No if you are prompted to save changes to an open document.

The map with eleven selected parcels displays.

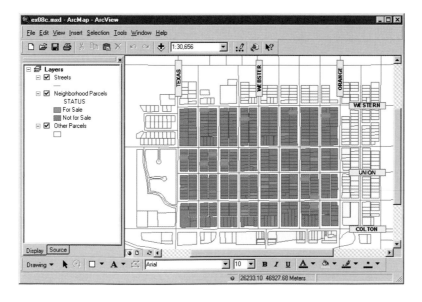

2 Click the Tools menu, point to Reports, and click Create Report. The Report Properties dialog opens with the Fields tab selected.

The Layer/Table drop-down list specifies the layer or table you will work with. The Available Fields scrolling box lets you choose the attributes to include in the report.

3 Click the Layer/Table drop-down arrow and click Neighborhood Parcels.

Your clients will want to have street addresses and information on sale price, square footage, and number of bathrooms. You don't need to include the number of bedrooms—all the houses are known to have three.

4 In the Available Fields list, click ADDRESS. Click the Add fields button (right arrow) in the middle of the dialog. The ADDRESS field moves from the Available Fields list to the Report Fields list.

The ADDRESS field also appears in the Report Viewer Contents Field drop-down list. That means it will be displayed when you preview the report.

5 In the Available Fields list, double-click SALE_PRICE to add it to the Report Fields list. Do the same for the SQ_FT and BTH_RMS fields. Since you want the report to contain data only for the eleven selected parcels, make sure the Use Selected Set check box is checked.

Next, you will use the Sorting tab to arrange the eleven lots according to sale price.

6 Click the Sorting tab. In the Sort column, click the SALE_PRICE value of None and click Ascending from the popup list. In the report, the houses will appear from least expensive to most expensive.

Next, you will change the default appearance of the report.

7 Click the Display tab.

Report settings are grouped in categories (such as Report, Elements, and Background) in the Settings window on the left. Each setting has several properties. For example, the Field Names setting has properties for Border, Font, Height, and so on. Each property, in turn, has several possible values. For example, a font may be Times New Roman, Arial, Courier, or something else.

By default, the Elements setting is displayed and the Field Names element is checked. This means that the field names you added will be displayed in the report.

You will give the report a title and make the title bigger.

8 Under Elements, check Title. In the right-hand window, title properties and their values display. Click on the Report Title value. In the pop-up text box, replace the text with **Available Three Bedroom Houses**. Make sure the dialog matches the following graphic, then click on Text in the Property column to close the text box.

9 Click on the Times New Roman value. An Ellipsis button (...) appears at the right edge of the column.

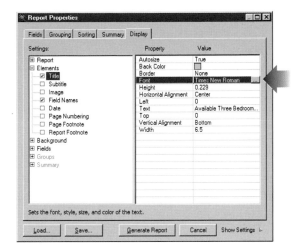

10 Click the Ellipsis button to open the Font dialog. In the Size scrolling box, click 26.

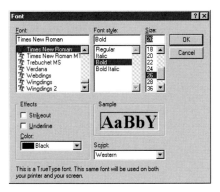

11 Click OK.

Because the address information in your report is long, you'll widen the Address field.

12 In the Settings box, click the plus sign next to Fields, then click ADDRESS. Click the Width value of 1.184 and replace it with **3** to allow three inches for addresses on the printed page. Press the Enter key.

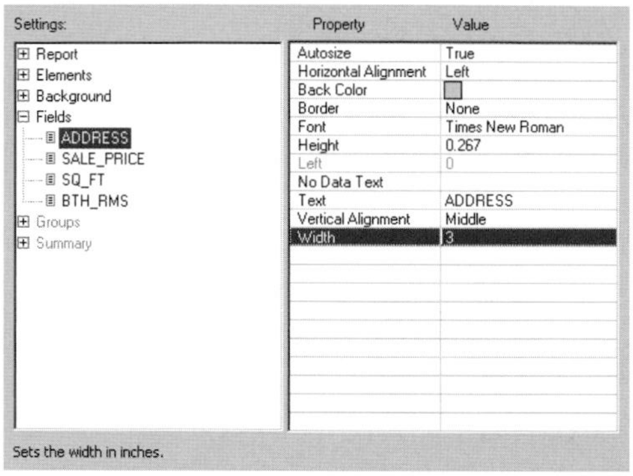

With the additional width, the report will probably look better if you change the page orientation from portrait (vertical) to landscape (horizontal).

13 In the Settings box, click the plus sign next to Report. Click the Page Setup property. An Ellipsis button appears at the edge of the Value column.

14 Click the Ellipsis button to open the Page Setup dialog. In the Orientation frame, click Landscape, as shown in the following graphic, then click OK.

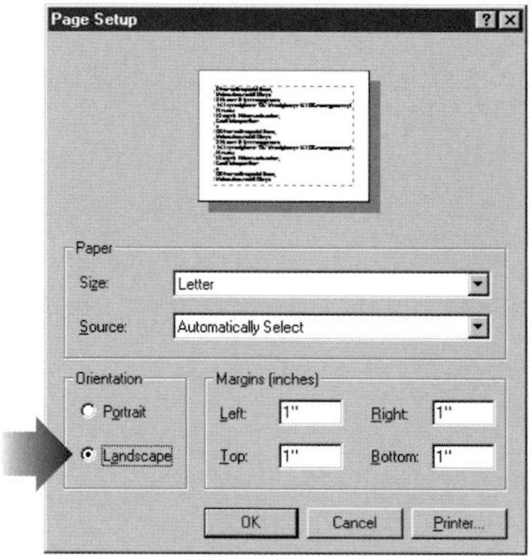

You are ready to preview the results.

15 At the bottom of the Report Properties dialog, click Generate Report.

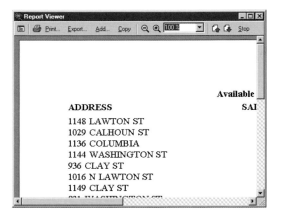

The size of your dialog may be different, but you probably can't see the whole report. The drop-down list at the top of the dialog lets you change the preview scale. (It doesn't change the printed size of the report.)

16 Click the drop-down arrow and click 50%. If necessary, resize the window to see the entire report.

If your computer is connected to a printer, you can print the report.

17 At the top of the dialog, click the Print button.

18 Click OK to print the report.

19 Close the Report Viewer dialog. On the Report Properties dialog, click Close.

You are prompted to save the report.

20 If you want to save the report, click Yes. In the Save Report dialog, navigate to **C:\GTKArcGIS\Chapter08\MyData**. Name the file **my_report** and click Save. If you don't want to save the report, click No.

There is no need to save the map document. You haven't made any changes to it.

ADDING REPORTS TO LAYOUTS

Within a map document, you can add a report to a layout by clicking the Add button in the Report Viewer dialog. If you have saved a report to disk, you can add it to any map layout by loading it from the Report Properties dialog. For more information, click the Contents tab in ArcGIS Desktop Help and navigate to *ArcMap > Creating reports > Creating a simple report* and *ArcMap > Creating reports > Saving and loading a report*.

---

21 If you are continuing with the next chapter, leave ArcMap open. Otherwise, click the File menu and click Exit. Click No if prompted to save your changes.

Joining and relating tables

Joining tables
Relating tables

In chapter 8, you learned how to get information from a layer attribute table. More information is available about most features, however, than is found in the attribute table. A world countries layer might have attributes like name, area, and population, but these are just a few kinds of information you might want to show on a map. Additional data—demographic, economic, cultural, physical—is available as tables from many sources. You can also create your own tables from information in atlases or fact books. These tables, which have no spatial properties themselves, can be associated with the layer attribute table. The information they contain can then be used to query and symbolize maps.

To associate a nonspatial table with a layer attribute table, there must be a way to match records in one with appropriate records in the other. This is done with an attribute common to both tables, such as a name or identification code.

Tables can be associated in one of two ways: they can be joined or related. A table join appends the attributes of the nonspatial table to the layer attribute table. A table relate does not append attributes. Instead, you select records in the layer attribute table to see the matching records in the nonspatial table. (Or you can do it the other way around—it works both ways.) Whether you use a join or a relate depends on what kind of relationship exists between records in the two tables.

Suppose you want to associate a nonspatial table of country capitals with a layer of countries. Because each country has just one capital, it is appropriate to join the tables. The attribute value "Paris" will be joined to the record for France, the value "Riyadh" to Saudi Arabia, and so on.

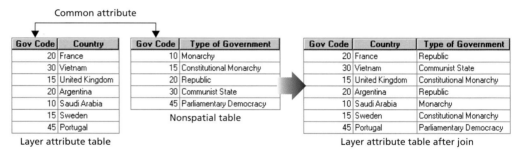

Common attribute

Country Code	Country
29	France
68	Saudi Arabia
106	Chad
248	Spain
199	Venezuela
9	United Kingdom
96	Philippines

Layer attribute table

Country Code	Capital
199	Caracas
96	Manila
68	Riyadh
29	Paris
106	N'Djamena
9	London
248	Madrid

Nonspatial table

Country Code	Country	Capital
29	France	Paris
68	Saudi Arabia	Riyadh
106	Chad	N'Djamena
248	Spain	Madrid
199	Venezuela	Caracas
9	United Kingdom	London
96	Philippines	Manila

Layer attribute table after join

The record relationship between the tables is one-to-one. For each country, there is only one capital. For each capital, there is only one country.

Or suppose you want to associate a nonspatial table describing systems of government with a layer of countries. Again, because each country has just one type of government, the tables can be joined. The attribute value "Republic" will be joined to the record for France, the value "Communist State" to Vietnam, and so on.

Common attribute

Gov Code	Country
20	France
30	Vietnam
15	United Kingdom
20	Argentina
10	Saudi Arabia
15	Sweden
45	Portugal

Layer attribute table

Gov Code	Type of Government
10	Monarchy
15	Constitutional Monarchy
20	Republic
30	Communist State
45	Parliamentary Democracy

Nonspatial table

Gov Code	Country	Type of Government
20	France	Republic
30	Vietnam	Communist State
15	United Kingdom	Constitutional Monarchy
20	Argentina	Republic
10	Saudi Arabia	Monarchy
15	Sweden	Constitutional Monarchy
45	Portugal	Parliamentary Democracy

Layer attribute table after join

The record relationship is many-to-one. For each country, there is only one type of government. A single type of government, however, may apply to many countries.

But now suppose you want to associate a nonspatial table of major cities with a layer of countries. Because each country has more than one major city, a join is not appropriate. If the attribute value "Paris" were joined to France, for example, such matching records as Lyon and Marseille could not be. In this situation, the tables should be related rather than joined.

Common attribute

Country Code	Country
29	France
68	Saudi Arabia
106	Chad
248	Spain
199	Venezuela
9	United Kingdom
96	Philippines

Layer attribute table

Country Code	City
129	Mombasa
129	Nairobi
29	Paris
29	Lyon
29	Marseille
60	Katmandu
248	Madrid
248	Barcelona
248	Valencia

Nonspatial table

The record relationship is one-to-many. For each country, there are many major cities. For each city, there is only one country. By selecting France in the layer attribute table, you can see all its major cities in the nonspatial table.

Joining tables

A table join is preserved only within a map document—the tables on disk are not changed. You can permanently append attributes by exporting a joined layer as a new data set. You'll learn how to export a layer in chapter 11.

Once tables are joined, you can use the appended attributes of the nonspatial table to symbolize, label, query, and analyze the features in a layer.

Common attribute

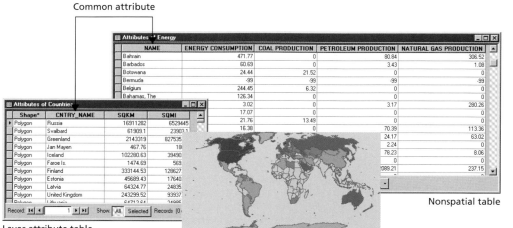

Nonspatial table

Layer attribute table

When a nonspatial table of world energy statistics is joined to a layer attribute table of countries, features can be symbolized by energy attributes. Here, a graduated color scheme of light orange to red shows per capita energy consumption in millions of BTUs.

Exercise 9a

Between 1993 and 1998, abandoned oil extraction sites (called pits) in coastal Louisiana were evaluated for their risk to the environment. The pits, dating back to 1906, include wells, storage tanks, and other equipment and structures that may leak oil and possibly contaminate nearby waterways. If these structures are exposed by erosion, as often happens, they may be struck by boats, risking an oil spill. During the study, each pit was given a hazard rating and most were assigned specific recommendations for cleanup.

As a GIS analyst for the state of Louisiana, you'll make a map that symbolizes the most hazardous pits according to the type of cleanup that has been recommended for them. The map will show how many sites need each kind of cleanup and which parishes have the most serious problems. The map will help lawmakers decide which sites to clean up first, and how much money needs to be spent in each parish to do the job.

1. Start ArcMap. In the ArcMap dialog, click the option to use an existing map. In the list of existing maps, double-click Browse for maps. (If ArcMap is already running, click the File menu and click Open.) Navigate to **C:\GTKArcGIS\Chapter09**. Click **ex09a.mxd** and click Open.

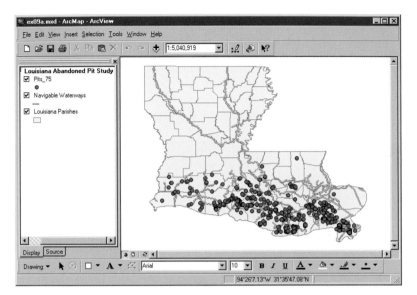

You see a map of Louisiana showing parishes, navigable waterways, and pits. The state boundary shows territorial jurisdiction, which extends 3 miles into the Gulf of Mexico.

Southern Louisiana has more than twenty-four thousand abandoned pits. Each has been given a hazard rating from 0 to 90. The Pits_75 layer in the table of contents has 606 pits, each with a hazard rating of 75 or higher.

2. Click the View menu, point to Bookmarks, and click Southern Louisiana. The view zooms to the southern part of the state.

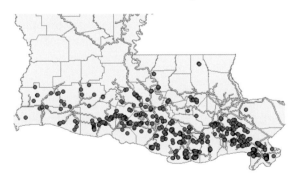

3 Right-click the Pits_75 layer and click Open Attribute Table.

	FID	Shape*	IDNUMBER	PIT_TYPE	STATUS	PARISH	CONTAINMT	CONT_COND
	0	Point	01_w_20669	WELL	ABANDONED/ INACTIVE	ACADIA	NONE	INADEQUATE
	1	Point	01_w_20714	WELL	ABANDONED/ INACTIVE	ACADIA	NONE	INADEQUATE
	2	Point	01_w_22317	WELL	ABANDONED/ INACTIVE	ACADIA	NONE	INADEQUATE
	3	Point	01_w_22318	WELL	ABANDONED/ INACTIVE	ACADIA	NONE	INADEQUATE
	4	Point	01_w_22331	WELL	ABANDONED/ INACTIVE	ACADIA	NONE	INADEQUATE
	5	Point	01_w_22398	WELL	ABANDONED/ INACTIVE	ACADIA	NONE	INADEQUATE
	6	Point	01_w_22900	WELL	ACTIVE	ACADIA	NONE	INADEQUATE
	7	Point	01_w_23121	WELL	ABANDONED/ INACTIVE	ACADIA	NONE	INADEQUATE
	8	Point	01_w_23122	WELL	ABANDONED/ INACTIVE	ACADIA	NONE	INADEQUATE
	9	Point	03_f_23326	FACILITY	ABANDONED/ INACTIVE	ASCENSION	NONE	INADEQUATE
	10	Point	03_f_3326	FACILITY	ABANDONED/ INACTIVE	ASCENSION	NONE	ADEQUATE
	11	Point	03_gf_23298	GATHERING FACILITY	ABANDONED/ INACTIVE	ASCENSION	NONE	INADEQUATE
	12	Point	03_tb_23433	TANK BATTERY	ACTIVE	ASCENSION	LEVEE	INADEQUATE
	13	Point	04_mh_23513	MANIFOLD HEADER	ACTIVE	ASSUMPTION	NONE	INADEQUATE
	14	Point	04_tb_23527	TANK BATTERY	ACTIVE	ASSUMPTION	LEVEE	INADEQUATE
	15	Point	04_tb_23571	TANK BATTERY	ACTIVE	ASSUMPTION	LEVEE	INADEQUATE
	16	Point	04_w_23735	WELL	ACTIVE	ASSUMPTION	NONE	INADEQUATE
	17	Point	04_w_23736	WELL	ABANDONED/ INACTIVE	ASSUMPTION	NONE	INADEQUATE
	18	Point	04_w_23743	WELL	ABANDONED/ INACTIVE	ASSUMPTION	NONE	INADEQUATE

Record: |◄ ◄| 1 |► ►| Show: All Selected Records (0 out of 606 Selected.) Options ▾

The IDNUMBER attribute identifies each pit and PARISH names the parish it's found in. Other attributes provide detailed information about the pits, but there is no attribute for the recommended cleanup. This information is stored in a nonspatial table that you'll join to the Pits_75 layer.

4 Close the Pits_75 table. On the Standard toolbar, click the Add Data button.

5 In the Add Data dialog, navigate to **C:\GTKArcGIS\Chapter09\Data**. Click on **Remedial_actions.dbf,** as shown in the following graphic, then click Add.

Add Data

Look in: Data

Metals.dbf
miss_buff.shp
navgeog3dkbts1.gif
navgeog3dlbts.shp
opageog3dxp71.gif
Pits_75.shp
pshgeog3dpdot.shp
pshgeog3dpdot1.gif
Remedial_actions.dbf

Name: Remedial_actions.dbf

Show of type: Datasets and Layers (*.lyr)

Add
Cancel

The Remedial_actions table is added to the table of contents. When a table is added to a map, the tab at the bottom of the table of contents switches from Display to Source, showing tables and paths to layers.

6 In the table of contents, right-click the Remedial_actions table and click Open.

OID	IDNUMBER	ACCESS_LND	ACCESS_WA	CONT_IN_RQ	CONT_RP_R	WELLH_P_A	INST_BARR	CLNUP_HAZ	
0	01_w_22317	y	n	n	n	y	n	None	Operator needs to submit plan to l
1	01_w_22318	y	n	n	n	y	n	None	Operator needs to submit plan to l
2	01_w_20669	y	n	n	n	y	n	None	Operator needs to submit plan to l
3	01_w_20714	y	n	n	n	y	n	None	Operator needs to submit plan to l
4	01_w_22398	y	n	n	n	y	n	None	Operator needs to submit plan to l
5	01_w_22900	y	n	n	n	n	n	None	Operator needs to submit plan to l
6	01_w_23121	y	n	n	n	y	n	None	Operator needs to submit plan to l
7	01_w_23122	y	n	n	n	y	n	None	Operator needs to submit plan to l
8	03_f_23326	y	n	n	n	n	n	None	Operator needs to submit plan to l
9	03_gf_23298	y	n	n	n	n	n	None	Monitor Site.
10	03_tb_23433	y	n	n	n	n	n	None	Operator needs to submit plan to l
11	04_mh_23513	y	n	n	n	n	n	None	Operator needs to submit plan to l
12	04_tb_23527	y	n	n	n	n	n	None	Operator needs to submit plan to l
13	04_tb_23571	y	n	n	n	n	n	None	Operator needs to submit plan to l
14	04_w_23735	n	y	n	n	y	n	None	Operator needs to submit plan to l
15	04_w_23736	n	y	n	n	y	n	None	Operator needs to submit plan to l
16	04_w_23743	n	y	n	n	y	n	None	Operator needs to submit plan to l
17	04_w_23748	n	y	n	n	y	n	None	Operator needs to submit plan to l
18	04_w_23844	n	y	n	n	y	n	None	Operator needs to submit plan to l

Record: 1   Show: All Selected   Records (0 out of 472 Selected.)   Options ▾

The IDNUMBER attribute identifies pits and is the common attribute that will be used to join the tables. (The field name of the common attribute is the same in both tables, but it doesn't have to be. What matters is that the values identify the same pits; for example, that Pit 01_w_22317 in the Remedial_actions table is the same pit as Pit 01_w_22317 in the Pits_75 table.)

7 In the Attributes of Remedial_actions table, right-click on the IDNUMBER field heading. On the context menu, click Freeze/Unfreeze Column.

8 Scroll all the way to the right. The IDNUMBER field does not move.

IDNUMBER	CLNUP_HAZ	CLEANUP
01_w_22317	None	Operator needs to submit plan to LADNR for clean-up procedure for approval.
01_w_22318	None	Operator needs to submit plan to LADNR for clean-up procedure for approval.
01_w_20669	None	Operator needs to submit plan to LADNR for clean-up procedure for approval.
01_w_20714	None	Operator needs to submit plan to LADNR for clean-up procedure for approval.
01_w_22398	None	Operator needs to submit plan to LADNR for clean-up procedure for approval.
01_w_22900	None	Operator needs to submit plan to LADNR for clean-up procedure for approval.
01_w_23121	None	Operator needs to submit plan to LADNR for clean-up procedure for approval.
01_w_23122	None	Operator needs to submit plan to LADNR for clean-up procedure for approval.
03_f_23326	None	Operator needs to submit plan to LADNR for clean-up procedure for approval.
03_gf_23298	None	Monitor Site.
03_tb_23433	None	Operator needs to submit plan to LADNR for clean-up procedure for approval.
04_mh_23513	None	Operator needs to submit plan to LADNR for clean-up procedure for approval.
04_tb_23527	None	Operator needs to submit plan to LADNR for clean-up procedure for approval.
04_tb_23571	None	Operator needs to submit plan to LADNR for clean-up procedure for approval.
04_w_23735	None	Operator needs to submit plan to LADNR for clean-up procedure for approval.
04_w_23736	None	Operator needs to submit plan to LADNR for clean-up procedure for approval.
04_w_23743	None	Operator needs to submit plan to LADNR for clean-up procedure for approval.
04_w_23748	None	Operator needs to submit plan to LADNR for clean-up procedure for approval.
04_w_23844	None	Operator needs to submit plan to LADNR for clean-up procedure for approval.

Record: 0 Show: All Selected Records (0 out of 472 Selected.) Options ▾

The recommended cleanup is the last field in the table.

9 Scroll down through the table.

IDNUMBER	CLNUP_HAZ	CLEANUP
51_w_17672	None	Repair or removal of structure.
51_w_17705	None	Operator needs to submit plan to LADNR for clean-up procedure for approval.
53_tb_12075	None	Operator needs to submit plan to LADNR for clean-up procedure for approval.
53_tb_13647	None	Operator needs to submit plan to LADNR for clean-up procedure for approval.
53_w_12074	None	Monitor Site.
55_p_135		Vacuum and remove to permitted facility. On-site biological treatment. On-site thermal treatment.
55_w_2000	None	None
55_w_206		Vacuum and remove to permitted facility. On-site biological treatment. On-site thermal treatment.
55_w_207		Vacuum and remove to permitted facility. On-site biological treatment. On-site thermal treatment.
55_w_25342	None	Repair or removal of structure.
55_w_2814	None	Repair or removal of structure.
55_w_2825	None	Repair or removal of structure.
55_w_2861	None	Repair or removal of structure.
55_w_2868	None	Repair or removal of structure.
55_w_2875	None	Repair or removal of structure.
55_w_2880	None	Repair or removal of structure.
55_w_2885	None	Repair or removal of structure.
55_w_2887	None	Repair or removal of structure.
55_w_309		Vacuum and remove to permitted facility. On-site biological treatment. On-site thermal treatment.

Record: 0 Show: All Selected Records (0 out of 472 Selected.) Options ▾

The cleanups range from none to on-site biological and thermal treatment.

Both the Remedial_actions table and the Pits_75 layer attribute table contain one record for each pit. The record relationship between the tables is therefore one-to-one. For each record in the Pits_75 table, there is no more than one matching record in the Remedial_actions table.

The Remedial_actions table has fewer records (472) than the Pits_75 table (606). It may be that cleanup recommendations have not yet been made for the other 134 pits. Records that don't have matches in the Remedial_actions table will have blank attribute values appended to them.

10 Close the Attributes of Remedial_actions table. In the table of contents, right-click on the Pits_75 layer. On the context menu, point to Joins and Relates, then click Join.

11 In the drop-down list at the top of the Join Data dialog, make sure "Join attributes from a table" is selected. In drop-down list number 1, click the drop-down arrow and click IDNUMBER. This specifies IDNUMBER as the common attribute in the Pits_75 table.

12 In drop-down list number 2, click the drop-down arrow and click Remedial_actions. In number 3, click the drop-down arrow and click IDNUMBER. This specifies IDNUMBER as the common attribute in the Remedial_actions table. Make sure your dialog matches the following graphic, then click OK.

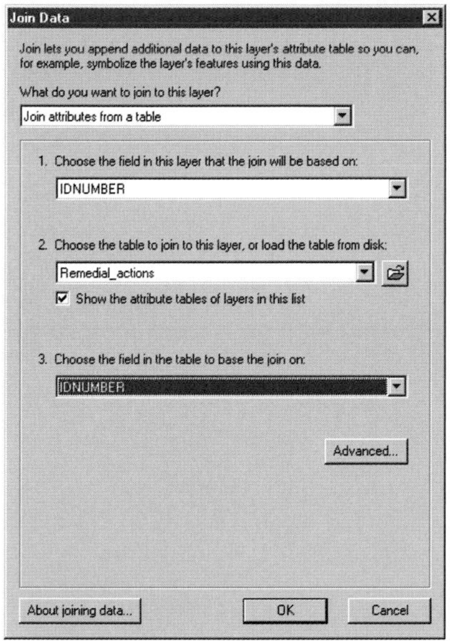

ArcMap joins the attributes in the Remedial_actions table to the Pits_75 table, matching the records by their ID numbers.

13 In the table of contents, right-click the Pits_75 layer and click Open Attribute Table. Scroll to the right until you see field names with the Remedial_actions prefix.

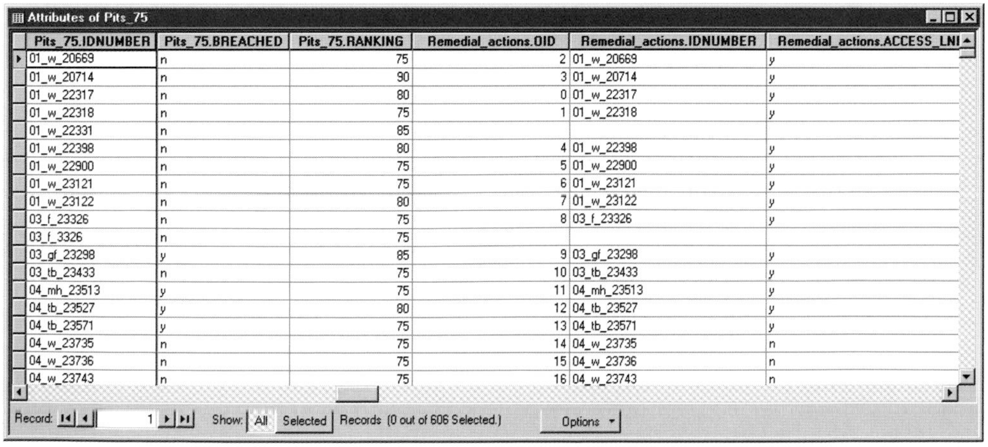

Pits_75.IDNUMBER	Pits_75.BREACHED	Pits_75.RANKING	Remedial_actions.OID	Remedial_actions.IDNUMBER	Remedial_actions.ACCESS_LNI
01_w_20669	n	75	2	01_w_20669	y
01_w_20714	n	90	3	01_w_20714	y
01_w_22317	n	80	0	01_w_22317	y
01_w_22318	n	75	1	01_w_22318	y
01_w_22331	n	85			
01_w_22398	n	80	4	01_w_22398	y
01_w_22900	n	75	5	01_w_22900	y
01_w_23121	n	75	6	01_w_23121	y
01_w_23122	n	80	7	01_w_23122	y
03_f_23326	n	75	8	03_f_23326	y
03_f_3326	n	75			
03_gf_23298	y	85	9	03_gf_23298	y
03_tb_23433	n	75	10	03_tb_23433	y
04_mh_23513	y	75	11	04_mh_23513	y
04_tb_23527	y	80	12	04_tb_23527	y
04_tb_23571	y	75	13	04_tb_23571	y
04_w_23735	n	75	14	04_w_23735	n
04_w_23736	n	75	15	04_w_23736	n
04_w_23743	n	75	16	04_w_23743	n

Record: 1   Show: All Selected   Records (0 out of 606 Selected.)   Options

The joined table contains the attributes of both the Pits_75 table and the Remedial_actions table. The field name prefixes identify which table the attribute comes from.

14 Scroll all the way to the right. The Remedial_actions.CLEANUP field contains the recommended cleanup for each pit.

The values are blank wherever a pit does not have a matching record in the Remedial_actions table. When you symbolize the pits on the CLEANUP attribute, features with blank records will not be displayed on the map.

15 Close the table. In the table of contents, double-click on the Pits_75 layer to open the Layer Properties dialog. Click the Symbology tab.

16 In the Show box, click Categories. Click the Value Field drop-down arrow, scroll to the bottom of the list, and click Remedial_actions.CLEANUP. Click Add All Values.

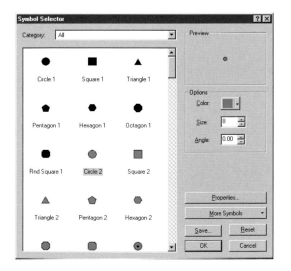

In the Value column, the five cleanup procedures are listed, though some of the descriptions are cut off. The Count column shows the number of sites corresponding to each type of cleanup.

17 Click the Symbol column heading and click Properties for All Symbols. The Symbol Selector dialog opens. In the scrolling box, click Circle 2. Highlight the default size and type **8**. Make sure your dialog matches the following graphic, then click OK.

18 On the Symbology tab, uncheck the <all other values> check box. Click the Color Scheme drop-down arrow and click the Basic Random scheme, the first one in the list. Make sure your dialog matches the following graphic (your colors may be different) and click OK.

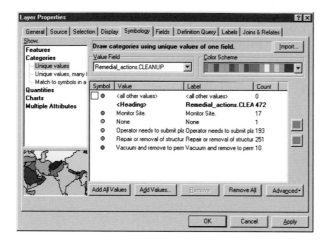

The symbology is applied to the map.

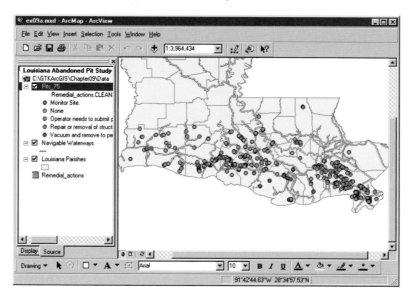

19 In the table of contents, place the mouse pointer over labels to see their full descriptions.

Pits that need to be repaired, removed, or treated are mostly located in a few parishes in the southeastern tip of the state.

20 If you want to save your work, click the File menu and click Save As. Navigate to **C:\GTKArcGIS\Chapter09\MyData**. Rename the file **my_ex09a.mxd** and click Save.

21 If you are continuing with the next exercise, leave ArcMap open. Otherwise, click the File menu and click Exit. Click No if prompted to save your changes.

Relating tables

Tables should be associated by a relate instead of a join when a record in the layer attribute table may have many matches in the nonspatial table (a one-to-many relationship). When tables are related, you can highlight records in either table to see matching records in the other.

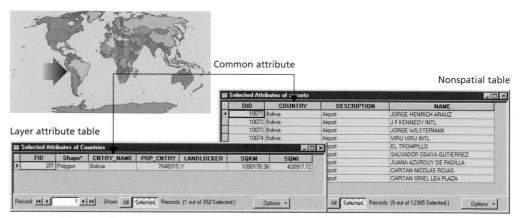

Common attribute

Nonspatial table

Layer attribute table

A nonspatial table of world airports is related to a layer attribute table of countries. You can select a country on the map to see the names of all its airports. You can also select a record in the nonspatial table to highlight a feature on the map.

Exercise 9b

Oil leaks and spills are not the only dangers posed by abandoned pits. The pits often contain toxic metals—barium, lead, and zinc among others—that should not contaminate water. Soil and water samples taken during the pit study have been analyzed for the presence of these metals. In this exercise, you'll relate tables to see the metals analysis for pits within a half mile of the Mississippi River.

Besides examining individual pits for the metals they contain, it would be useful to have a series of maps showing the distribution of particular metals for all hazardous pits—a map of pits containing barium, another of pits containing chromium, and so on. You will not go that far in this exercise, but you will relate tables to select all pits that contain lead.

1 Start ArcMap. In the ArcMap dialog, click the option to use an existing map. In the list of existing maps, double-click Browse for maps. (If ArcMap is already running, click the File menu and click Open.) Navigate to **C:\GTKArcGIS\Chapter09**. Click **ex09b.mxd** to highlight it and click Open.

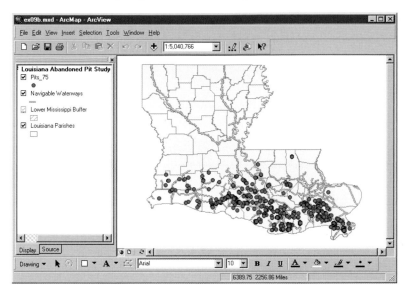

You see the map of Louisiana with abandoned pits, navigable waterways, and parishes. There is also a scale-dependent layer called Lower Mississippi Buffer.

2 Click the View menu, point to Bookmarks, and click Mississippi.

The view zooms to a stretch of the Mississippi River. The Lower Mississippi Buffer layer is now visible, showing a half-mile buffer on either side of the river as it runs through southern Louisiana. The red rectangle on the state map shows you the area you're zoomed to.

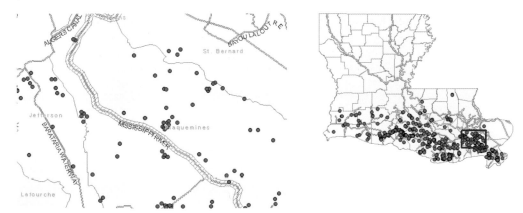

Relating tables

Of the pits in the Pits_75 layer, only two are within a half mile of the Mississippi. You'll check the toxic metals in each.

3 Click the View menu, point to Bookmarks, and click Site 1. At this scale, the pits are labeled with their ID numbers.

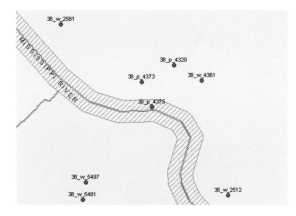

4 On the Tools toolbar, click the Identify tool.

5 Click on pit 38_p_4375 to identify it.

The attributes of the Pits_75 layer do not include an analysis of metals found on-site. This information is stored in a separate table, which you'll add to the map document.

6 Close the Identify Results window. On the Standard toolbar, click the Add Data button.

7 In the Add Data dialog, navigate to **C:\GTKArcGIS\Chapter09\Data**. Click on **Metals.dbf**, as shown in the following graphic, then click Add.

The Metals table is added to the table of contents and the Source tab is selected.

8 In the table of contents, right-click the Metals table and click Open.

OID	IDNUMBER	SAMPID	ANALYSISID	CREWID	METAL	SAMP_TYPE	CONC_NUM	CONC_SOIL	COP
0	03_tb_23433	1	03_tb_23433/1	(C-12)	Ba	s	545.5	545.5	
1	03_tb_23433	1	03_tb_23433/1	(C-12)	Zn	s	72.7	72.7	
2	04_mh_23513	1	04_mh_23513/1	(C-13)	Ba	s	1176.5	1176.5	
3	04_mh_23513	1	04_mh_23513/1	(C-13)	Zn	s	376.5	376.5	
4	04_tb_23527	1	04_tb_23527/1	(C-14)	Ba	s	74.1	74.1	
5	04_tb_23527	1	04_tb_23527/1	(C-14)	Zn	s	348.1	348.1	
6	04_tb_23571	1	04_tb_23571/1	(C-15)	Ba	s	175.4	175.4	
7	04_tb_23571	1	04_tb_23571/1	(C-15)	Zn	s	78.9	78.9	
8	10_tb_19015	1	10_tb_19015/1	(S-6)	Ba	s	342.6	342.6	
9	10_tb_19015	1	10_tb_19015/1	(S-6)	Zn	s	12	12	
10	10_tb_19015	2	10_tb_19015/2	(S-7)	Ba	s	144.9	144.9	
11	10_w_19357	1	10_w_19357/1	(A-9)	Ba	s	2639.9	2639.9	
12	10_w_19357	1	10_w_19357/1	(A-9)	Zn	s	77.3	77.3	
13	17_tb_24319	1	17_tb_24319/1	(C-17)	Ba	w	0.1	0	
14	17_tb_24330	1	17_tb_24330/1	(C-18)	Ba	s	271.4	271.4	
15	17_tb_24330	1	17_tb_24330/1	(C-18)	Zn	s	62.9	62.9	
16	23_tb_15130	1	23_tb_15130/1	(C-1)	Ba	w	0.7	0	
17	23_tb_15130	1	23_tb_15130/1	(C-1)	Zn	w	3.21	0	
18	23_w_15134	1	23_w_15134/1	(C-6)	Ag	s	3.9	3.9	

Record: 1 Show: All Selected Records: (0 out of 148 Selected.) Options ▾

The table's attributes include METAL, which shows the chemical symbol for each metal sampled; SAMP_TYPE, either soil or water; and CONC_NUM, the concentration of the metal in the sample (in milligrams per kilogram for soil and milligrams per liter for water). The common attribute for the Metals and Pits_75 tables is IDNUMBER.

The Metals table has many records with the same ID number because there is a unique record for every sample taken at a pit. At most pits, several metals have been analyzed, and sometimes more than one sample of a metal has been taken.

Because the Pits_75 table contains one record per pit and the Metals table may contain several, the Pits_75 table has a one-to-many relationship to the Metals table. If you joined the tables, ArcMap would find the first matching record in the Metals table, join its attributes to the Pits_75 table, and ignore any further matching records. To preserve the one-to-many relationship, you must relate the tables instead.

9 Close the Attributes of Metals table. In the table of contents, right-click the Pits_75 layer, point to Joins and Relates, and click Relate.

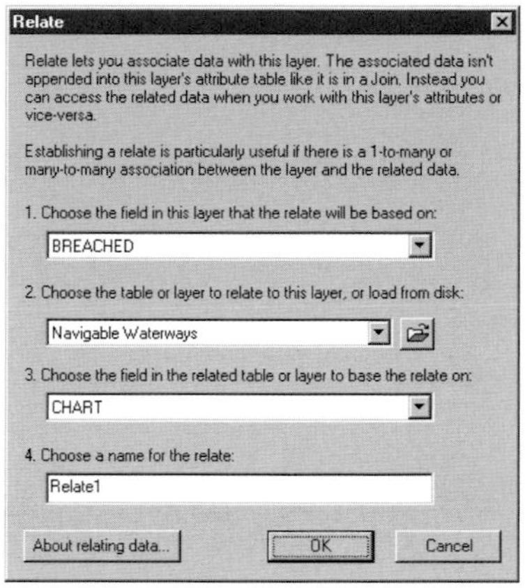

10 In drop-down list number 1 of the Relate dialog, click the drop-down arrow and click IDNUMBER. This specifies IDNUMBER as the common attribute in the Pits_75 table.

11 In drop-down list number 2, click the drop-down arrow and click Metals. In number 3, click the drop-down arrow and click IDNUMBER. This specifies IDNUMBER as the common attribute in the Metals table.

12 In drop-down list number 4, highlight the default name and type **Metals analysis**. Make sure your dialog matches the following graphic, then click OK.

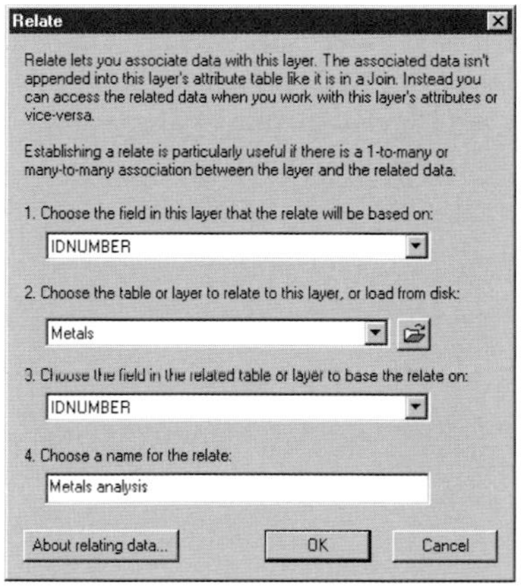

A relate is established between the two tables.

13 Click the Selection menu and click Set Selectable Layers. Uncheck all layers except Pits_75, as shown in the following graphic, then click Close.

14 On the Tools toolbar, click the Select Features tool.

15 On the map, click on pit 38_p_4375 to select it.

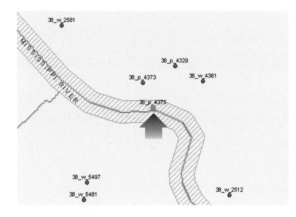

16 In the table of contents, right-click on the Pits_75 layer and click Open Attribute Table. At the bottom of the table, click Selected to show selected records.

17 At the bottom of the table, click Options. On the context menu, point to Related Tables and click Metals analysis : Metals.

18 The Attributes of Metals table opens. (You may have to move the Pits_75 table out of the way to see it.) Click its title bar to bring it forward. At the bottom of the table, click Selected.

OID	IDNUMBER	SAMPID	ANALYSISID	CREWID	METAL	SAMP_TYPE	CONC_NUM	CONC_SOIL	CONC
102	38_p_4375	1	38_p_4375/1	A-39	Ba	s	361.7	361.7	
103	38_p_4375	1	38_p_4375/1	A-39	Zn	s	63.8	63.8	
104	38_p_4375	2	38_p_4375/2	A-40	Ba	s	232.6	232.6	
105	38_p_4375	2	38_p_4375/2	A-40	Zn	s	62.8	62.8	

Record: 1   Show: All | Selected   Records (4 out of 148 Selected.)   Options ▾

Four records in the Metals table match the record for Pit 38_p_4375. Two soil samples (SAMPID values 1 and 2) were taken from the pit and each sample was analyzed for barium and zinc (Ba and Zn in the METAL field). The concentration levels (CONC_NUM) are relatively low—barium samples for all pits have a mean value of 5,116 while zinc samples have a mean value of 410.

Now you'll check the levels at the other pit.

19 Close both tables. Click the View menu, point to Bookmarks, and click Site 2.

20 Make sure the Select Features tool is still selected on the Tools toolbar and click on pit 38_p_4565.

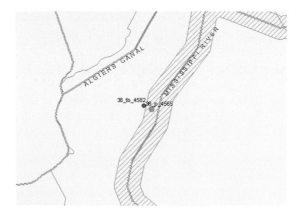

21 In the table of contents, right-click on the Pits_75 layer and click Open Attribute table. At the bottom of the table, click Selected.

FID	Shape*	IDNUMBER	PIT_TYPE	STATUS	PARISH	
216	Point	38_p_4565	PIT	ABANDONED/ INACTIVE	PLAQUEMINES	LEVEE

Selected Attributes of Pits_75

Record: 1   Show: All Selected   Records (1 out of 606 Selected.)   Options ▾

22 Click Options, point to Related Tables, and click Metals analysis : Metals.

23 The Attributes of Metals table opens. Click its title bar to bring it forward. Click Selected.

Selected Attributes of Metals

OID	IDNUMBER	SAMPID	ANALYSISID	CREWID	METAL	SAMP_TYPE	CONC_NUM	CONC_SOIL	CONC
106	38_p_4565	1	38_p_4565/1	B-20	Ba	s	712.9	712.9	
107	38_p_4565	1	38_p_4565/1	B-20	Zn	s	92.1	92.1	

Record: 1   Show: All Selected   Records (2 out of 148 Selected.)   Options ▾

The pit has two matching records in the Metals table—a soil sample of barium and a soil sample of zinc. Again, both concentrations are relatively low.

Your final task is to locate all pits that contain lead. To do this, you must use the relate in the other direction: first making a selection on the Metals table and then seeing which features in the Pits_75 layer are selected.

24 At the bottom of the Metals table, click All to show all records. Click Options. On the context menu, click Select By Attributes.

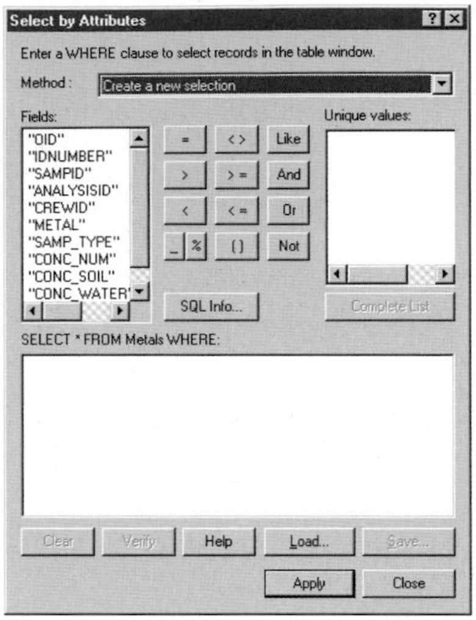

25 Make sure the Method is set to Create a new selection. In the Fields scrolling box, double-click "METAL" to add it to the expression box. Click the equals (=) button. In the Unique sample values list, double-click 'Pb', the symbol for lead. (If you don't see 'Pb' in the sample values list, click Complete List.) Make sure your expression matches the one in the following graphic, then click Apply.

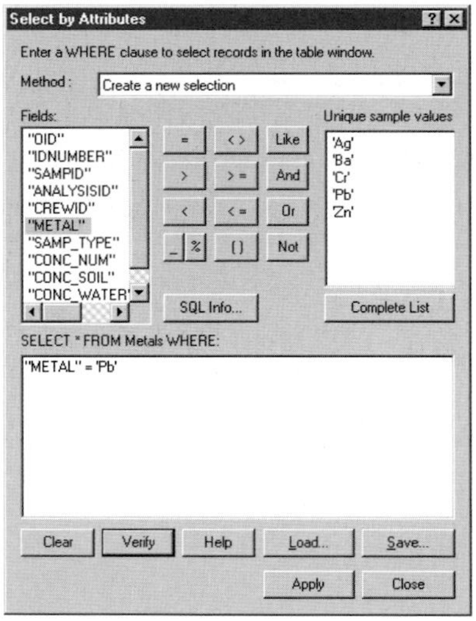

26 In the Attributes of Metals table, click Selected to show the selected records.

	OID	IDNUMBER	SAMPID	ANALYSISID	CREWID	METAL	SAMP_TYPE	CONC_NUM	CONC_SOIL	CONC.
▶	20	23_w_15134	1	23_w_15134/1	(C-6)	Pb	s	752.5	752.5	
	32	29_p_158	1	29_p_158/1	29P158	Pb	s	350	350	
	115	50_w_26291	1	50_w_26291/1	(D-6)	Pb	s	1225	1225	

Selected Attributes of Metals

Record: 1 Show: All | Selected Records (3 out of 148 Selected.) Options ▾

There are three records for lead samples. By comparing the ID numbers, you can see that each lead sample was taken from a different pit.

27 In the Selected Attributes of Metals table, click Options, point to Related Tables, and click Metals analysis : Pits_75.

The Selected Attributes of Pits_75 table updates. Click its title bar to bring it forward.

	FID	Shape*	IDNUMBER	PIT_TYPE	STATUS	PARISH	
▶	59	Point	23_w_15134	WELL	ACTIVE	IBERIA	NONE
	130	Point	29_p_158	PIT	ABANDONED/ INACTIVE	LAFOURCHE	LEVEE
	408	Point	50_w_26291	WELL	ABANDONED/ INACTIVE	ST. MARTIN	NONE

Selected Attributes of Pits_75

Record: 1 Show: All | Selected Records (3 out of 606 Selected.) Options ▾

You see the records for the three pits that contain lead.

28 Close both tables. (The Select By Attributes dialog closes by itself.) In the table of contents, right-click the Pits_75 layer, point to Selection, and click Zoom To Selected Features.

ArcMap zooms to the smallest extent that shows all selected features.

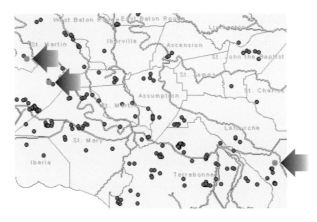

To make a map of pits containing lead, you would create a layer from the selected features. You'll learn how to create a selection layer in chapter 11.

An interesting follow-up to your work would be to join the Remedial_actions table to the Pits_75 table, then relate the Metals table to the joined table. You could then see which cleanup options have been recommended for the three sites that contain lead.

29 If you want to save your work, click the File menu and click Save As. Navigate to **C:\GTKArcGIS\Chapter09\MyData**. Rename the file **my_ex09b.mxd** and click Save.

When you save a map document, joins and relates are saved with it and are restored the next time you open the document. If you want to remove a join, right-click the layer with joined attributes, point to Joins and Relates, point to Remove Join(s), and click the name of the join. To remove a relate, point to Remove Relate(s) and click the name of the relate.

30 If you are continuing to the next chapter, leave ArcMap open. Otherwise, click the File menu and click Exit. Click No when prompted to save your changes.

Selecting features by location

Using location queries
Combining attribute and location queries

In chapter 8, you selected features according to their attribute values—for example, houses with three bedrooms. In this chapter, you'll select features by location, that is, according to their spatial relationship to other features, whether in another layer or in the same layer.

The spatial relationships that can be used are distance, containment, intersection, and adjacency.

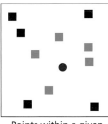

Points within a given distance of the red point are selected.

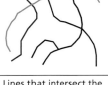
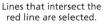

Points contained by the red polygon are selected.

Lines that intersect the red line are selected.

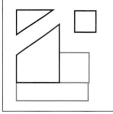

Polygons adjacent to the red polygon are selected.

ArcGIS defines eleven spatial relationships, each a variation on one of the four types. For example, there is containment (where the contained feature may touch the boundary of the containing feature) and complete containment (where the boundaries may not touch).

Using location queries

To select features by location, you specify a selection method, a selection layer, a spatial relationship, a reference layer, and sometimes a distance buffer. In the following example, cities are selected if they lie within 1 mile of rivers.

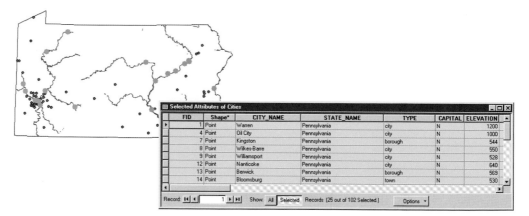

ArcMap measures the distances from cities to rivers and selects cities that meet the condition.

For more information, click the Contents tab in ArcGIS Desktop Help and navigate to *ArcMap > Querying maps > Selecting features according to their location*.

Exercise 10a

You work for a small chain of gourmet food stores that is scouting locations for a new store in Riverside, California.

The location should be close to a freeway so it is accessible to shoppers in nearby cities and people coming home from work. It should be in or near a shopping center to be convenient for people running other errands. And because your products are expensive, the store should be in an area with a large number of affluent households.

Some data in this chapter has been fictionalized to fit the scenario.

You'll begin by selecting neighborhoods that contain shopping centers and are close to freeways.

1 Start ArcMap. In the ArcMap dialog, click the option to use an existing map. In the list of existing maps, double-click Browse for maps. (If ArcMap is already running, click the File menu and click Open.) Navigate to **C:\GTKArcGIS\Chapter10**. Click **ex10a.mxd** and click Open.

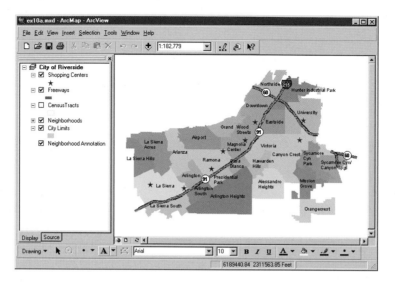

The map extent is the city limits of Riverside. Layers include neighborhoods, state and interstate freeways, and shopping centers.

First, you'll select neighborhoods near freeways.

2 Click the Selection menu and click Select By Location.

By default, the selection method is "select features from." Use this whenever you want to create a new selected set.

3 In the scrolling list of selection layers, check Neighborhoods.

4 In the list of spatial relationships, click the drop-down arrow and click "are within a distance of."

5 In the list of reference layers, click the drop-down arrow and click Freeways.

The check box to apply a buffer to the features in the Freeways layer is checked. These buffers, which are not drawn on the map, define the distance around freeways within which features will be selected.

6 Replace the current distance value with **0.5**. Click the distance units drop-down arrow and click Miles.

You have specified that you want to select all neighborhoods within half a mile of a freeway. A neighborhood will be selected if any part of it is within this distance.

7 Make sure your dialog matches the following graphic, then click Apply and move it away from the map.

The neighborhoods are selected on the map.

Now you'll refine the selection by choosing those neighborhoods from the currently selected set that also contain a shopping center.

8 In the Select By Location dialog, click the selection method drop-down arrow and click "select from the currently selected features in." In the list of selection layers, leave Neighborhoods checked.

9 In the list of spatial relationships, click the drop-down arrow and click "contain."

10 In the list of reference layers, click the drop-down arrow and click Shopping Centers. The check box to apply a buffer should stay unchecked.

If you applied a buffer to the shopping centers, only neighborhoods that contained the entire buffer area would be selected.

11 Make sure your dialog matches the following graphic. Click Apply, then click Close.

The neighborhoods are selected on the map.

Six neighborhoods meet your criteria. In the next exercise, you'll narrow the search further by looking for the affluent ones.

12 If you want to save your work, click the File menu and click Save As. Navigate to **C:\GTKArcGIS\Chapter10\MyData**. Rename the file **my_ex10a.mxd** and click Save.

13 If you are continuing with the next exercise, leave ArcMap open. Otherwise, click the File menu and click Exit. Click No if prompted to save your changes.

Combining attribute and location queries

Location and attribute queries can be used together to solve a problem. For example, if you're doing emergency planning, you might want to select cities of 100,000 or more (an attribute query) that lie within 10 miles of major fault lines (a location query).

Exercise 10b

You have found neighborhoods that are close to freeways and contain shopping centers. You also want to locate your store in an affluent neighborhood. The Neighborhoods layer has no demographic information, but the Census Tracts layer does. You'll do an attribute query to select the census tracts that meet your criteria. Then you'll create a location query to select the neighborhoods that substantially overlap these census tracts. Once you decide on a neighborhood, you'll add zoning and building data to help you choose a specific location for the new store.

1 Start ArcMap. In the ArcMap dialog, click the option to use an existing map. In the list of existing maps, double-click Browse for maps. (If ArcMap is already running, click the File menu and click Open.) Navigate to **C:\GTKArcGIS\Chapter10**. Click **ex10b.mxd** and click Open.

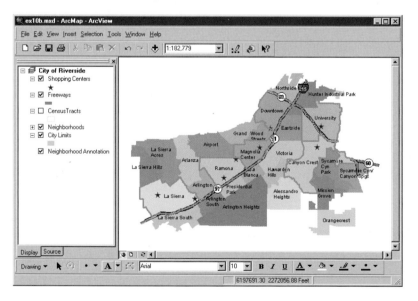

The map displays the city of Riverside and the neighborhoods selected in the previous exercise.

2 In the table of contents, turn on the Census Tracts layer.

The census tracts are outlined in pale orange. Some tracts cross neighborhood boundaries and some neighborhoods include more than one tract.

3 In the table of contents, right-click on the Census Tracts layer and click Open Attribute Table.

OBJECTID*	Shape*	TRACT	POP_99	HH_99	MEDINC_99	AVGINC_99	Shape_Length	Shape_Area
1	Polygon	06065042300	6778	2213	35122	39063	40716.688832	21223272.178006
2	Polygon	06065030100	7574	2332	37158	41377	34609.158488	47805294.841587
3	Polygon	06065042203	11756	5427	22372	27404	47968.772721	77029688.539122
4	Polygon	06065042204	14090	4663	53257	63986	17544.540765	9893983.229287
5	Polygon	06065042204	14090	4663	53257	63986	43066.162108	49341412.147733
6	Polygon	06065042204	14090	4663	53257	63986	15179.959301	1065123.183422
7	Polygon	06065030200	5505	2186	33981	57869	52138.381742	58008433.917904
8	Polygon	06065040200	13803	4249	33405	39474	12619.789946	3904301.958263
9	Polygon	06065030500	11428	3149	26193	38979	36024.297831	46255465.622958
10	Polygon	06065030300	6789	2014	21152	26811	29292.194688	28809584.560391
11	Polygon	06065030400	7140	1811	26405	34768	23817.855922	29532904.588090
12	Polygon	06065042202	2592	359	22356	30414	36706.353913	47895598.659127
13	Polygon	06065030700	6148	2425	39208	45690	23237.445678	26653424.253939
14	Polygon	06065030800	6907	2625	44216	50210	34673.422698	47515121.563171
15	Polygon	06065041000	12605	3582	49178	55991	52273.327647	98763487.435985
16	Polygon	06065030900	3289	897	45383	53698	36712.639836	66495323.657643
17	Polygon	06065042201	15688	6078	58830	79475	70783.875694	248939781.612226
18	Polygon	06065031100	5137	1932	42697	47100	25483.661692	31990493.598680
19	Polygon	06065030600	12165	4075	86072	129351	80344.938205	222079945.138311
20	Polygon	06065031000	10363	3613	34297	42504	27665.952424	34446105.694697

Record: 1   Show: All Selected   Records (0 out of 37 Selected.)   Options ▾

You'll use the number of households (HH_99) and the average household income (AVGINC_99) as criteria for locating your business.

4 At the bottom of the table, click Options and click Select By Attributes.

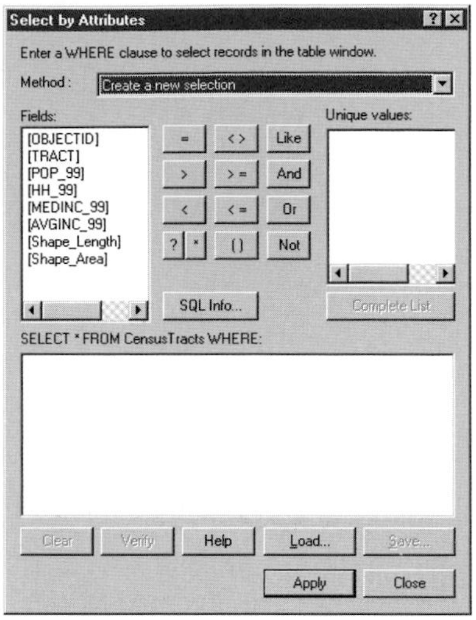

The Method drop-down list is set to Create a new selection, which is what you want.

5 In the Fields box, double-click on [HH_99]. Click the > (greater than) button. Press the space bar and type **4000**. Click the And button. In the Fields box, double-click [AVGINC_99]. Click the > button. Press the space bar and type **65000**.

Your expression will select census tracts with more than four thousand households and an average yearly income over $65,000.

6 Make sure your dialog matches the following graphic, then click Apply. Move the attribute table out of the way, if necessary, and click Close on the dialog.

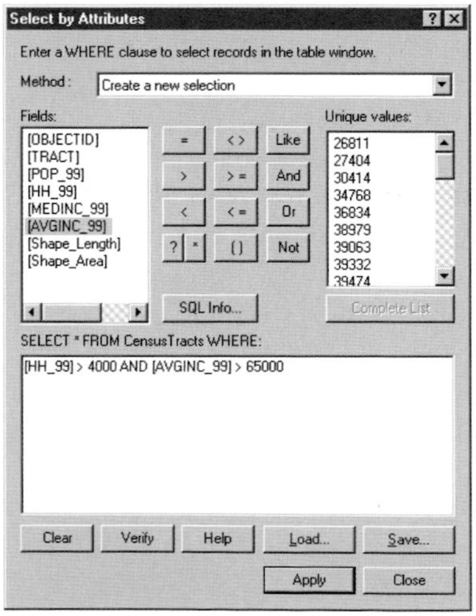

In the table, three census tracts are selected.

7 Close the Attributes of Census Tracts table.

It's hard to pick out the selected tracts because they are highlighted in the same color as the neighborhoods.

8 In the table of contents, turn off the Neighborhoods layer.

The three tracts are located in the southeastern part of the city.

9 In the table of contents, turn the Neighborhoods layer back on.

You'll use the selected census tracts to select the neighborhoods they overlap.

10 Click the Selection menu and click Select By Location.

11 In the Select By Location dialog, click the selection method drop-down arrow and click "select from the currently selected features in."

12 In the list of selection layers, scroll down and click the Neighborhoods check box.

13 In the list of spatial relationships, click the drop-down arrow and click "have their center in."

Neighborhoods with centers in one of the selected census tracts will be selected. This method will find those neighborhoods that overlap the selected census tracts enough to share their demographic characteristics.

14 In the list of reference layers, click the drop-down arrow and click Census Tracts.

Underneath the last drop-down list, the check box to use selected features is checked. This means that only the three selected features in the Census Tracts layer will be used in the spatial selection.

The check box to apply a buffer to the features in Census Tracts should stay unchecked. If you applied a buffer, neighborhoods would be selected if their center lay anywhere within the buffer.

15 Make sure your dialog matches the following graphic, then click Apply. When the selection is finished, click Close.

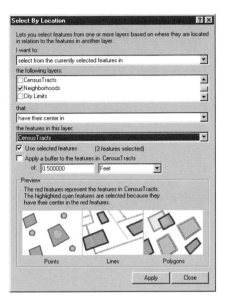

16 In the table of contents, turn off the Census Tracts layer.

A single neighborhood, Canyon Crest, is selected. It is populous, affluent, contains a major shopping center, and is close to a freeway.

17 In the table of contents, right-click on the Neighborhoods layer, point to Selection, and click Zoom To Selected Features.

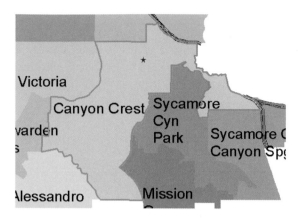

The map zooms to the Canyon Crest neighborhood. To look for sites in this neighborhood, you'll add two new layers to the map. One shows which parts of the neighborhood are zoned for commercial use. The other shows buildings within those districts.

18 On the Standard toolbar, click the Add Data button.

19 In the Add Data dialog, navigate to **C:\GTKArcGIS\Chapter10\Data \RiversideCityData.mdb**. Click on CCbuildings. Press the Ctrl key and click CCzoning. Make sure your dialog matches the following graphic, then click Add.

The two new layers are added to the map. (Your colors may be different.) The layers contain zoning and building data clipped to the Canyon Crest neighborhood. You'll learn how to clip data in the next chapter.

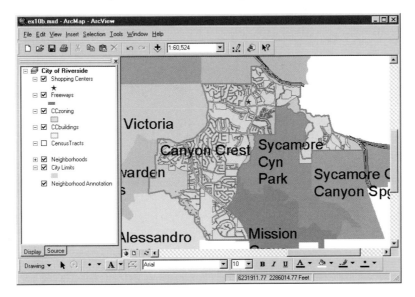

20 In the table of contents, double-click the CCzoning layer. Click the Definition Query tab.

A definition query resembles an attribute query in that you write an expression to find features with particular attributes. The difference is that features satisfying an attribute query are selected, while features satisfying a definition query are displayed and the rest are hidden.

Since you're interested only in commercial property, you'll write a query to display only those features in the CCzoning layer that are zoned for commercial use.

21 On the Definition Query tab, click Query Builder.

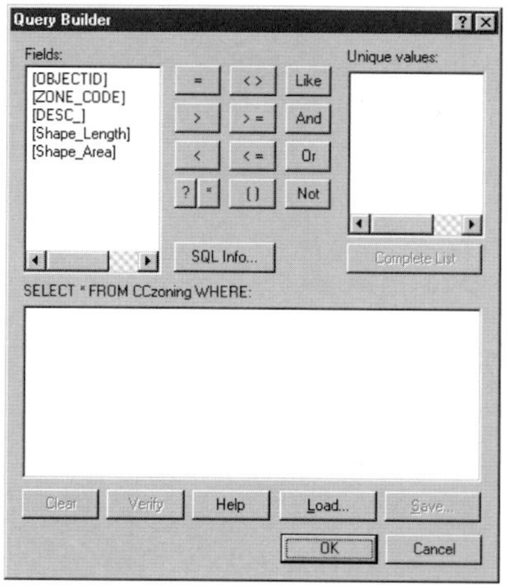

22 In the Fields box, double-click [DESC_] to add it to the expression box. (This attribute contains zoning code descriptions.) Click the equals (=) button. In the Unique values box, double-click 'Commercial'. Make sure that your dialog matches the following graphic, then click OK.

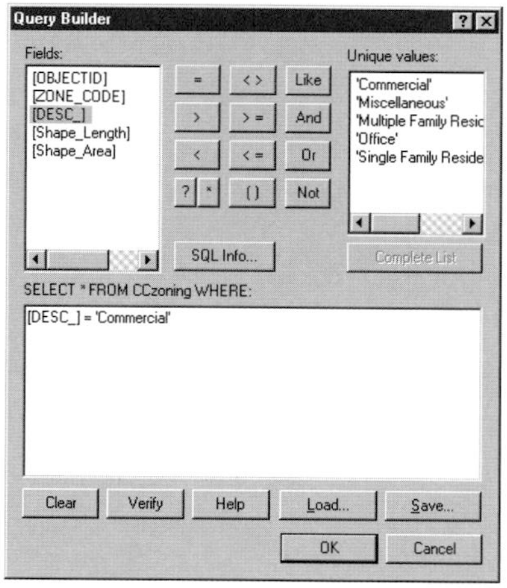

The query is displayed in the Definition Query box.

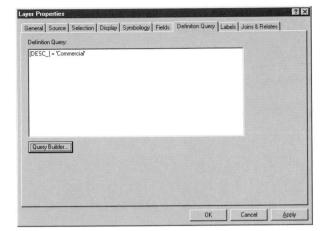

23 Click OK on the Layer Properties dialog.

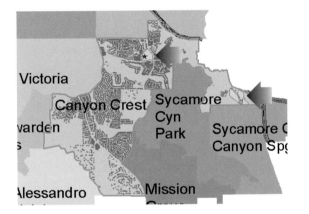

Now the only features displayed in the layer are those zoned for commercial use. Because the other features are hidden, the features from the CCbuildings layer beneath it show through.

Of the two commercial areas, shown by arrows in the previous graphic, you prefer the one that contains the shopping center.

24 On the Tools toolbar, click the Zoom In tool.

25 Zoom to the commercial area containing the shopping center.

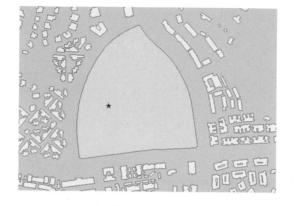

To see the buildings, you need to change the drawing order of the layers.

26 In the table of contents, drag CCbuildings above CCzoning.

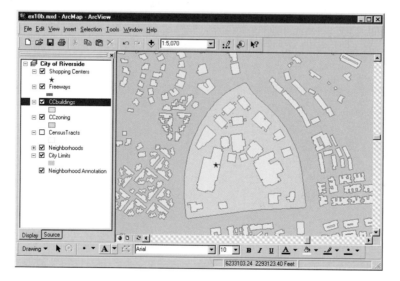

The commercially zoned buildings vary in size. You need 4,000 to 6,000 square feet for your store. You can identify the buildings and get their square footage from the Shape_Area field in the layer attribute table. Since you don't know what the buildings look like or whether they are available, your next step might be to drive out to the area and then call a real estate agent.

27 If you want to save your work, click the File menu and click Save As. Navigate to **C:\GTKArcGIS\Chapter10\MyData**. Rename the file **my_ex10b.mxd** and click Save.

28 If you are continuing to the next chapter, leave ArcMap open. Otherwise, click the File menu and click Exit. Click No when prompted to save your changes.

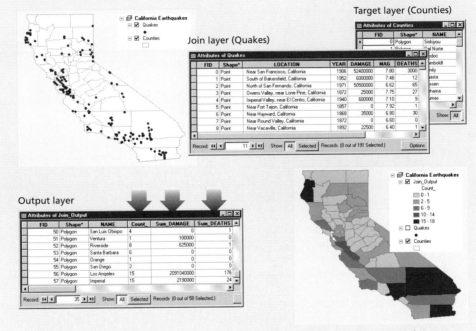

JOINING ATTRIBUTES BY LOCATION

In this chapter, you selected features in one layer according to their spatial relationships to features in other layers. You can use the same kinds of spatial relationships (containment, distance, intersection) to join the attributes of features in one layer to features in another. This operation, called a spatial join, may also create new attributes, such as a count of the features in one layer that are contained by features in another layer or distance measurements between features in two layers.

Here, a layer of earthquake points is spatially joined to a layer of California counties. The output gives county-by-county totals for such earthquake attributes as damage and deaths.

This spatial join is based on containment. The output table has the attributes of the Counties layer plus three new ones. For each county, you can see how many earthquakes there have been, how much damage has been done, and how many people have died. In the map at the right, the counties are symbolized by number of earthquakes.

Continued on next page

JOINING ATTRIBUTES BY LOCATION (continued)

Here, the same layer of earthquake points is spatially joined to a layer of cities to find the distance from each city to the earthquake nearest it.

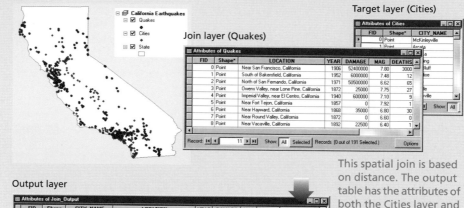

Target layer (Cities)

Join layer (Quakes)

Output layer

This spatial join is based on distance. The output table has the attributes of both the Cities layer and the Quakes layer. The LOCATION attribute from the Quakes layer shows the nearest earthquake to each city. The new Distance attribute shows how far away the quake was (in meters).

You do a spatial join in much the same way as the table join you did in chapter 9. In the table of contents, right-click the target layer (the one you are joining attributes to), point to Joins and Relates, and click Join. In the Join Data dialog, choose "Join data from another layer based on spatial location," then select the join layer. The output layer attributes vary according to the spatial relationship between the target and join layers and the options you choose in the dialog. For more information, click the Contents tab in ArcGIS Desktop Help and navigate to *ArcMap > Querying maps > Joining the attributes of features by their location.*

Preparing data for analysis

Dissolving features
Creating graphs
Clipping layers
Exporting data

Data sets are seldom in exactly the condition you need for a project. If you lack the data to support your analysis, there's not much to do except start looking. Sometimes, however, the problem is one of too much data—you may have thousands of features cluttering your map with unnecessary detail, or data that covers a greater area than you're interested in.

You can simplify a data set by dissolving several features in a layer into one. You can trim a data set to your area of interest by using features in one layer to clip features in another. You can work with fewer features by making a selection on a layer and creating a new layer from it. This layer may be saved with the map or saved to disk as a new data set.

Dissolving features

A dissolve creates a new data set in which all features in an input layer that have the same value for a specified attribute become a single feature. In the following example, states are dissolved by sales region.

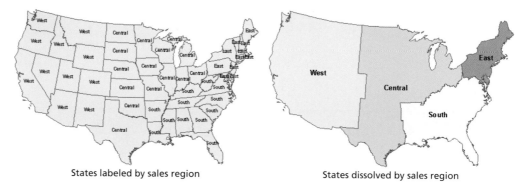

States labeled by sales region   States dissolved by sales region

Apart from geometry and ID, the new data set has just two attributes by default: the attribute used in the dissolve (sales region) and the number of features dissolved to make each new feature. You can include other attributes as well. In the sales region example, the input table has an attribute storing the number of customers per state. In the output table, these values can be summed for each region.

Attributes of States

FID	Shape*	STATE_NAME	STATE_ABBR	SALES_REGION	CUSTOMERS	POP1999	HOUSEHO
41	Polygon	Alabama	AL	South	19	4382953	150(
35	Polygon	Arizona	AZ	West	33	4790311	136(
45	Polygon	Arkansas	AR	South	27	2557924	89(
23	Polygon	California	CA	West	46	33090214	1038(
30	Polygon	Colorado	CO	West	22	4049168	128:
17	Polygon	Connecticut	CT	East	18	3279409	123(
27	Polygon	Delaware	DE	East	10	751747	24:
26	Polygon	District of Columbia	DC	East	14	514869	24:
47	Polygon	Florida	FL	South	50	15163069	513(
43	Polygon	Georgia	GA	South	48	7804377	236(
7	Polygon	Idaho	ID	West	9	1250247	36(

Record: 0 Show: All Selected Records (0 out of 49 Selected.) Options

Input sales region table

Attributes of Sales Regions

FID	Dissolve_Shape*	SALES_REGION	Count_REGION	Sum_CUSTOMERS
0	Polygon	Central	14	394
1	Polygon	East	12	321
2	Polygon	South	12	352
3	Polygon	West	11	252

Record: 1 Show: All Selected Records (0 out of 4 Selected.) Options

Output sales region table

Exercise 11a

You work for a lumber company that plans to harvest timber in the Tongass National Forest in southeastern Alaska. Forest land can be divided into stands—groups of trees with something in common, such as type, age, or size. In a national forest, stands can be grouped into larger areas and leased to private companies by the U.S. Forest Service. Restrictions are placed on logging in sensitive parts of the lease areas, such as endangered animal habitat.

The Forest Service is presently considering leasing five adjacent areas.

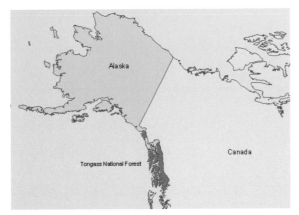

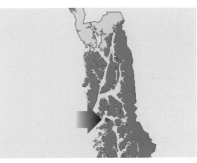

The Tongass National forest, shown in dark green, covers 16,800,000 acres (about 68,000,000 square kilometers) of the Alaska panhandle.

Lease areas under consideration are shown in purple.

As your company's GIS analyst, your job in this and the following chapter is to calculate the timber values of the potential lease areas. Your analysis will help your company decide how much to bid for each area.

You have a polygon layer of forest stands provided by the Forest Service. Its attributes include the estimated value of each stand and the lease area each stand belongs to.

In this exercise, you'll dissolve the stands into the five lease areas. You'll total the stand values to get a preliminary estimate of how much each lease area is worth. In chapter 12, you'll refine this estimate by eliminating areas that can't be harvested.

1 Start ArcMap. In the ArcMap dialog, click the option to use an existing map. In the list of existing maps, double-click Browse for maps. (If ArcMap is already running, click the File menu and click Open.) Navigate to **C:\GTKArcGIS\Chapter11**. Click **ex11a.mxd** and click Open.

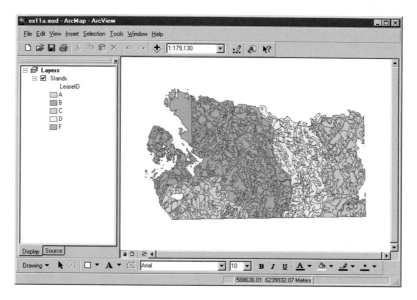

The map shows a layer of forest stands, symbolized by the lease area they belong to.

2 In the table of contents, right-click on the Stands layer and click Open Attribute Table.

OBJECTID	Shape*	LeaseID	StandValue	ValuePerMeter	StandID	Shape_Length	Shape_Area
1	Polygon	A	1.003531	64	6224	769.689245	15680.172005
2	Polygon	A	7.380322	42	1164	2164.996611	175721.964087
3	Polygon	A	0.936683	63	6223	650.045632	14867.984924
4	Polygon	A	10.568293	30	1169	5261.256657	352276.409512
5	Polygon	A	1.974707	63	1171	776.790314	31344.562658
6	Polygon	A	4.238298	63	1178	1307.944741	67274.578893
7	Polygon	A	5.056288	53	1198	1768.194060	95401.656306
8	Polygon	A	2.726222	52	1209	946.578676	52427.342690
9	Polygon	A	1.472038	53	1216	714.853307	27774.296188
10	Polygon	A	8.734157	25	1229	4421.968632	349366.263451
11	Polygon	A	1.022995	43	1233	687.696463	23790.580300
12	Polygon	A	7.126407	26	1259	3003.696897	274092.559487

Record: 1   Show: All   Selected   Records (0 out of 1405 Selected.)   Options

The StandValue attribute contains the dollar value of each stand in millions of dollars. It was obtained by multiplying ValuePerMeter by Shape_Area. (Shape_Area stores the size of each feature in square meters.)

3 Close the table. Click the Tools menu and click GeoProcessing Wizard.

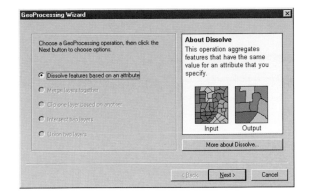

The first panel of the wizard presents five operations. The only one available is to dissolve features. The others require more than one layer.

4 Click Next to advance to the second panel.

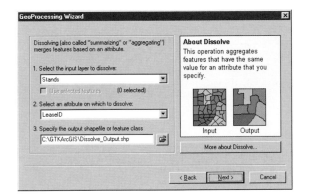

On this panel you select a layer to dissolve, an attribute to dissolve on, and an output data set.

5 In the first drop-down list, Stands is selected. (It's the only layer in the map.) In the second drop-down list, make sure that LeaseID is selected.

The output data can be saved as a shapefile or as a geodatabase feature class. You'll save it as a geodatabase feature class because the rest of the Tongass data is in this format. To leave the Tongass geodatabase intact, you'll save the output to a geodatabase called MyTongass that has been created for you.

6 Click the Browse button next to the third drop-down list. In the Saving Data dialog, click the Save as type drop-down arrow and click Personal Geodatabase feature classes.

Dissolving features

7 Navigate to **C:\GTKArcGIS\Chapter11\MyData**. Double-click on **MyTongass.mdb**.

8 In the Name box, replace Dissolve_Output with **Leases**. Make sure your dialog matches the following graphic, then click Save.

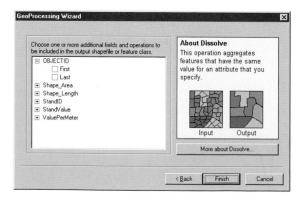

The output file information is updated in the wizard panel.

9 Click Next.

ArcMap can summarize the attribute values of features that are dissolved and include the summary values in the output attribute table. Numeric attributes can be summarized by minimum, maximum, average, sum, standard deviation, or variance.

10 Click the plus sign next to StandValue to see these summary operations. Check the box next to Sum, as shown in the following graphic, then click Finish.

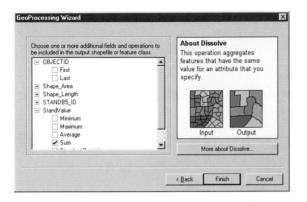

When the stands are dissolved, the new Leases layer is added to the map. Your color may be different.

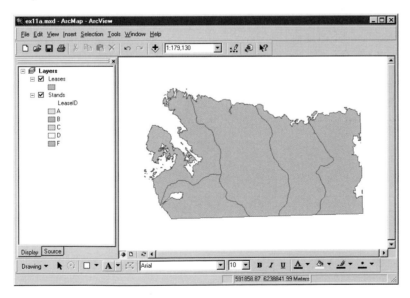

Dissolving features

11 In the table of contents, right-click on the Leases layer and click Open Attribute Table.

12 Scroll through the table.

LeaseID is the attribute you dissolved on. Count_LeaseID, added by ArcMap, tells you how many input features were dissolved to make each output feature. Sum_StandValue is the attribute you checked in the GeoProcessing Wizard. It contains the sum of all stand values (in millions of dollars) in each lease area. The value of lease A, for instance, is about 626 million dollars.

Shape_Length and Shape_Area are measurement attributes automatically maintained by ArcMap for geodatabase feature classes. (Shape_Length, for a polygon feature class, measures feature perimeters.)

13 Close the table.

14 If you want to save your work, click the File menu and click Save As. Navigate to **C:\GTKArcGIS\Chapter11\MyData**. Rename the file **my_ex11a.mxd** and click Save.

15 If you are continuing with the next exercise, leave ArcMap open. Otherwise, click the File menu and click Exit. Click No if prompted to save your changes.

Creating graphs

The ArcGIS Graph Wizard lets you create many different kinds of graphs, including column, pie, area, and scatter graphs. You can set properties for such elements as titles, axes, and graph markers (the bars in a bar graph, for instance). Graphs can be saved with a map document or as files with a .grf extension that can be added to any map document.

Exercise 11b

You have dissolved the forest stands into lease areas and summed their harvestable values. In this exercise, you'll present the values in a chart and add the chart to a map layout.

1 Start ArcMap. In the ArcMap dialog, click the option to use an existing map. In the list of existing maps, double-click Browse for maps. (If ArcMap is already running, click the File menu and click Open.) Navigate to **C:\GTKArcGIS\Chapter11**. Click **ex11b.mxd** and click Open.

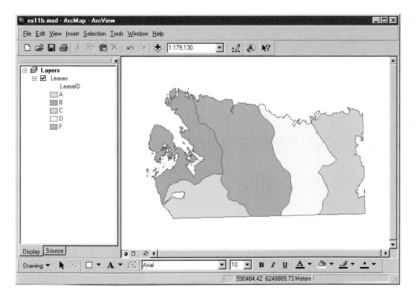

The map shows the lease areas you created in the previous exercise.

2 Click the Tools menu, point to Graphs, and click Create. The Graph Wizard opens.

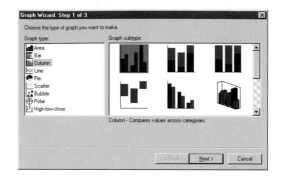

In the first panel, you'll accept the default graph type (a column graph) and subtype (one that compares values across categories).

3 Click Next.

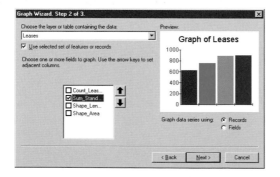

In the second panel, you choose a layer and check the attributes you want to graph.

4 Leases is the selected layer. In the box of attributes, uncheck Count_LeaseID and check Sum_StandValue. (The full attribute name appears if you hold the mouse pointer over it.) Make sure your dialog matches the following graphic, then click Next.

In the third panel, you'll add a title and label the x-axis. (To change fonts, colors, and other properties, you would click Advanced Options.) The graph preview updates as you make changes.

5 In the Title box, replace Graph of Leases with **Lease Values**. In the Sub title box, type **In millions of dollars**.

6 Check Label X Axis With and make sure its drop-down list is set to LeaseID.

7 Uncheck Show Legend. The LeaseID values display on the x-axis. Make sure your dialog matches the following graphic, then click Finish.

The graph displays in a window that floats on the application window. The graph makes it easy to compare the lease area values. Lease F, the most valuable, is worth about 1.5 billion dollars.

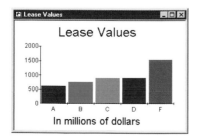

You'll add the graph to the map layout.

8 Right-click on the graph title bar. On the context menu, click Show on Layout.

The map switches automatically to layout view.

9 Close the graph window.

The graph displays in the middle of the virtual page, marked with blue selection handles. Other elements, such as the map title and labels, have been added for you.

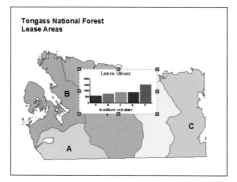

10 On the Tools toolbar, make sure the Select Elements tool is selected.

11 Drag the graph to the upper right corner of the layout, as shown in the following graphic. Click outside the virtual page to unselect the graph.

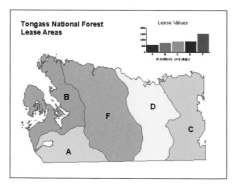

12 Click the View menu and click Data View.

13 If you want to save your work, click the File menu and click Save As. Navigate to **C:\GTKArcGIS\Chapter11\MyData**. Rename the file **my_ex11b.mxd** and click Save.

14 If you are continuing with the next exercise, leave ArcMap open. Otherwise, click the File menu and click Exit. Click No if prompted to save your changes.

Clipping layers

Clipping trims features in one layer at the boundaries of features in another layer. This lets you work with layers that have a common spatial extent, making it easier to navigate in your map. Clipping is often important for analysis. Suppose you want to determine the amount of wetland area in a county. Since wetlands may cross county boundaries, you would have to clip the wetland polygons at the county boundaries to get an accurate measurement.

In the following example, a layer of interstate highways is clipped at the boundaries of the state of Oklahoma.

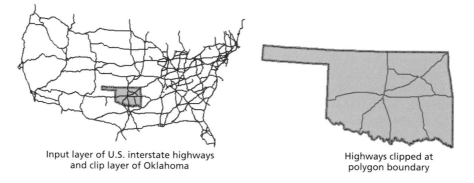

Input layer of U.S. interstate highways
and clip layer of Oklahoma

Highways clipped at
polygon boundary

Exercise 11c

The Forest Service has just determined that, of the five lease areas, only lease F is mature enough for harvest. Your company will direct its attention to making a bid for lease F.

Not every square meter of the lease area is harvestable. Logging is prohibited near streams and goshawk nests. (Goshawks are a protected bird species.) You have layers of streams and goshawk nests that cover all five lease areas, but now you'd like to work with data sets that cover only the area of lease F.

In this exercise, you'll clip a layer of streams to the boundary of lease F.

CHAPTER 11 • PREPARING DATA FOR ANALYSIS

1 Start ArcMap. In the ArcMap dialog, click the option to use an existing map. In the list of existing maps, double-click Browse for maps. (If ArcMap is already running, click the File menu and click Open.) Navigate to **C:\GTKArcGIS\Chapter11**. Click **ex11c.mxd** and click Open.

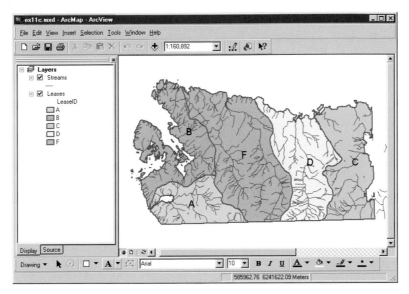

The map displays lease areas and streams.

To clip the streams to the lease F boundary, you must first select lease F. You'll turn the selection into a new layer so you can look at lease F apart from the others.

2 Click the Selection menu and click Set Selectable Layers. Uncheck Streams, as shown in the following graphic, then click Close.

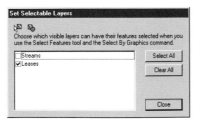

3 On the Tools toolbar, click the Select Features tool.

4 Click on lease F to select it. It is outlined in cyan.

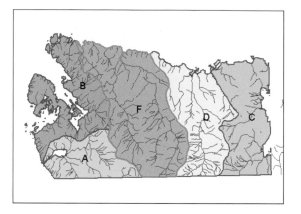

5 In the table of contents, right-click on the Leases layer, point to Selection, and click Create Layer From Selected Features.

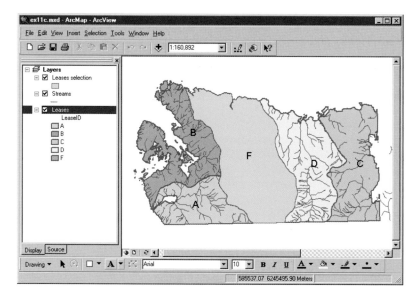

A layer called "Leases selection" is added to the top of the table of contents. (Your color may be different.) This layer exists only in the map document. It is not stored on disk.

6 Turn off the Leases layer and drag the Leases selection layer to the bottom of the table of contents.

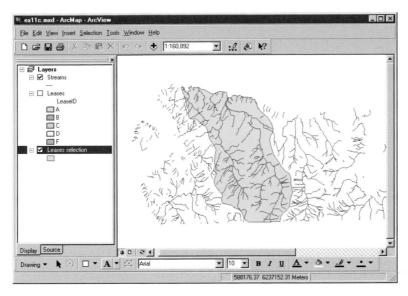

You'll use the GeoProcessing Wizard to clip the streams to the boundary of this layer.

7 Click the Tools menu and click GeoProcessing Wizard. On the first panel, click the operation to clip one layer based on another, then click Next.

On the second panel you'll select the layer to be clipped, the layer to clip with, and the output data set.

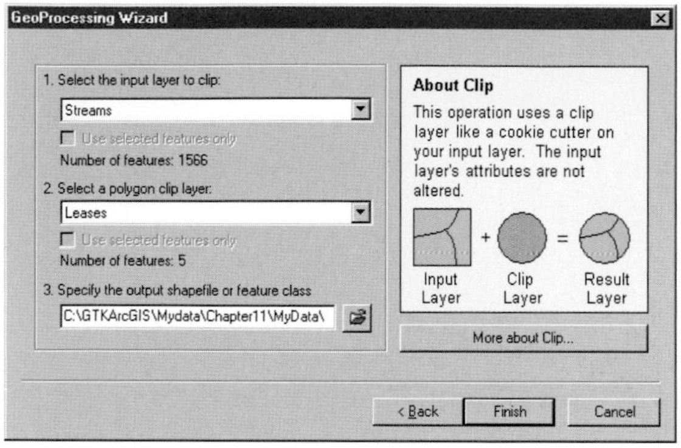

8 In the first drop-down list, click Streams. In the second drop-down list, click Leases selection.

9 Click the Browse button next to the third drop-down list. In the Saving Data dialog, click the Save as type drop-down arrow and click Personal Geodatabase feature classes.

10 Navigate to **C:\GTKArcGIS\Chapter11\MyData** and double-click on **MyTongass.mdb**.

11 In the Name box, replace Clip_Output with **StreamsF**. Make sure your dialog matches the following graphic, then click Save.

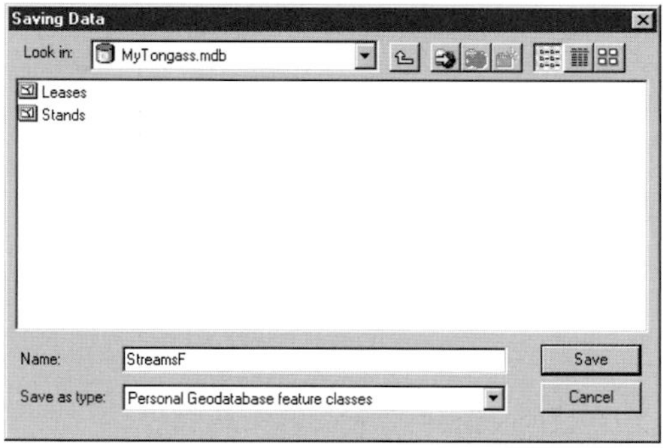

The output file information is updated in the wizard panel.

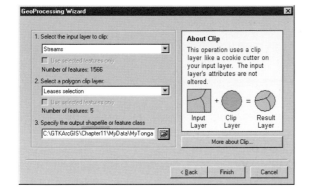

12 Click Finish.

When the operation is finished, the StreamsF layer is added to the map. Your color may be different.

13 In the table of contents, turn off the Streams layer.

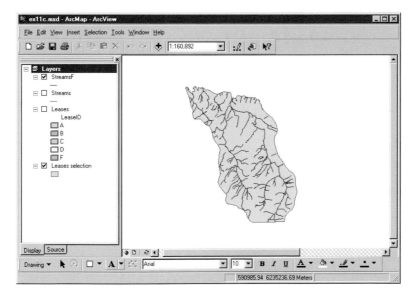

The stream features are clipped to the boundary of lease F.

14 If you want to save your work, click the File menu and click Save As. Navigate to **C:\GTKArcGIS\Chapter11\MyData**. Rename the file **my_ex11c.mxd** and click Save.

15 If you are continuing with the next exercise, leave ArcMap open. Otherwise, click the File menu and click Exit. Click No if prompted to save your changes.

Exporting data

Operations like dissolve and clip create new data sets automatically. Another way to make a new data set from an existing one is to make a selection on a layer and export the selected features.

Exercise 11d

In addition to the streams layer, you have a layer of goshawk nests covering all five lease areas. You could clip this layer just as you did the streams. Unlike the streams, however, the nests are points and don't cross polygon boundaries. (In the map it will look as if they do, but that is an effect of symbology.) Because nests are contained within polygons, you can use Select By Location to select the nests in lease F and then export the selected set.

1 Start ArcMap. In the ArcMap dialog, click the option to use an existing map. In the list of existing maps, double-click Browse for maps. (If ArcMap is already running, click the File menu and click Open.) Navigate to **C:\GTKArcGIS\Chapter11**. Click **ex11d.mxd** and click Open.

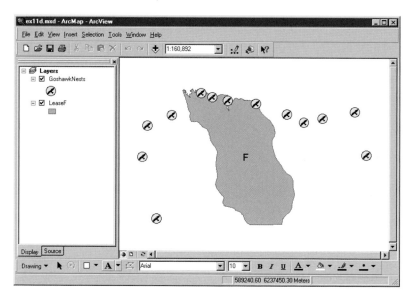

The map contains a layer of goshawk nests and a layer of lease F.

2 Click the Selection menu and click Select By Location.

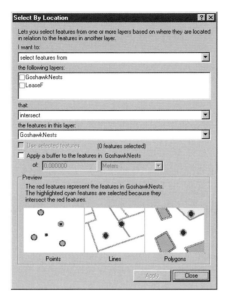

By default, the first drop-down list is set to "select features from."

3 In the scrolling box of layers, check GoshawkNests.

4 In the next drop-down list, click "are contained by."

5 In the list of layers, click LeaseF. Make sure your dialog matches the following graphic, then click Apply. Click Close.

On the map, four nests are selected.

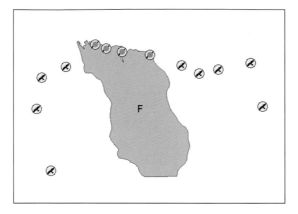

In the table of contents, right-click the GoshawkNests layer, point to Data, and click Export Data.

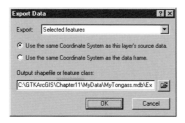

The Export drop-down list is correctly set to Selected features. The option to use the same coordinate system as the layer's source data is also correct. (You'll learn more about coordinate systems in chapter 13.)

7 Click the Browse button next to the Output shapefile or feature class box.

8 In the Saving Data dialog, make sure the Save as type drop-down list is set to Personal Geodatabase feature classes. Navigate to **C:\GTKArcGIS\Chapter11 \MyData** and double-click on **MyTongass.mdb**.

9 In the Name box, replace Export_Output with **NestsF**. Make sure your dialog matches the following graphic, then click Save.

10 Click OK in the Export Data dialog.

ArcMap exports the feature to a new feature class and prompts you to add the exported data to the map.

11 Click Yes.

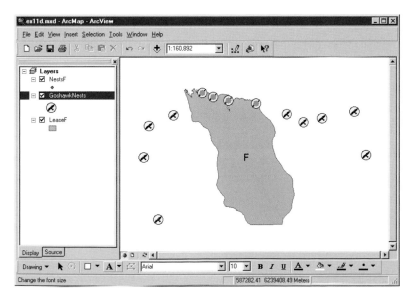

12 In the table of contents, turn off the GoshawkNests layer.

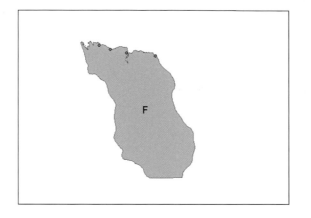

The new layer contains only goshawk nests within lease F. The default symbols are not as informative as the ones in the GoshawkNests layer.

13 In the table of contents, double-click on the NestsF layer. In the Layer Properties dialog, click the Symbology tab and click Import.

The Import Symbology dialog opens.

You want to import symbology from another layer in the map, so the first option is set correctly. The Layer drop-down list is also correctly set. Because you are symbolizing a point layer (NestsF), ArcMap assumes you want to import symbology from another point layer (GoshawkNests).

14 Click OK.

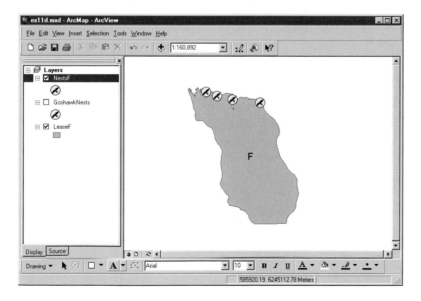

15 Click OK in the Layer Properties dialog.

You have prepared the data for your analysis. In the next chapter, you'll create exclusion zones around the streams and goshawk nests in lease F. You'll use these zones to figure out how much timberland in the lease area is harvestable and how much it's worth.

16 If you want to save your work, click the File menu and click Save As. Navigate to **C:\GTKArcGIS\Chapter11\MyData**. Rename the file **my_ex11d.mxd** and click Save.

17 If you are continuing to the next chapter, leave ArcMap open. Otherwise, click the File menu and click Exit. Click No when prompted to save your changes.

Analyzing spatial data

Buffering features
Overlaying data
Calculating attribute values

Most of the problems you solve with GIS involve examining spatial relationships among features. Although even something as simple as measuring the distance between two points can be called spatial analysis, the term is usually applied to operations that create new spatial data sets from existing ones.

In this chapter, you'll use two common spatial analysis tools, buffers and overlays. A buffer is an area drawn at a uniform distance around a feature.

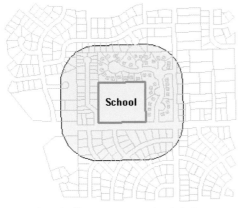

A 500-foot buffer around a school defines an area where billboard advertising is prohibited.

Overlays identify areas where features in two layers overlap (have coincident geometry) and create features in a new data set from these overlaps. In a union overlay, non-overlapping areas are also included in the new data set. In an intersect overlay, only the coincident geometry is preserved.

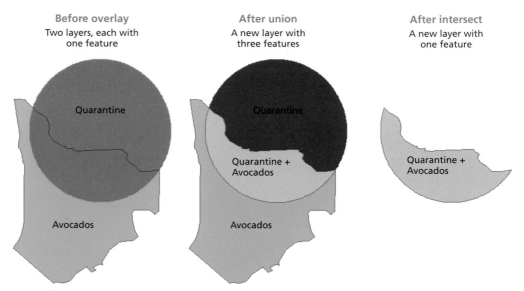

A fruit fly quarantine zone overlaps avocado groves (left). Overlay analysis—whether union or intersect—creates new features where input layers overlap. In this case, the analysis identifies areas where avocados must be destroyed.

Buffering features

Buffers are usually created as a new polygon data set, but they can also be drawn as graphics on a map. Buffers can be drawn at a constant distance, such as 100 meters, around every feature in a layer, or at a distance that varies according to attribute values. For example, buffers representing the range of radio signals from a transmitter might vary according to an attribute describing the transmitter strength. Buffers can also be concentric rings representing multiple distances, such as the areas within 100, 500, and 1,000 meters of a well.

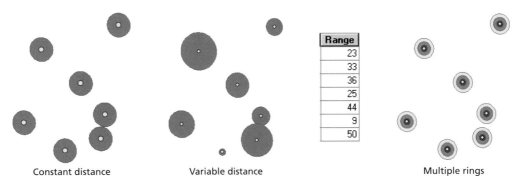

Range
23
33
36
25
44
9
50

Constant distance   Variable distance   Multiple rings

If features are close together, their buffers may overlap. You can preserve the overlaps or remove them.

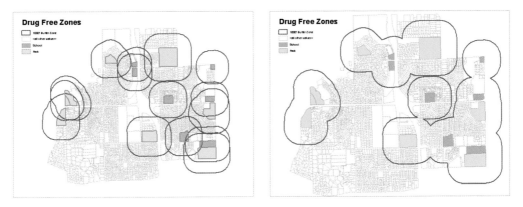

Exercise 12a

Your goal is to determine the value of harvestable land in lease F so that your lumber company can make a bid. In chapter 11, you dissolved forest stands into leases. Then you clipped streams and selected goshawk nests within lease F. In this exercise, you'll buffer the nest and stream layers to show where logging is prohibited. According to government regulations, no trees may be cut within 800 meters of a goshawk nest, the range of goshawk fledglings. Nor can trees be cut within 50 meters of a stream. Logging near streams leads to erosion of the stream banks, adding sediment to the water. This kills aquatic plant life and disrupts the food chain. The prohibition on logging is increased to 100 meters from streams where salmon spawn.

1 Start ArcMap. In the ArcMap dialog, click the option to use an existing map. In the list of existing maps, double-click Browse for maps. (If ArcMap is already running, click the File menu and click Open.) Navigate to **C:\GTKArcGIS\Chapter12**. Click **ex12a.mxd** and click Open.

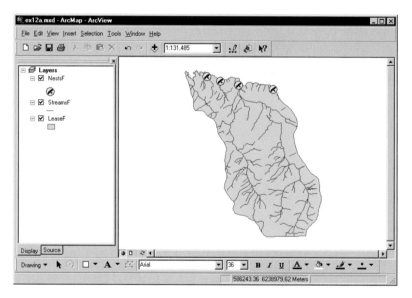

The map shows lease F, goshawk nests, and streams. You'll begin by buffering the goshawk nests.

2 Click the Tools menu and click Buffer Wizard.

3 In the first panel, the option to buffer the features of a layer is selected. Click the drop-down arrow and click NestsF.

4 Click Next. In the second panel, click the option to create buffers at a specified distance. Type **800** as the distance value. At the bottom of the dialog, click the distance units drop-down arrow and click Meters.

5 Click Next. In the final panel, make sure that the option to dissolve barriers between buffers is set to Yes.

6 Make sure that the option to save buffers in a new layer is selected. Click the Browse button.

7 In the Saving Data dialog, click the Save as type drop-down arrow and click Personal Geodatabase feature classes. Navigate to **C:\GTKArcGIS\Chapter12\MyData**. Double-click **MyTongass.mdb**.

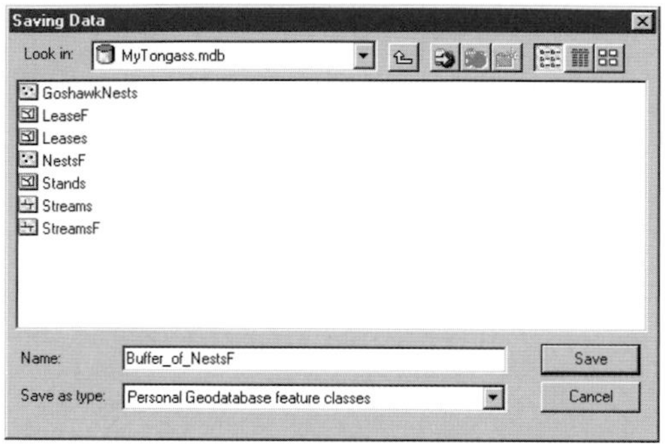

More feature classes have been added to the MyTongass geodatabase to make it complete.

8 Click Save to accept the default name, Buffer_of_NestsF. Make sure that your panel matches the following graphic, then click Finish.

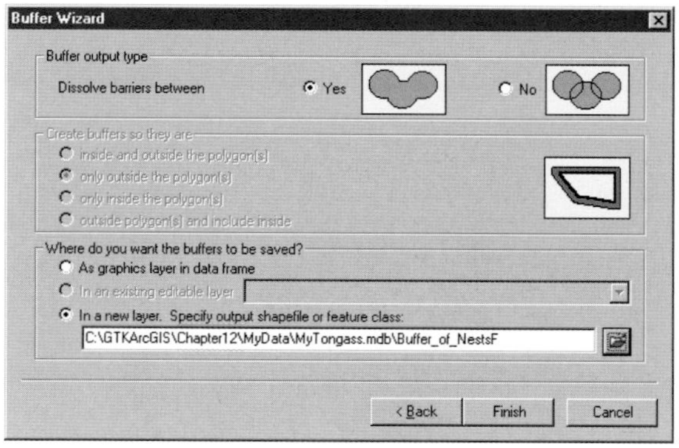

The new layer is added to the table of contents and displayed on the map. (New buffers always draw in brown.) Where buffers overlap, the barriers between them have been removed, as specified in step 5.

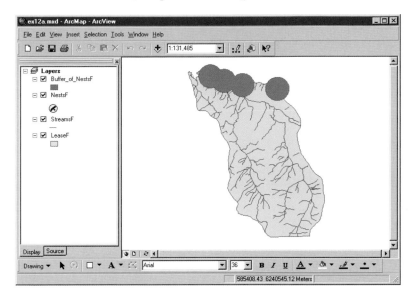

9 In the table of contents, right-click on the Buffer_of_NestsF layer and click Open Attribute Table.

ObjectID*	Shape*	Shape_Length	Shape_Area	BufferDist
1	Polygon	10358.700025	5458199.615650	800
2	Polygon	5095.711094	2065650.395009	800

Record: 1   Show: All Selected Records (0 out of 2 Selected.)   Options ▾

The table contains a record for each buffer polygon. Buffers with dissolved barriers form a single feature, so there are just two records. The attributes include the buffer length (perimeter), area, and distance from buffered features.

Now you'll buffer the Streams layer. The buffers for this layer will vary according to whether or not salmon spawn in a stream.

10 Close the Attributes of Buffer_of_NestsF table. In the table of contents, right-click the StreamsF layer and click Open Attribute Table.

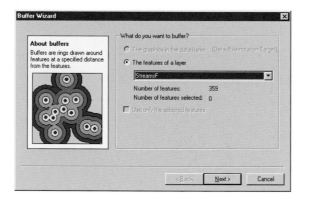

The HasSpawning field shows whether or not a stream has spawning salmon. The Distance field values of 50 and 100 correspond to the No and Yes values in the HasSpawning field.

11 Close the table. In the table of contents, turn off the Buffer_of_NestsF and NestsF layers.

12 Click the Tools menu and click Buffer Wizard.

13 In the first panel, the option to buffer the features of a layer is selected. Click the drop-down arrow and click StreamsF.

14 Click Next. In the second panel, click the option to create buffers based on a distance from an attribute. Make sure the drop-down list is set to the Distance field. Make sure that the distance units are meters.

15 Click Next. In the final panel, click No so that barriers between buffers are not dissolved.

If you dissolved barriers for variable-width buffers, buffers of different sizes would be combined into a single feature and ArcMap would not create a BufferDist attribute. But you'll need this attribute later in the chapter to help you figure out which land is harvestable.

16 Make sure that the option to save buffers in a new layer is selected and that the output feature class is **C:\GTKArcGIS\Chapter12\MyData\MyTongass.mdb \Buffer_of_StreamsF**. If it isn't, click the Browse button and navigate to this location. Make sure the dialog matches the following graphic, then click Finish.

The new layer is added to the top of the table of contents. At this scale, it may be hard to see that the buffers have different widths.

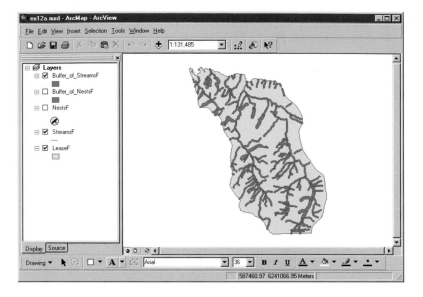

17 Click the View menu, point to Bookmarks, and click Streams Closeup. Drag the StreamsF layer to the top of the table of contents.

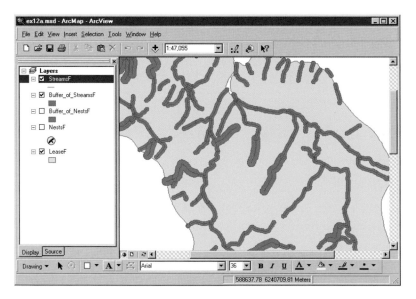

The difference between the 50- and 100-meter buffers is more pronounced.

18 In the table of contents, right-click on the Buffer_of_StreamsF layer and click Open Attribute Table. The BufferDist field contains values of 50 and 100.

ObjectID*	Shape*	Shape_Length	Shape_Area	BufferDist
1	Polygon	783.236733	31763.637617	50
2	Polygon	1234.204969	92898.503655	100
3	Polygon	434.498524	13950.399047	50
4	Polygon	839.726192	34510.560743	50
5	Polygon	1337.490696	103320.152215	100
6	Polygon	428.599463	13652.707846	50
7	Polygon	401.353126	12276.009128	50
8	Polygon	1209.367376	53252.393229	50

Attributes of Buffer_of_StreamsF

Record: 1   Show: All Selected   Records (0 out of 359 Selected.)   Options ▾

19 Close the table. Turn off the StreamsF layer. Turn on the Buffer_of_NestsF layer. In the table of contents, only the two buffer layers and the LeaseF layer should be turned on.

20 In the table of contents, right-click on the LeaseF layer and click Zoom to Layer.

The two buffer layers define the areas where trees cannot be cut. In the next exercise, you'll use overlays to define the areas where they can be cut.

21 If you want to save your work, click the File menu and click Save As. Navigate to **C:\GTKArcGIS\Chapter12\MyData**. Rename the file **my_ex12a.mxd** and click Save.

22 If you are continuing with the next exercise, leave ArcMap open. Otherwise, click the File menu and click Exit. Click No if prompted to save your changes.

Overlaying data

An overlay creates a new data set by superimposing one layer on another. The output data has the attributes of both input layers.

An overlay can be a union or an intersect of the input layers. In a union, the total area from both input layers is included in the output layer.

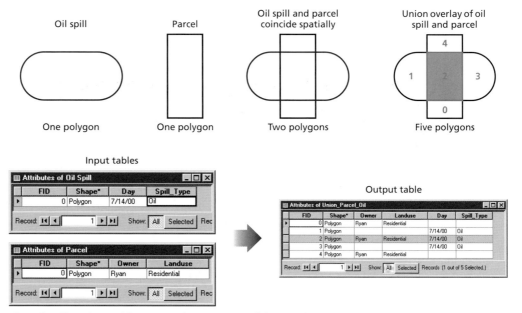

The Oil Spill and Parcel layers overlap. A union of the two layers creates a new layer with five features. Values in the output table are populated or blank depending on whether or not an output feature coincides with an input feature. Only feature 2 has all its attributes populated.

In an intersect, only the area common to both input layers is included in the output layer.

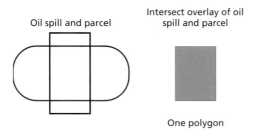

A union requires that both input layers be polygons. In an intersect, a polygon layer can overlay a polygon or a line layer. In the latter case, the output is a line layer.

Exercise 12b

In this exercise, you'll union the nest and stream buffer layers from the previous exercise to create a single layer of the land that cannot be harvested. Then you'll union this layer with a layer of stands in lease F. Because new features will be created wherever stand polygons cross buffers, every output feature will be entirely inside or entirely outside a buffer. The set of features lying outside buffers represents harvestable land.

1 Start ArcMap. In the ArcMap dialog, click the option to use an existing map. In the list of existing maps, double-click Browse for maps. (If ArcMap is already running, click the File menu and click Open.) Navigate to **C:\GTKArcGIS\Chapter12**. Click **ex12b.mxd** and click Open.

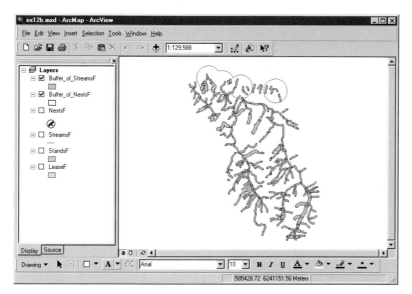

The map shows the buffers for streams and goshawk nests. The other layers are turned off.

2 Click the Tools menu and click GeoProcessing Wizard. In the first panel, click the operation to union two layers.

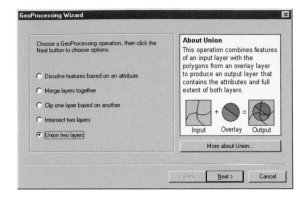

3 Click Next.

In the second panel you specify the two input layers and the output data set.

4 Make sure the input layer to union is set to Buffer_of_StreamsF and the polygon overlay layer is set to Buffer_of_NestsF.

As long as these are the two layers, it doesn't matter which is the input and which the overlay. The results will be the same.

5 Click the Browse button next to the output file name.

6 In the Saving Data dialog, make sure the Save as type drop-down list is set to Personal Geodatabase feature classes. Navigate to **C:\GTKArcGIS\Chapter12\MyData**. Double-click on **MyTongass.mdb**. Replace the default file name of Union_Output with **NestAndStream**.

Saving Data

Look in: MyTongass.mdb

- Buffer_of_NestsF
- Buffer_of_StreamsF
- GoshawkNests
- LeaseF
- Leases
- NestsF
- Stands
- Streams
- StreamsF

Name: NestAndStream   Save

Save as type: Personal Geodatabase feature classes   Cancel

7 Click Save. Make sure that your panel matches the following graphic, then click Finish.

GeoProcessing Wizard

1. Select the input layer to union:

Buffer_of_StreamsF

☐ Use selected features only

Number of features: 359

2. Select a polygon overlay layer:

Buffer_of_NestsF

☐ Use selected features only

Number of features: 2

3. Specify the output shapefile or feature class

C:\GTKArcGIS\Chapter12\MyData\MyTonga

About Union

This operation combines features of an input layer with the polygons from an overlay layer to produce an output layer that contains the attributes and full extent of both layers.

Input   Overlay   Output

More about Union...

< Back   Finish   Cancel

When the layers have been unioned, the new NestAndStream layer is added to the map. (Your color may be different.)

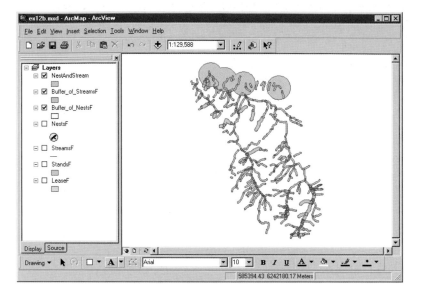

8 In the table of contents, right-click the NestAndStream layer and click Open Attribute Table.

ObjectID*	Shape*	BufferDist	BufferDist_1	Shape_Length	Shape_Area
1	Polygon	50	0	480.387353	14518.928
2	Polygon	100	0	129.945072	772.083
3	Polygon	50	0	156.728503	566.585
4	Polygon	100	0	156.728503	566.585
5	Polygon	100	0	156.728503	566.585
6	Polygon	50	0	640.983015	23557.564
7	Polygon	50	0	8.345423	0.328
8	Polygon	50	0	8.345423	0.328
9	Polygon	100	0	8.345423	0.328
10	Polygon	50	0	6.635253	0.039
11	Polygon	50	0	6.635253	0.039
12	Polygon	100	0	6.635253	0.039
13	Polygon	50	0	6.635253	0.039
14	Polygon	50	0	76.651907	83.216
15	Polygon	100	0	76.651907	83.216
16	Polygon	50	0	76.651907	83.216
17	Polygon	50	0	151.513075	1131.084
18	Polygon	100	0	151.513075	1131.084
19	Polygon	50	0	81.711475	135.180

Record: 1   Show: All Selected Records (0 out of *2000 Selected.)   Options

The table contains buffer distance attributes from both input layers. To avoid a conflict, ArcMap changed the name of one of the BufferDist fields to BufferDist_1. Every record in the table has a nonzero value in at least one of the BufferDist fields. Features lying within both a stream buffer and a goshawk nest buffer have nonzero values in both fields.

9 Close the table. Turn on the StandsF layer.

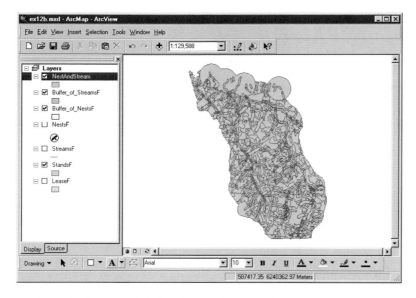

To find the harvestable land, you'll union the NestAndStream layer with the StandsF layer.

10 Click the Tools menu and click GeoProcessing Wizard. In the first panel, click to union two layers.

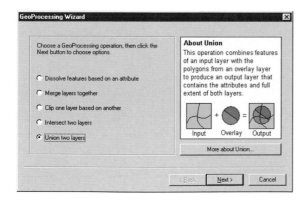

11 Click Next. In the second panel, make sure NestAndStream is selected as the input layer to union. For the polygon overlay layer, click the drop-down arrow and click StandsF.

12 Click the Browse button next to the output file name.

13 In the Saving Data dialog, make sure the Save as type drop-down list is set to Personal Geodatabase feature classes. If necessary, navigate to **C:\GTKArcGIS \Chapter12\MyData\MyTongass.mdb**. Replace the default file name of Union_Output with **Final**.

14 Click Save. Make sure that your panel matches the following graphic, then click Finish.

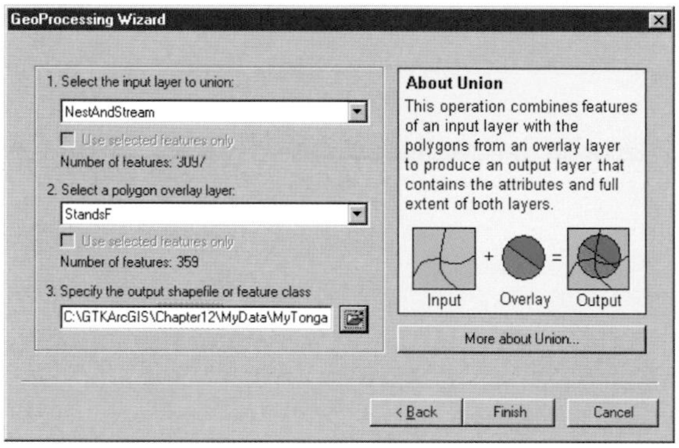

When the layers have been unioned, the new Final layer is added to the map. (Your color may be different.)

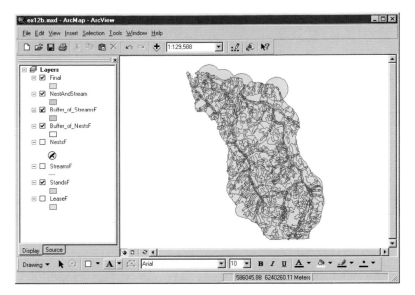

15 In the table of contents, right-click the Final layer and click Open Attribute Table.

ObjectID*	Shape*	BufferDist	BufferDist_1	LeaseID	StandValue	ValuePerMeter	StandID
1	Polygon	0	0	F	0.033645	27	191
2	Polygon	50	0		0	0	
3	Polygon	0	0	F	0.072730	52	696
4	Polygon	0	0	F	0.036905	54	696
5	Polygon	50	0		0	0	
6	Polygon	0	0	F	0.262797	43	189
7	Polygon	50	0	F	0.262797	43	189
8	Polygon	0	0	F	0.302535	27	187
9	Polygon	50	0	F	5.553224	3	143
10	Polygon	50	0	F	2.459511	26	180
11	Polygon	50	0	F	0.302535	27	187

Record: [◄] [◄] [1] [►] [►|]   Show: All Selected   Records (0 out of *2000 Selected.)   Options ▾

To create a layer in which no stands cross buffers, ArcMap has had to make more than six thousand features. (ArcMap does not show all the records at once. If you want to see the total, scroll to the bottom of the table or click the Move to end of table button in the lower left part of the dialog.)

Features in protected areas have a nonzero value for one or both BufferDist attributes. Only features with zeros for both attributes are in harvestable areas.

16 Scroll all the way to the right.

	LeaseID	StandValue	ValuePerMeter	StandID	Shape_Length	Shape_Area
▶	F	0.033645	27	1911	204.706195	1246.090602
		0	0	0	261.730256	4029.654667
	F	0.072730	52	6961	261.575061	1398.655795
	F	0.036905	54	6963	262.955436	683.420444
		0	0	0	301.142121	4492.249970
	F	0.262797	43	1890	298.408409	4759.361232
	F	0.262797	43	1890	173.410013	1352.187092
	F	0.302535	27	1878	260.681814	3419.062125
	F	5.553224	3	1434	7.613404	2.545098
	F	2.459511	26	1801	233.822944	1776.061452
	F	0.302535	27	1878	352.675299	7099.941043

Attributes of Final

Record: 1   Show: All Selected   Records (0 out of *2000 Selected.)   Options ▾

Along with the buffer attributes, the table includes the attributes from the StandsF layer.

ArcMap maintains Shape_Length and Shape_Area values for every feature in a geodatabase feature class. It does not, however, automatically update attributes that are based on length or area, such as StandValue (ValuePerMeter times Shape_Area). In the next exercise, you'll recalculate the StandValue attribute to get an accurate total value for harvestable land.

17 Close the table.

18 If you want to save your work, click the File menu and click Save As. Navigate to **C:\GTKArcGIS\Chapter12\MyData**. Rename the file **my_ex12b.mxd** and click Save.

19 If you are continuing with the next exercise, leave ArcMap open. Otherwise, click the File menu and click Exit. Click No if prompted to save your changes.

Calculating attribute values

You can write an expression to calculate attribute values for all records in a table or just for selected ones. For numeric attributes, the expression can include constants, functions, or values from other fields in the table. For text attributes, the expression can include character strings that you type or text values from other fields.

Exercise 12c

The graph you made in chapter 11 showed that the timber value of lease F was about 1.5 billion dollars. In this exercise, you'll adjust that value to take into account only harvestable areas. You'll create a definition query to display just these areas, then you'll recalculate stand values to determine how much the total harvestable area is worth.

1 Start ArcMap. In the ArcMap dialog, click the option to use an existing map. In the list of existing maps, double-click Browse for maps. (If ArcMap is already running, click the File menu and click Open.) Navigate to **C:\GTKArcGIS\Chapter12**. Click **ex12c.mxd** and click Open.

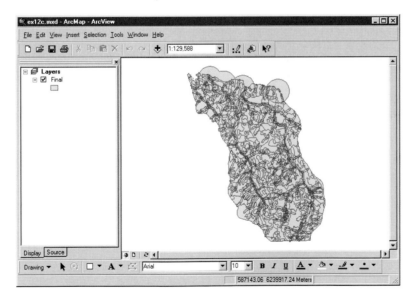

The map contains the Final layer you created in the last exercise.

2 In the table of contents, right-click the Final layer and click Open Attribute Table.

ObjectID*	Shape*	BufferDist	BufferDist_1	LeaseID	StandValue	ValuePerMeter	StandID	Shape_Length	Shape_Area
1	Polygon	0	0	F	0.033645	27	1911	204.706195	1246.090602
2	Polygon	50	0		0	0	0	261.730256	4029.654667
3	Polygon	0	0	F	0.072730	52	6961	261.575061	1398.655795
4	Polygon	0	0	F	0.036905	54	6963	262.955436	683.420444
5	Polygon	50	0		0	0	0	301.142121	4492.249970
6	Polygon	0	0	F	0.262797	43	1890	298.408409	4759.361232
7	Polygon	50	0	F	0.262797	43	1890	173.410013	1352.187092
8	Polygon	0	0	F	0.302535	27	1878	260.681814	3419.062125
9	Polygon	50	0	F	5.553224	3	1434	7.613404	2.545098
10	Polygon	50	0	F	2.459511	26	1801	233.822944	1776.061452
11	Polygon	50	0	F	0.302535	27	1878	352.675299	7099.941043
12	Polygon	50	0	F	5.553224	3	1434	265.085585	2924.195350
13	Polygon	50	0	F	0.302535	27	1878	137.842543	685.996045
14	Polygon	100	0	F	0.302535	27	1878	137.842543	685.996045
15	Polygon	0	0	F	4.238982	43	1812	239.050170	1813.393853
16	Polygon	0	0	F	0.191679	27	1875	447.336331	7099.222143
17	Polygon	0	0	F	2.504689	42	1814	440.930252	8646.222751
18	Polygon	0	0	F	5.553224	3	1434	297.576835	4885.853106
19	Polygon	0	0	F	5.553224	3	1434	56.801183	137.531078
20	Polygon	0	0	F	5.553224	3	1434	1175.584726	42584.099130

Record: 1 Show: All Selected Records (0 out of *2000 Selected.) Options ▾

Any feature with zeros in both BufferDist fields is harvestable.

3 Close the table. In the table of contents, double-click the Final layer. In the Layer Properties dialog, click the Definition Query tab.

4 Click Query Builder to open the Query Builder dialog.

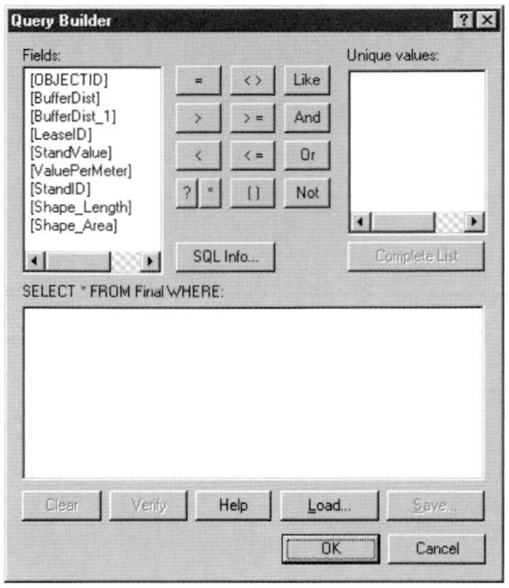

5 In the Fields box, double-click [BufferDist] to add it to the expression box. Click the equals (=) button. In the Unique sample values box, double-click 0.

[BufferDist] = 0

6 Click the And button. In the Fields box, double-click [BufferDist_1], then click the equals (=) button. In the Unique sample values box, double-click 0. Make sure your expression matches the following graphic, then click OK.

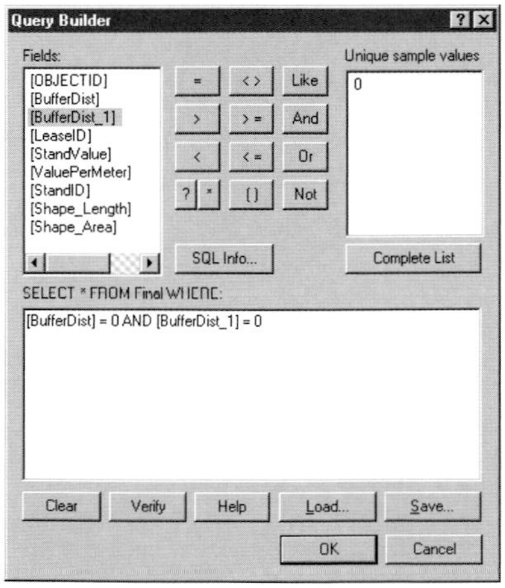

The query displays in the Definition Query box.

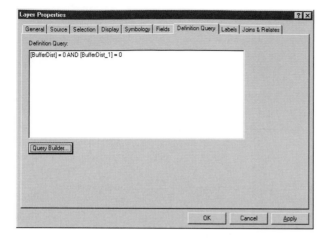

7 Click OK on the Layer Properties dialog.

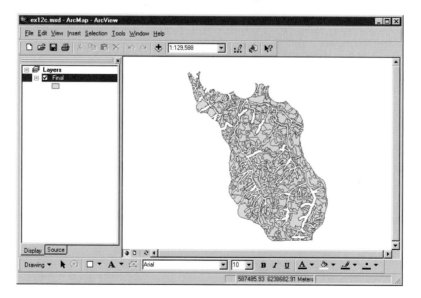

On the map, only features satisfying the query—that is, features representing harvestable land—are displayed. Now you'll update the StandValue attribute for these features.

8 In the table of contents, right-click on the Final layer and click Open Attribute Table.

The table includes only records for features shown by the definition query—699 records, rather than the original 6,181.

9 Right-click on the field name StandValue and click Calculate Values.

A message box informs you that you are about to make changes to a table outside an editing session.

10 Click Yes. The Field Calculator dialog opens.

11 In the Fields scrolling list, click Shape_Area to add it to the expression box. Click the multiplication (*) button. In the Fields scrolling list, click ValuePerMeter.

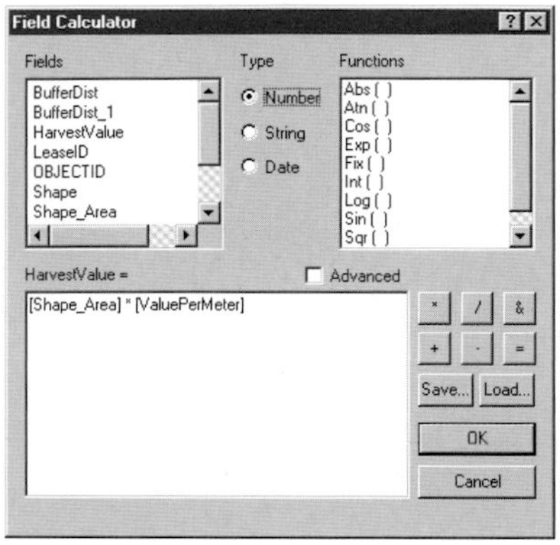

This expression will give you the updated stand values in dollars. In the table, however, the stand values are expressed in millions of dollars.

12 Click at the beginning of the expression and type an opening parenthesis "(" followed by a space. Click at the end of the expression and type a space followed by a closing parenthesis ")". Click the division (/) button. Type a space and type **1000000**. Make sure your expression matches the one in the following graphic, then click OK.

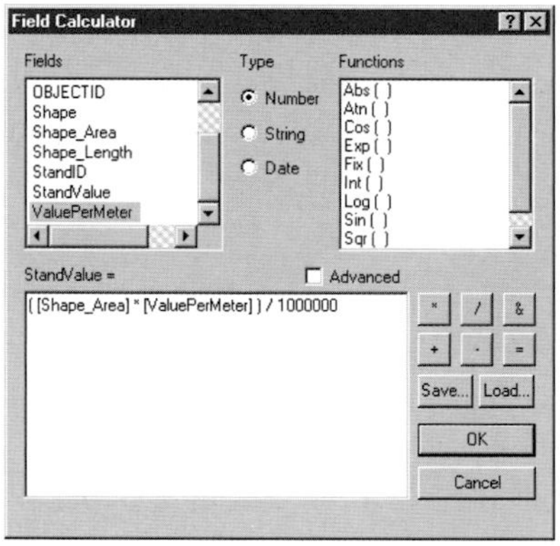

The values in the StandValue field are recalculated.

13 Right-click on the StandValue field name and click Statistics.

The sum of the values is 1,044.924747. The harvestable value of lease F is therefore just over a billion dollars—about two thirds of the original calculation shown in your graph from exercise 11b, step 7.

14 Close the Statistics window and the table.

Your company will use this information to make a competitive bid. It's a big invest-ment, but tree harvesting is expensive. You have to move heavy equipment into the area, supply the labor force, and construct roads.

A more detailed analysis would consider additional factors, such as the locations of existing roads, the slope of the land, and other protected areas like stands of old-growth trees.

15 If you want to save your work, click the File menu and click Save As. Navigate to **C:\GTKArcGIS\Chapter12\MyData**. Rename the file **my_ex12c.mxd** and click Save.

In the next chapter, you'll launch ArcMap from ArcCatalog. So even if you are con-tinuing, you should exit ArcMap now.

16 Click the File menu and click Exit. Click No if prompted to save your changes.

Projecting data in ArcMap

Projecting data for display

Defining a projection

The location of any given place can be defined with reference to lines of latitude and longitude, which create an imaginary mesh over the world.

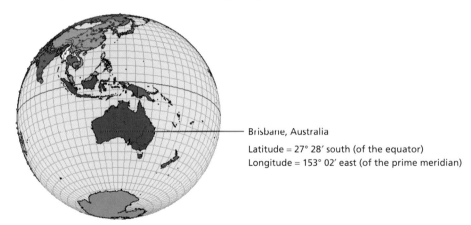

Brisbane, Australia

Latitude = 27° 28′ south (of the equator)

Longitude = 153° 02′ east (of the prime meridian)

Latitude and longitude values belong to a spherical coordinate system—a system for defining locations and making measurements on a sphere, or something close to a sphere (a spheroid), like the earth.

The latitude–longitude value of a point depends on the assumptions you make about the earth's shape. The earth isn't perfectly round. It bulges at the equator and is flattened at the poles. Technically, this makes it an oblate spheroid.

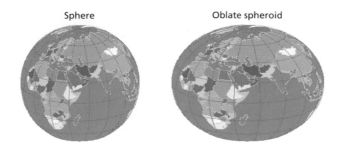

Sphere   Oblate spheroid

Besides being not quite round to begin with, the surface of the earth has various bumps and indentations. Determining the exact shape of the earth is not a simple matter. There are many different models—ArcMap recognizes almost three hundred of them.

To make a map, one of these models of the earth (or some part of it) must be represented on a flat surface. This is accomplished by a mathematical transformation called a map projection.

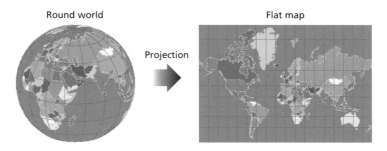

Round world   Projection   Flat map

Just as location on a sphere is defined by latitude and longitude, location on a map is defined by Cartesian coordinates, which assign values to points according to their positions on a horizontal x-axis and a vertical y-axis. As opposed to a spherical coordinate system, this is a planar coordinate system.

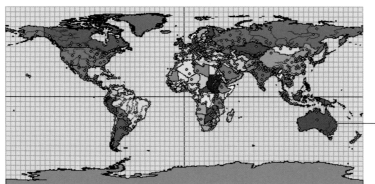

Brisbane, Australia

x = 17,015,699
(meters along the x-axis)

y = −3,052,928
(meters along the y-axis)

The exact location of a point on a map varies according to the map projection used. There are about fifty commonly used projections and many variations on each.

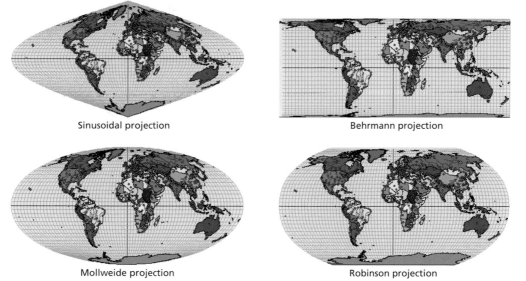

Sinusoidal projection

Behrmann projection

Mollweide projection

Robinson projection

Four world projections. Many projections are made for individual continents, countries, parts of countries, or strips of land that may cross national boundaries.

Every spatial data set in a GIS stores latitude–longitude coordinates for its features. These coordinates make up its *geographic coordinate system* (GCS). A data set that has been projected also stores Cartesian coordinates for its features. These make up its projected coordinate system (PCS).

When you work with unprojected data (data that has only a geographic coordinate system), any measurements or calculations you make are based on a sphere or spheroid. This is problematic because degrees of latitude do not have constant length. A degree of latitude at the 30th parallel (30 degrees north of the equator) is longer than a degree of latitude at the 60th parallel. Both represent 1/360th of a circle, but the circles have different circumferences.

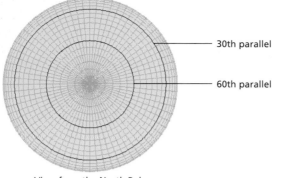

30th parallel

60th parallel

View from the North Pole

Since degrees of latitude are not constant, they can't be used to make meaningful measurements of distance and area.

This problem is overcome with map projections. On a flat surface, units of measurement (meters or feet, for example) are constant, which means you can make meaningful area and distance measurements. There is another difficulty, however. Since the world is a sphere and maps are flat, you can't go from one to the other without changing the proportions of features on the surface. Map projections distort shape, area, distance, and direction. Some projections preserve one of these properties at the expense of others, some compromise on all of them, and some preserve properties for one part of the world and not others.

The Mercator projection, for example, preserves direction but distorts area. The sinusoidal projection preserves area but distorts shape.

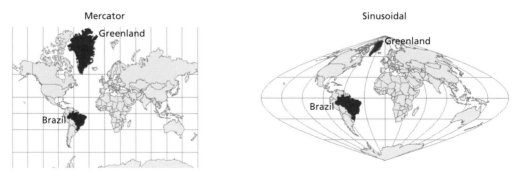

In the Mercator projection, Greenland looks larger than Brazil, although Brazil is four times its size. Because direction is preserved, Brazil correctly appears due south of Greenland. In the sinusoidal projection, the proportional sizes of Greenland and Brazil are correct. Their shapes, however, are distorted—Greenland is too narrow and Brazil too wide. (Brazil is still due south of Greenland. The sinusoidal projection represents direction as a curve rather than a straight line.)

Your choice of a map projection allows you to control the type of distortion in a map for your area of interest. If you are working with a fairly small area and using an appropriate projection, the effects of distortion are insignificant. If you are working with the whole world, there is bound to be significant distortion of some spatial property.

For more information about choosing projections, and about coordinate systems in general, refer to the ArcGIS documentation *Understanding Map Projections*. For more information, click the Contents tab in ArcGIS Desktop Help and navigate to *ArcMap > Creating maps > About coordinate systems* and *ArcMap > Creating maps > Specifying a coordinate system*.

Projecting data for display

When you add a layer to a map, both its appearance and the results of measurements and calculations you make depend on its coordinate system.

You can find a data set's coordinate system in its spatial metadata.

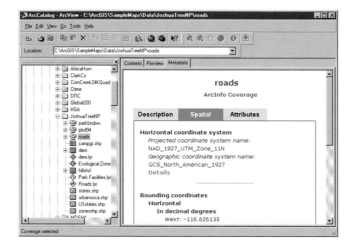

When data sets that have the same coordinate system are added to a data frame, the features in each layer are correctly positioned with respect to each other. If you subsequently add a data set that has a different coordinate system, ArcMap changes it to match the others in a process called "on-the-fly" projection. This new, temporary projection is applied only within a particular data frame; the data set's native coordinate system (the one shown in its spatial metadata) does not change.

By default, layers are projected on the fly to the coordinate system of the first layer added to a data frame (even if the layer is later removed). This coordinate system is stored as a property of the data frame and can be changed. You can project all layers in a data frame to any coordinate system ArcMap supports.

Source data

Cities in sinusoidal PCS

Data frame

Sinusoidal PCS

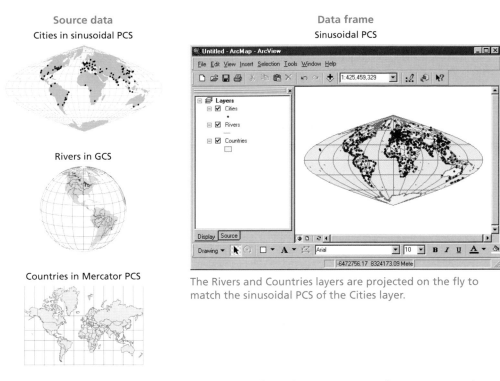

Rivers in GCS

Countries in Mercator PCS

The Rivers and Countries layers are projected on the fly to match the sinusoidal PCS of the Cities layer.

To project a layer on the fly, ArcMap uses the information stored in its geographic coordinate system. On-the-fly projection works best when all layers in the map have the same GCS (in other words, when they all use the same model of the earth). If you add a layer, projected or not, that has a different geographic coordinate system from other layers, you'll see this warning:

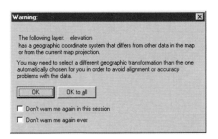

ArcMap will add and project the layer anyway. Because the differences among geographic coordinate systems are fairly small, the display is usually fine.

On-the-fly projections are less mathematically rigorous than permanent projections (which change the native coordinate system of a data set). If you plan to use data sets in an exacting analysis, you should project them permanently to the same coordinate system with the ArcToolbox Projection Wizard. With ArcView, you can do this for shapefiles and geodatabase feature classes; with ArcEditor and ArcInfo, for other data formats as well.

Exercise 13a

You work for the United States Census Bureau and are creating a map of the United States that shows population change between 1990 and 2000. The map will have three data frames: one for the lower forty-eight states, one for Alaska, and one for Hawaii. You will use the same geographic shapefile of U.S. states in all three frames and apply a suitable projection to each.

1 Start ArcCatalog. In the ArcCatalog tree, double-click the connection to **C:\GTKArcGIS**. Double-click the **Chapter13** folder. Double-click the **Data** folder.

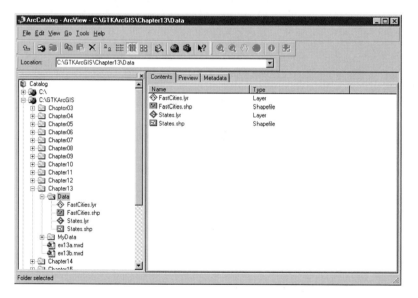

There are two shapefiles: FastCities and States. Each has a corresponding layer file. In this exercise, you'll use the States data. You'll work with FastCities, which contains the fastest-growing city in each state, in the next exercise.

2 In the catalog window, click on **States.lyr** and click the Preview tab.

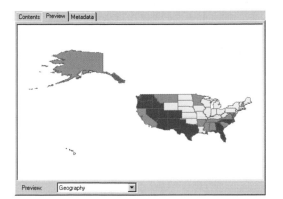

The layer has been symbolized with a color ramp that shows population change. The shapes of the states are somewhat distorted. The northern boundary of the United States is a straight line, for instance, while Alaska looks short and wide. This appearance is characteristic of unprojected data in ArcMap.

3 Click the Preview drop-down arrow and click Table. Scroll to the right.

STATE_NAME	POP1990	POP2000	NumChange	PctChange
Washington	4866692	7078516	1027429	21.1
Montana	799065	902195	103130	12.9
Maine	1227928	1274923	46995	3.8
North Dakota	638800	642200	3400	0.5
South Dakota	696004	754844	58840	8.5
Wyoming	453588	7078516	40194	8.9
Wisconsin	4891769	7078516	471906	9.6
Idaho	1006749	1293953	287204	28.5
Vermont	562758	608827	46069	8.2
Minnesota	4375099	4919479	544380	12.4
Oregon	2842321	3421399	579078	20.4
New Hampshire	1109252	1235786	126534	11.4
Iowa	2776755	2926324	149569	5.4
Massachusetts	6016425	6349097	332672	5.5

Record: 1 Show: All Selected Records (of 50)

Preview: Table

The table has 1990 and 2000 population figures for each state, as well as the population change in raw numbers and percentages. Every state grew during the decade. The layer is classified and symbolized on the PctChange attribute.

You'll confirm that the States shapefile has a geographic coordinate system.

4 In the catalog tree, click on States.shp. In the display, click the Metadata tab.

5 In the metadata window, click the Spatial tab.

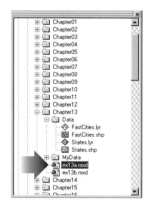

The metadata shows a geographic coordinate system called GCS_North_American_1983. There is no projected coordinate system. If there were, it would be listed here, too.

Next, you'll start ArcMap and add the States layer file to a map document.

6 In the catalog tree, double-click **ex13a.mxd**.

ArcMap opens in layout view.

chapter

10
11
12

13

The map contains three empty data frames: Hawaii, Alaska, and Lower 48. Lower 48 is active. A title and legend have already been added to the map.

You'll add the States layer to each data frame and zoom to a different location in each. Then you'll select an appropriate coordinate system for each data frame. By default, empty data frames have no coordinate system defined.

7 Position the ArcCatalog and ArcMap windows so you can see the catalog tree and the ArcMap table of contents.

8 In the catalog tree, click States.lyr and drag it to the bottom of the ArcMap table of contents. Make ArcMap the active application.

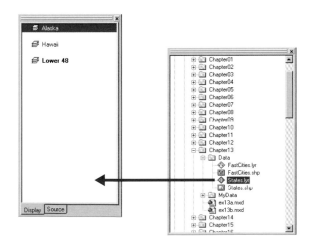

The layer is added to the table of contents and displays in the data frame. It looks as it did when you previewed it in ArcCatalog. You'll use a bookmark to zoom in to the lower forty-eight states.

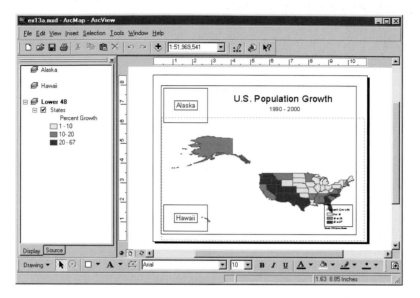

9 Click the View menu, point to Bookmarks, and click Lower 48.

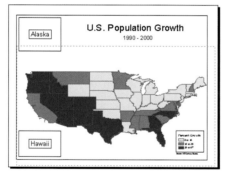

You'll apply a new coordinate system to the data frame.

10 In the table of contents, right-click the Lower 48 data frame and click Properties. In the dialog, click the Coordinate System tab.

The data frame's current coordinate system is GCS_North_American_1983.

11 In the Select a coordinate system box, click the plus sign next to Predefined.

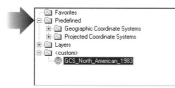

12 Click the plus sign next to Projected Coordinate Systems, the plus sign next to Continental, then the plus sign next to North America.

The projected coordinate systems for continental North America are listed. You'll select an equal-area projection. Equal-area projections maintain the spatial property of size (the areas of states are correct). Other spatial properties are distorted to some extent.

13 Click North America Albers Equal Area Conic. (Hold the mouse pointer over a name to see all of it.) The details of the projection appear in the Current coordinate system box. Make sure that your dialog matches the following graphic, then click OK.

The layer is reprojected on the fly. You'll use a bookmark to zoom in a little closer.

14 Click the View menu, point to Bookmarks, and click Lower 48 after Projection.

The states are displayed in the Albers projection. The projection is applied only within the data frame. On disk, the States shapefile still has a geographic coordinate system.

You'll copy the States layer to the other two data frames and apply coordinate systems to them.

15 In the table of contents, right-click the States layer and click Copy. In the table of contents, right-click on the Hawaii data frame and click Paste Layer. Again in the table of contents, right-click on the Alaska data frame and click Paste Layer.

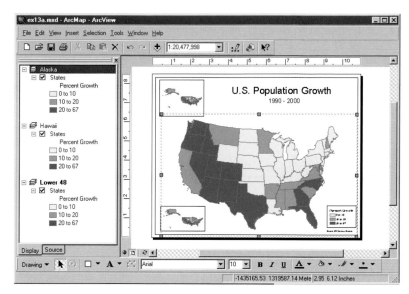

The States layer now displays in all three data frames.

16 In the table of contents, right-click the Alaska data frame and click Activate.

17 Again in the table of contents, right-click the Alaska data frame and click Properties. If necessary, click the Coordinate System tab.

Again, the current coordinate system is set to GCS_North_American_1983. You'll select an Albers projection developed for Alaska.

18 In the Select a coordinate system box, click the plus sign next to Predefined, the plus sign next to Projected Coordinate Systems, the plus sign next to Continental, and the plus sign next to North America.

19 Click Alaska Albers Equal Area Conic. Make sure that your dialog matches the following graphic, then click OK.

The layer is reprojected on the fly. You'll zoom in to Alaska using a bookmark.

20 Click the View menu, point to Bookmarks, and click Alaska.

21 In the table of contents, right-click the Hawaii data frame and click Activate.

22 Click the View menu, point to Bookmarks, and click Hawaii.

At this scale, Hawaii's shape and relative size don't appear distorted. You'll leave the data frame's coordinate system, GCS_North_American_1983, as is. Each of the three data frames now has a different coordinate system. You'll return to this map later.

23 If you want to save your work, click the File menu and click Save As. Navigate to **C:\GTKArcGIS\Chapter13\MyData**. Rename the file **my_ex13a.mxd** and click Save.

24 If you are continuing with the next exercise, minimize ArcMap by clicking on the left button in the upper right corner of the ArcMap application title bar. Otherwise, click the File menu and click Exit. Click No if prompted to save your changes.

25 In ArcCatalog, click the File menu and click Exit.

In the next exercise, you'll work with ArcToolbox first, then ArcMap.

Defining a projection

ArcMap can examine the coordinates of a data set and tell whether or not it has a projected coordinate system, because the x,y values of projected data are distinct from the latitude–longitude values of unprojected data. ArcMap cannot determine on its own, however, *which* projection a data set is in.

To find out, it reads coordinate system information stored with the data. For shapefiles, this information is kept in a file with the extension .prj. (For a shapefile called Streets.shp, it would be Streets.prj.) Geodatabases store it as a table within the database.

Every data set has a coordinate system, but it may be missing the information that identifies it. If the information is available somewhere, such as in a document describing the data, you should try to get it. Once you have the information, you can add it to a data set using the Define Projection Wizard in ArcToolbox.

If you add a layer that is in a projected coordinate system to ArcMap, and the coordinate system information is missing, you'll get the following warning:

Much of the time this is not a problem. You can still display and work with this data as long as ArcMap does not need to project it on the fly. ArcMap will not be able, however, to align this data with data in a different coordinate system.

Exercise 13b

In this exercise, you'll add a layer of the fastest growing cities in each state to your map. You have acquired a shapefile of projected data and its corresponding layer file from a colleague at the Census Bureau. Unfortunately, the shapefile doesn't have a projection (.prj) file so ArcMap can probably not align it with other layers in a data frame. After e-mailing your colleague, you have received the following reply:

"Sorry that the projection wasn't defined. The FastCities shapefile is in the *North America Lambert conformal conic* projected coordinate system."

You'll add this coordinate system information to the shapefile with the Define Projection wizard.

1 Start ArcToolbox by double-clicking the ArcToolbox icon on your computer desktop. (Alternatively, click the Start button on the Windows taskbar, point to Programs, point to ArcGIS, and click ArcToolbox.)

The ArcToolbox application window opens. It has three tool sets: Conversion Tools, Data Management Tools, and My Tools. (MyTools has no tools in it. You can put the tools you use most frequently here.)

2 Click the plus sign next to Data Management Tools. Click the plus sign next to Projections.

The Define Projection wizards apply coordinate system information to data sets. The Project Wizard reprojects input data and saves it as a new data set.

3 Double-click the Define Projection Wizard (shapefiles, geodatabase) to open it.

In the first panel of the wizard, you select the data set to define.

4 Click the Browse button. In the Add Data dialog, navigate to **C:\GTKArcGIS \Chapter13\Data** and click on FastCities.shp, as shown in the following graphic. Click Add.

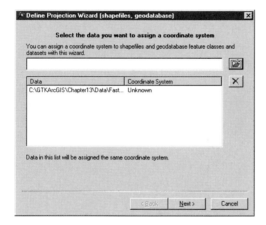

The shapefile name is added to the dialog. Its coordinate system is unknown.

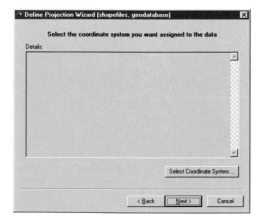

5 Click Next.

In this panel, you select the coordinate system to apply.

6 Click Select Coordinate System.

In the Spatial Reference Properties dialog, you can select a predefined coordinate system, import a coordinate system from another data set, or create a new coordinate system.

7 Click Select.

You'll locate the North America Lambert conformal conic projected coordinate system.

8 Double-click the Projected Coordinate Systems folder, the Continental folder, and the North America folder. Click on North America Lambert Conformal Conic.prj. Make sure that your dialog matches the following graphic, then click Add.

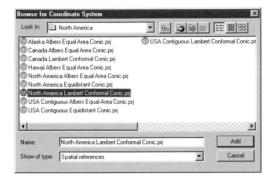

The Spatial Reference Properties dialog is updated with the details of this coordinate system.

9 Click OK.

The details are displayed in the wizard panel.

Defining a projected coordinate system automatically defines a geographic coordinate system as well.

10 Click Next.

The final wizard panel lists the input data set and the coordinate system.

11 Click Finish.

12 In ArcToolbox, click the Tools menu and click Exit.

Now that the coordinate system has been defined, the data can be added to your map document. ArcMap will reproject it on the fly in each data frame.

13 Start ArcMap. In the ArcMap dialog, click the option to use an existing map. In the list of existing maps, double-click Browse for maps. (If ArcMap is already running and you minimized it, click on the ArcMap application on your taskbar to open it. Click the File menu and click Open.) Navigate to **C:\GTKArcGIS\Chapter13**. Click **ex13b.mxd** and click Open.

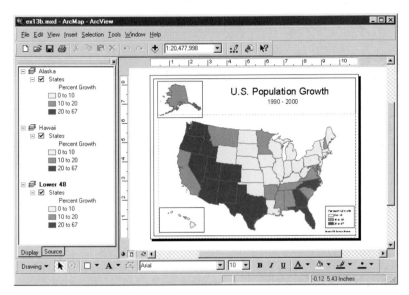

The map opens in layout view. The Lower 48 data frame is active.

14 On the Standard toolbar, click the Add Data button.

15 In the Add Data dialog, navigate to **C:\GTKArcGIS\Chapter13\Data** and click FastCities.lyr, as shown in the following graphic. Click Add.

The layer file, which shows the fastest growing city in each state, is added to the active data frame.

ArcMap reprojects the FastCities layer on the fly from North America Lambert conformal conic to North America Albers equal-area conic, the projection of the Lower 48 data frame. (The .lyr file uses the spatial reference of the .shp file it references.)

Now you'll add the layer to the Alaska and Hawaii data frames.

16 In the table of contents, right-click FastCities.lyr and click Copy.

17 In the table of contents, right-click on the Hawaii data frame and click Paste Layer. Again in the table of contents, right-click on the Alaska data frame and click Paste Layer.

Anchorage and Honolulu appear in their respective data frames.

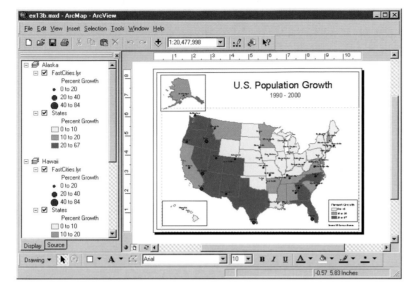

In the Alaska data frame, ArcMap reprojects the FastCities layer to Alaska Albers equal-area conic. In the Hawaii data frame, the FastCities layer is unprojected and its geographic coordinate system is applied. This is GCS_North_American_1983, the same GCS as that of the States layer. (If the two geographic coordinate systems didn't match, you would have seen a warning message.)

18 On the Layout toolbar, click the Zoom to 100% button.

You see a section of the map at the size it would be on a printed page.

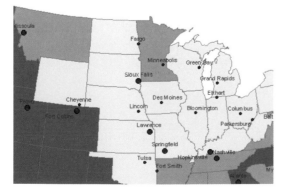

19 On the Layout toolbar, click the Pan tool.

20 Pan the layout to see other parts of the map, such as Alaska or Hawaii.

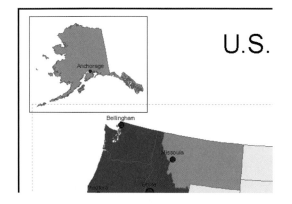

21 When finished, click the Zoom Whole Page button on the Layout toolbar.

Your map shows which states and cities have experienced the most growth between 1990 and 2000.

22 If you want to save your work, click the File menu and click Save As. Navigate to **C:\GTKArcGIS\Chapter13\MyData**. Rename the file **my_ex13b.mxd** and click Save.

In the next chapter, you will work exclusively with ArcCatalog, so you'll exit ArcMap now.

23 Click the File menu and click Exit. Click No if prompted to save your changes.

Building geodatabases

Creating a personal geodatabase
Creating feature classes
Adding fields and domains

Spatial data comes in a variety of formats that can be managed in ArcCatalog and added as layers to ArcMap. The geodatabase is a new spatial data format, designed specifically for ArcGIS.

Many common formats, such as shapefiles, coverages, CAD files, and geodatabases, organize spatial data into feature classes. A feature class is a group of points, lines, or polygons representing similar geographic objects. A group of lines representing rivers is a feature class. A group of polygons representing national parks is a feature class. A group of points representing hippopotamus sightings is a feature class. A feature class may contain many features or few, but all its features have the same geometry—points, lines, or polygons.

A shapefile consists of a single feature class. Geodatabases, coverages, and CAD files may contain several feature classes.

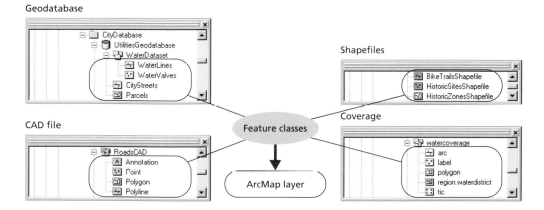

Geodatabases offer advantages over other spatial data formats. Many of the advantages enable coordinated relationships among feature classes. For instance, feature classes that are spatially dependent on each other can be organized into larger units called feature data sets. Water valves and water lines are physically attached and therefore spatially dependent. By making a feature data set of these two feature classes, you can ensure that if you move a water line, its water valves move with it automatically.

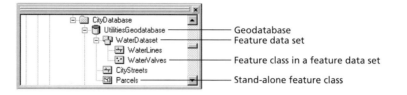

To make use of many advantages of the geodatabase format, you need an ArcEditor or ArcInfo license. Many others, however, are available in ArcView. One is the convenience of being able to store point, line, and polygon feature classes in a single file. Another, as you saw in chapter 7, is the ability to save labels as annotation feature classes that can be added to any map. A third is the ability to create domains for attributes. A domain establishes valid values or ranges of values for an attribute field and minimizes data entry mistakes by prohibiting invalid values. For example, if "Open" and "Closed" were the domain values for a water valve status field, it would be impossible to enter other values in the attribute table.

Geodatabases are either personal or multiuser. Personal geodatabases, like the ones in this book, are stored as Microsoft Access database files. Multiuser geodatabases (also called ArcSDE geodatabases) are used with relational database management systems such as Oracle, Informix, Microsoft SQL Server, or DB2.

Creating a personal geodatabase

You can create geodatabases, shapefiles, or coverages in ArcCatalog. (To create coverages you need an ArcEditor or ArcInfo license.) You can import and export data from one format to another in ArcCatalog, ArcToolbox, or ArcMap. In this exercise, you will create a personal geodatabase from ArcCatalog and import coverage and shapefile data into it.

Exercise 14a

You work in the GIS department of a medium-sized city in Kansas. You are part of a team that is deciding whether the city should convert its shapefile and coverage data to geodatabase format. One question that needs to be answered is how difficult the process would be. To find out, you will create a personal geodatabase and import a land parcels coverage, a water valves shapefile, and a fire hydrants shapefile.

1 Start ArcCatalog. In the ArcCatalog tree, double-click **C:\GTKArcGIS**. Double-click Chapter14. Right-click MyData, point to New, and click Personal Geodatabase.

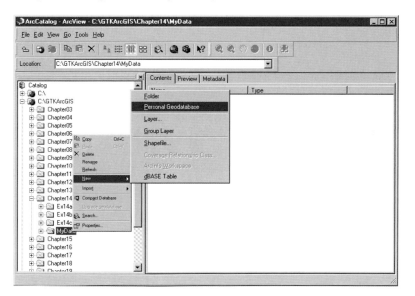

A new personal geodatabase is created in the MyData folder.

Contents	Preview	Metadata

Name	Type	
New Personal Geodatabase.mdb	Personal Geodatabase	

You will give the geodatabase a more descriptive name.

2 Make sure the name New Personal Geodatabase.mdb is highlighted inside a black rectangle. (If it isn't, right-click on it and click Rename.) Type **CityData** and then press Enter on the keyboard.

The geodatabase is now named CityData.mdb.

Contents	Preview	Metadata

Name	Type	
CityData.mdb	Personal Geodatabase	

If you don't see the .mdb file extension, click the Tools menu, click Options, click the General tab, uncheck Hide file extensions, and click OK. If your CityData icon looks different from the graphic, click the Details button on the Standard toolbar.

Next, you'll import the polygon feature class from a land parcels coverage to the new CityData geodatabase.

3 In the ArcCatalog display window, right-click on **CityData.mdb**, point to Import, and click Coverage to Geodatabase Wizard.

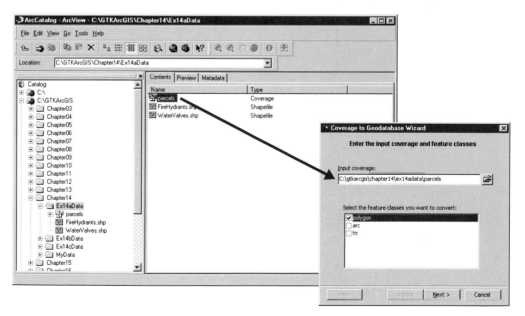

The first panel of the wizard asks which coverage you want to import.

4 Move the wizard panel away from ArcCatalog. In the ArcCatalog tree, double-click **Ex14aData**. In the display window, drag the parcels coverage to the Input Coverage box of the wizard panel.

The data path is added to the Input coverage box and the coverage's feature classes appear in the wizard panel window. By default, ArcCatalog assumes that you want to convert the polygon feature class.

5 In the wizard panel, click Next.

On the second panel, you specify which geodatabase you want to import the data to. Because you right-clicked on the CityData geodatabase in step 3, it is already selected and can't be changed. You will accept the default option to convert the data to a stand-alone feature class.

6 Click Next.

On the third panel, you decide whether to accept the default spatial parameters or to specify them yourself. Specifying the parameters yourself would allow you to change the coordinate system of the data, to omit selected attributes, or to rename fields. You will accept the default parameters.

7 Click Next.

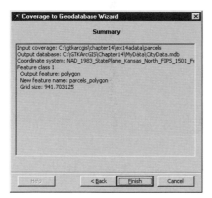

On the Summary panel, you can review the import information and click Back if you want to make changes.

8 Click Finish.

The coverage polygons are converted to a feature class in the CityData geodatabase.

9 In the ArcCatalog tree, double-click **MyData** and double-click **CityData.mdb**. The new feature class appears under the geodatabase. If you don't see it, click the View menu and click Refresh.

You will give the feature class a more natural sounding name.

10 In the ArcCatalog tree, right-click parcels_polygon and click Rename. Type **Parcels** and press Enter.

Now you will preview the data to make sure it looks okay.

11 In the ArcCatalog tree, make sure the Parcels feature class is selected. In the display window, click the Preview tab.

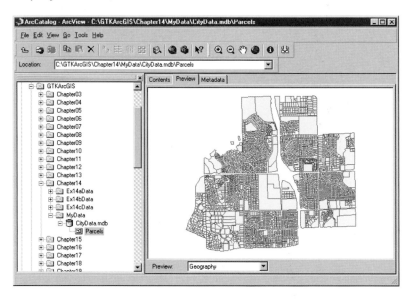

You still have two shapefiles to import into your geodatabase. All import operations can be done with either a wizard or a dialog. Once you are comfortable with data import, you may prefer the dialog because it's faster. It also lets you import several feature classes at once.

12 In the ArcCatalog display window, click the Contents tab. In the catalog tree, right-click on CityData.mdb, point to Import, and click Shapefile to Geodatabase. (This command is marked with a hammer to show that it opens a dialog. Wizards are marked with magic wands.)

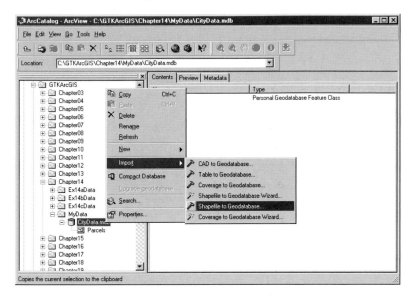

The Shapefile to Geodatabase dialog opens.

13 Move the dialog away from ArcCatalog. In the ArcCatalog tree, double-click Ex14aData, if necessary, to expand it. Drag the WaterValves.shp shapefile to the Input shapefile box of the dialog.

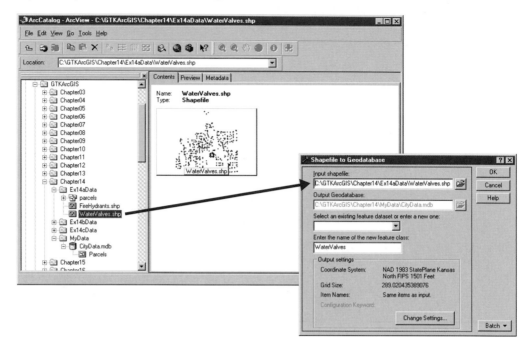

As before, the output geodatabase is already selected. A default feature class name (matching the shapefile name) is assigned automatically. The Output settings part of the dialog shows you the coordinate system and other information about the feature class. You do not need to change these settings.

You will add the second shapefile to the dialog.

14 In the Shapefile to Geodatabase dialog, click Batch.

The bottom of the dialog displays the WaterValves shapefile you just added.

15 In the dialog, click the Add Row button.

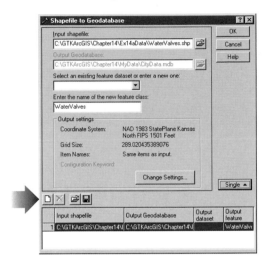

16 From the ArcCatalog tree, drag FireHydrants.shp to the Input shapefile box at the top of the dialog.

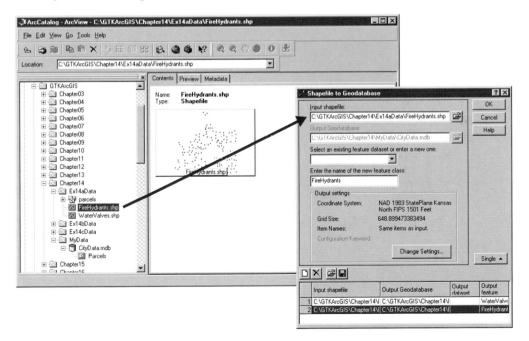

17 Click OK in the Shapefile to Geodatabase dialog.

First the water valves and then the fire hydrants shapefiles are imported.

18 In the ArcCatalog tree, double-click MyData and CityData.mdb. Click the Fire Hydrants feature class. In the display window, click the Preview tab to see the data. Click the WaterValves feature class to preview it as well.

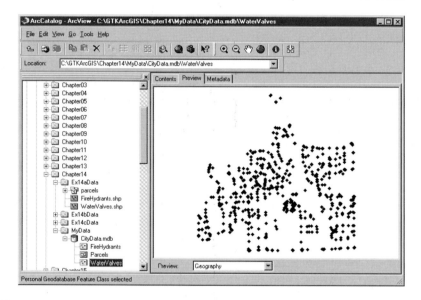

19 In the display window, click the Contents tab.

File management operations, including data import, are applied on execution and thus there is nothing to save.

20 If you are continuing to the next exercise, leave ArcCatalog open. Otherwise, click the File menu and click Exit.

Creating feature classes

When you imported data in the previous exercise, you accepted the default parameters of the existing data. When you create a new feature class, you have to define these parameters yourself. This means specifying the feature class geometry—point, line, or polygon—and the spatial reference.

A spatial reference is made up of a coordinate system, a spatial domain, and a precision. As you learned in chapter 13, a coordinate system is a framework for locating features on the earth's surface using either latitude–longitude or x,y values. A spatial domain defines the bounding coordinates for a feature class, beyond which features cannot be stored. Precision defines the smallest measurement that can be made in the coordinate system. For example, if the coordinate system units are feet, a precision of 12 allows you to make measurements as small as an inch. If the coordinate system units are kilometers, a precision of 1,000 allows you to make measurements as small as a meter.

The task of defining a spatial reference is simplified by the fact that you can select from a list of coordinate systems. ArcCatalog will set default domain and precision values for you. You can also import the spatial reference from another data set and modify it or use it as is.

Exercise 14b

You now know that you can convert the city's existing spatial data to a geodatabase. You also need to know how to create new data in the geodatabase format. In this exercise, you will make a feature class for water lines, although you won't put any features in it until the next chapter.

1 If you have completed exercise 14a, skip to step 2. Otherwise, start ArcCatalog. In the ArcCatalog tree, double-click **C:\GTKArcGIS**. Double-click **Chapter14**. Double-click **Ex14bData**. Right-click **CityData.mdb** and click Copy. Right-click **MyData** and click Paste.

2 Start ArcCatalog. In the ArcCatalog tree, double-click **C:\GTKArcGIS**. Double-click **Chapter14**, then double-click **MyData**. Right-click the CityData personal geodatabase, point to New, then click Feature Class.

The first panel of the New Feature Class wizard opens.

3 In the Name box, type **WaterLines**.

By default, the Type option is set to simple features (point, line, polygon), which is what you want. The feature classes listed in the other option require ArcInfo functionality and don't apply to what you're doing.

4 Click Next.

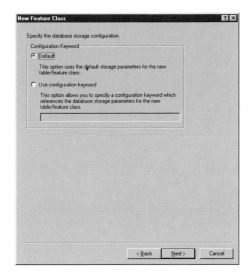

The Default option is the one you want. (The configuration keyword option applies only to multiuser geodatabases.)

5 Click Next.

The third panel displays the field names, data types, and field properties that belong to the new feature class. OBJECTID and SHAPE are required fields, automatically added by the software. The OBJECTID field stores a unique ID number for every feature in the class. The SHAPE field stores each feature's shape and its location in the coordinate system.

Depending on the type of feature class created, ArcGIS also creates and maintains measurement fields. A SHAPE_Length field is created for line feature classes. A SHAPE_Length and a SHAPE_Area field are created for polygon feature classes. The SHAPE_Length attribute for polygons stores perimeter lengths. These measurement fields only appear after the feature class is created.

You will set the geometry property for the SHAPE field to tell the geodatabase whether the new feature class is point, line, or polygon.

6 In the Field Name column, click SHAPE. The field properties for the SHAPE field are displayed.

The default Geometry Type is Polygon. Since you are creating a feature class of water lines, you'll change this to Line.

7 In the Field Properties list, next to Geometry Type, click on Polygon. A drop-down list of geometry types appears. Click Line.

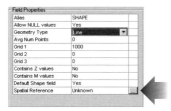

The Spatial Reference field property is set to Unknown. The water lines should have the same spatial reference as the parcels, the valves, and the fire hydrants that already belong to the geodatabase. You will apply the spatial reference from the Parcels feature class to the WaterLines class.

8 Click the Ellipsis button next to the Unknown value.

9 In the Spatial Reference Properties dialog, click the Coordinate System tab if necessary.

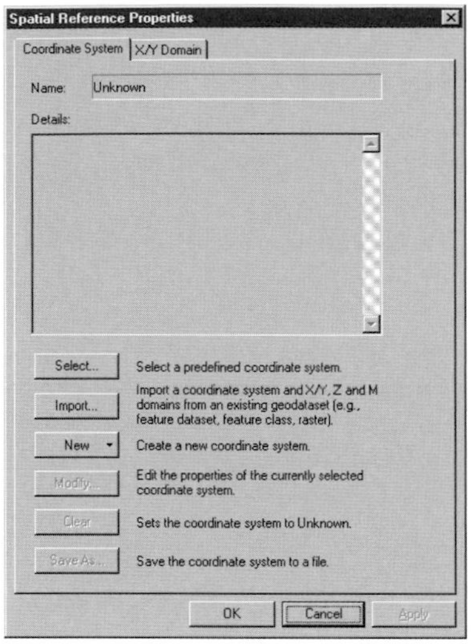

As no coordinate system has been selected, the Name is Unknown and the Details box is empty.

10 Click Import.

11 In the Browse for Dataset dialog, navigate to **C:\GTKArcGIS\Chapter14\MyData**. Double-click on CityData.mdb and click Parcels. Make sure that the dialog matches the following graphic, then click Add.

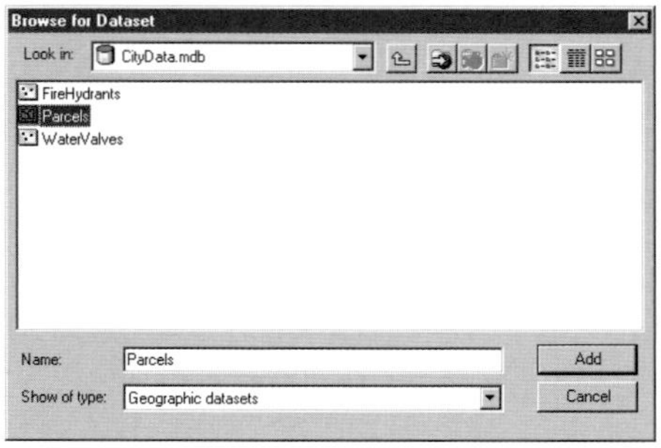

The Spatial Reference Properties dialog is updated with the coordinate system information. This is the same coordinate system that was displayed in the Summary wizard panel in step 7 of the previous exercise, but here all its details are shown.

12 Click OK in the Spatial Reference Properties dialog.

In the Field Properties list of the wizard panel, the Spatial Reference is updated.

13 Click Finish.

14 In the ArcCatalog tree, click, if necessary, the plus sign next to CityData.mdb. WaterLines has been added to the list of feature classes.

In the next exercise, you will add two new attributes to the WaterLines feature class: one for the date water lines are installed and one for the type of water line.

15 If you are continuing to the next exercise, leave ArcCatalog open. Otherwise, click the File menu and click Exit.

Adding fields and domains

When you create a feature class, you add fields to it to store attribute information. A field is defined by a name, a data type (for instance, text or integer), and properties that vary according to both the data type and the spatial data format. One such property, which can be defined for fields in geodatabases, is a domain.

A domain is either a list or a range of valid values for an attribute. Unlike other field properties, which apply exclusively to the field they are defined for, a domain can be applied to more than one field in a feature class and to more than one feature class within a geodatabase.

Exercise 14c

In this exercise, you will add two fields to the WaterLines feature class you created previously. One will store installation dates, the other the type of water line. There are three types of water lines: mains (which run under streets), domestic laterals (which run from mains to houses), and hydrant laterals (which run from mains to fire hydrants).

After you add the fields, you will create a domain and apply it to the field for water line type. The domain will ensure that no values other than the three valid ones can be entered in the attribute table. You will then specify one of those three to be the default.

chapter

14
15
16
17

1 If you have completed exercise 14b, skip now to step 2. Otherwise, start ArcCatalog. In the ArcCatalog tree, double-click **C:\GTKArcGIS**. Double-click **Chapter14**. Double-click **Ex14cData**. Right-click **CityData.mdb** and click Copy. Right-click **MyData** and click Paste.

2 Start ArcCatalog. In the ArcCatalog tree, double-click **C:\GTKArcGIS**. Double-click **Chapter14**. Double-click **MyData** and double-click **CityData.mdb**.

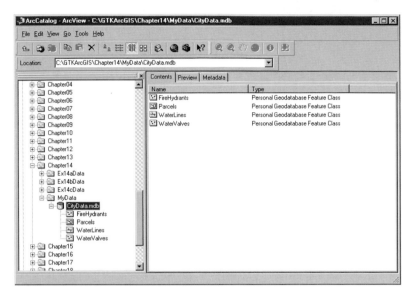

3 In the ArcCatalog tree, right-click **WaterLines** and click **Properties**. In the Feature Class Properties dialog, click the Fields tab.

4 In the Field Name column, type **Install_Date** in the first empty row. (Spaces are not allowed in field names.)

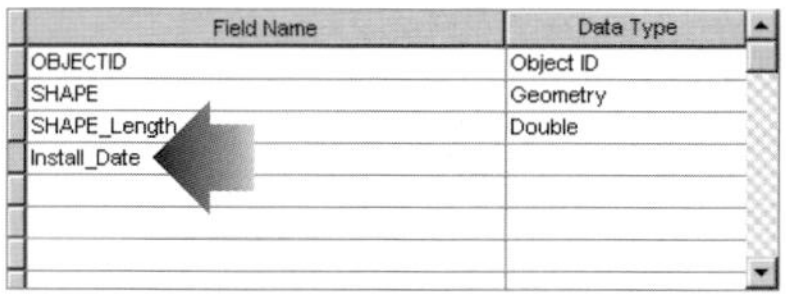

Field Name	Data Type
OBJECTID	Object ID
SHAPE	Geometry
SHAPE_Length	Double
Install_Date	

5 In the Data Type column, click the empty cell next to Install_Date. In the drop-down list that displays, click Date.

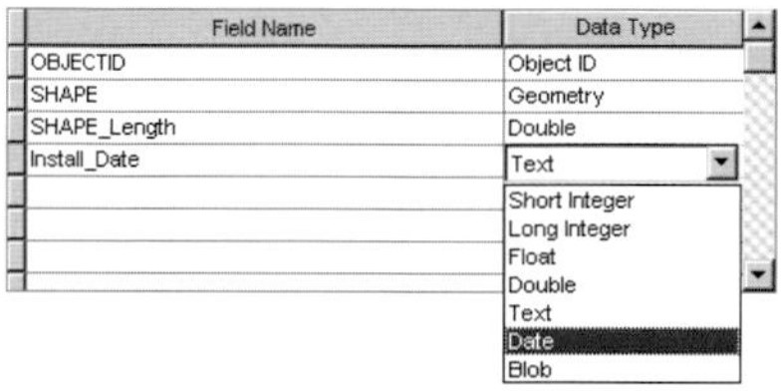

Field Name	Data Type
OBJECTID	Object ID
SHAPE	Geometry
SHAPE_Length	Double
Install_Date	Text
	Short Integer
	Long Integer
	Float
	Double
	Text
	Date
	Blob

6 In the Field Name column, type **Line_Type** in the next empty row. In the Data Type column, click the empty cell next to Line_Type. In the drop-down list, click Text. Make sure the dialog matches the following graphic, then click OK.

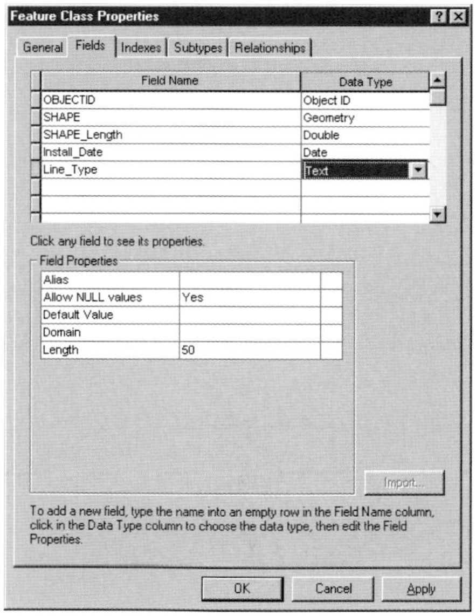

Feature Class Properties ? X

General | Fields | Indexes | Subtypes | Relationships |

Field Name	Data Type
OBJECTID	Object ID
SHAPE	Geometry
SHAPE_Length	Double
Install_Date	Date
Line_Type	Text

Click any field to see its properties.

Field Properties

Alias	
Allow NULL values	Yes
Default Value	
Domain	
Length	50

Import...

To add a new field, type the name into an empty row in the Field Name column, click in the Data Type column to choose the data type, then edit the Field Properties.

OK | Cancel | Apply

Now that you have added the two attribute fields, you will create a domain and apply it to the Line_Type field.

7 In the ArcCatalog tree, right-click CityData.mdb and click Properties to display the Database Properties dialog.

8 In the Domain Name column, type **WaterLineType** in the first cell. Click the first cell in the Description column and type **Type of water line installed**.

In the Domain Properties list, the default Field Type value is Long Integer. The domain field type must match the data type of the feature class it is being applied to. Since you made Line_Type a text field in step 6, you must do the same here.

9 Click on the Long Integer value. In the drop-down list, click Text.

The domain type changes automatically from Range to Coded Values.

Domain types can be either Coded Values or Range. In a Coded Values domain, a code—either numeric or non-numeric—stands for a description. In this case, because the Field Type is text, the code will be non-numeric. A Range domain is used for quantitative attribute values. It sets minimum and maximum limits for the numbers that can be input.

10 In the Coded Values list at the bottom of the dialog, click the first empty cell in the Code column. Type **M**. Click the first cell in the Description column and type **Main**.

11 In the next empty cell in the Code column, type **DL**. Type **Domestic Lateral** as its description.

12 Type **HL** in the next empty Code column cell. Type **Hydrant Lateral** as its description. Make sure the dialog matches the following graphic, then click OK.

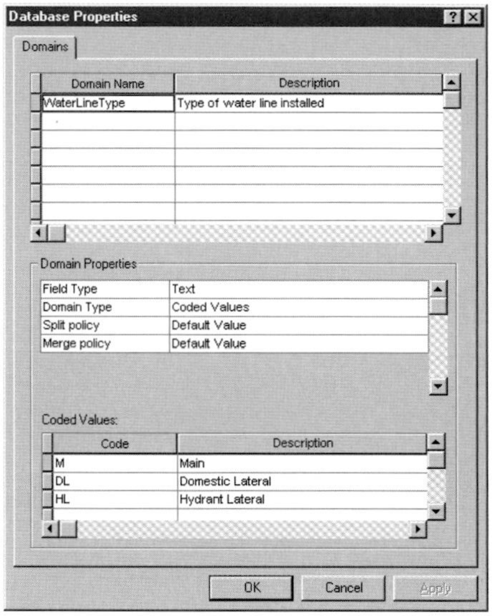

After a Coded Value domain has been applied to a feature class, you will pick from a drop-down list of the descriptions when you enter attribute values. The coded values are stored in the geodatabase, but you only see the descriptions in the attribute table.

Now that you have created the domain, you will apply it to the Line_Type field of the WaterLines feature class.

13 In the ArcCatalog tree, right-click the WaterLines feature class and click Properties. In the Feature Class Properties dialog, click the Fields tab if necessary.

14 In the Field Name column, click Line_Type. Its properties display.

15 In the Field Properties list, click the empty cell next to Domain. In the drop-down list, click WaterLineType.

You have created a domain and applied it to the Line_Type field. Finally, you will assign the field a default value. Mains are the most common type of water lines, so you'll make "Main" the default. Whenever a water line is added to the feature class, it will automatically get this value in the Line_Type field. As you'll see in the next chapter, you can easily change it if the line is a lateral.

16 In the Field Properties frame, click the empty cell next to Default Value and type **M**, the code for mains. Make sure the dialog matches the following graphic, then click OK.

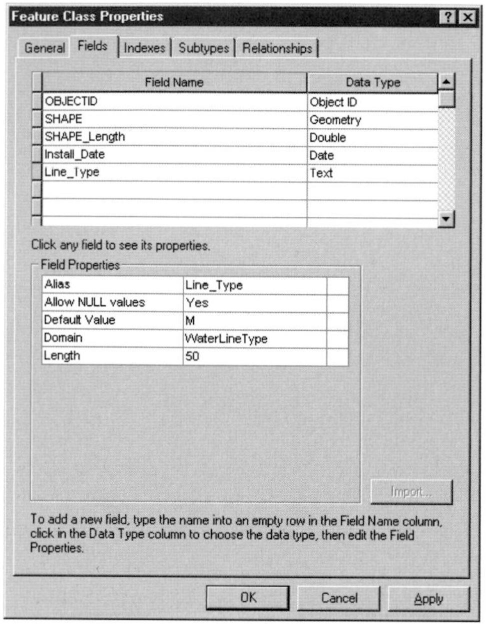

You can set a default value for a field without creating a domain. If a domain is applied, however, the default value must also be a valid domain value.

17 In ArcCatalog, click the File menu and click Exit.

Creating features

Drawing features
Using feature construction tools

Most of the vector spatial data used in a GIS has been digitized from paper maps and aerial or satellite photographs. Digitizing data involves placing a map or photo on a digitizing tablet (a drawing table connected to a computer) and tracing features with a puck, which is a device similar to a mouse. In a variation called heads-up digitizing, features are drawn with a mouse directly on the computer screen by tracing an aerial photo, a scanned map, or other spatial data.

Oregon's Crater Lake digitized heads-up from a satellite image.

Features can also be digitized without tracing. ArcGIS has several tools for creating circles, rectangles, curves, and other shapes of exact dimensions. You can specify the angles and lengths of line segments. You can also specify that line segments be parallel or perpendicular to other segments.

Points are features with no parts. They can be digitized with a single click. Lines, however, are more complicated. They begin, end, and often change direction. Polygons are lines that return to their origins.

The points where a line begins and ends are called endpoints. The points where a line changes direction or is intersected by another line are called vertices. The segments between vertices are called edges.

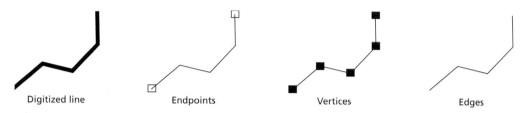

| Digitized line | Endpoints | Vertices | Edges |

When you look at line or polygon features on a map, you don't see them as edges, vertices, and endpoints, but when you create or edit features, you may. When you see a feature in this way, you are looking at its *edit sketch*. A new feature exists only as an edit sketch until it is saved.

In ArcGIS, all digitizing—whether to create new features or modify existing ones—is done in the course of an edit session. An edit session begins when you click the Start Editing menu command on the Editor toolbar and ends when you click the Stop Editing command. After starting an edit session, you specify three settings on the Editor toolbar. The *task* is the operation you want to carry out, such as creating new features. The *target* is the layer in which features are being digitized. The *tool* is a software function for completing the task.

Tool   Task   Target

The five tools for drawing edit sketches are grouped on a drop-down tool palette called the Sketch tool.

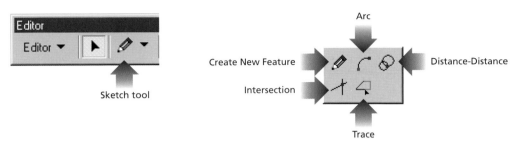

The Create New Feature tool draws point, line, or polygon features.

The Arc tool draws parametric, or true, curves—as opposed to curves that are a collection of very short line segments.

The Distance-Distance tool places a point at either of the two locations made by the intersection of two circles.

The Intersection tool places a point at the location where two lines would cross if they extended far enough.

The Trace tool creates features that follow the contours of selected lines or polygons.

When you digitize features, you sometimes make mistakes. You can undo mistakes with the Undo button on the Standard toolbar.

Drawing features

In this exercise, you will create water lines for the feature class you made in the CityData geodatabase in exercise 14b.

New features are often connected to existing features. For example, the boundaries of new land parcels may be adjacent to boundaries that have already been digitized. New streets intersect or extend to existing ones. New power lines run to and from poles. Making sure that features are connected would be difficult if it depended entirely on your eyesight.

ArcMap can automatically connect (or snap) features placed within a certain distance of each other. The rules specifying which features, and which feature parts, snap to others make up the snapping environment. The distance at which snapping occurs is called the snapping tolerance.

Exercise 15a

In a subdivision of your growing city, a contractor has laid new water lines, including an extension to a main and a line connecting a main to a fire hydrant. During construction, the city's project inspector recorded the locations of water valves and hydrants with a Global Positioning System (GPS) device. These locations have been imported as point feature classes in your geodatabase. As the city's GIS technician, you will use this point data and the ArcMap editing tools to digitize the new water lines.

1 Start ArcMap. In the ArcMap dialog, click the option to use an existing map. In the list of existing maps, double-click Browse for maps. (If ArcMap is already running, click the File menu and click Open.) Navigate to **C:\GTKArcGIS\Chapter15**. Click **ex15a.mxd** and click Open.

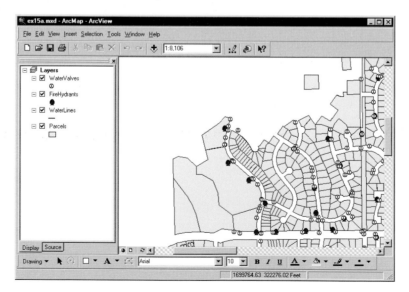

The map shows a subdivision under construction. Layers for water valves, fire hydrants, water lines, and parcels are listed in the table of contents. The WaterLines feature class you created in exercise 14b has no features in it yet. Before starting the edit session, you will zoom to the area where you are going to digitize water lines.

2 Click the View menu, point to Bookmarks, and click New Water Lines.

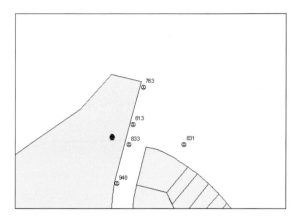

The display zooms to an area where there are several water valves and a fire hydrant. The field crew has laid three new water lines: from valve 763 to valve 813, from 813 to 831, and from 813 to the nearest fire hydrant. You will digitize these three lines.

First, you'll add the Editor toolbar and start an edit session.

3 On the Standard toolbar, click the Editor Toolbar button.

The Editor toolbar opens. The tools are disabled.

4 If necessary, move the Editor toolbar away from the map display. On the Editor toolbar, click the Editor menu and click Start Editing.

The editing tools are now enabled. The target defaults to the water valves layer, the first layer in the table of contents. You need to change the target to the water lines layer.

5 On the Editor toolbar, click the Target drop-down arrow and click WaterLines. Make sure the task is set to Create New Feature. (If not, click the Task drop-down arrow and click Create New Feature.)

Because the water lines must connect (snap) to each other and to other features, such as valves and hydrants, you'll set the snapping environment before you start digitizing.

6 On the Editor toolbar, click the Editor menu and click Snapping. The Snapping Environment dialog opens.

Layer	Vertex	Edge	End
WaterValves	☐	☐	☐
FireHydrants	☐	☐	☐
WaterLines	☐	☐	☐
Parcels	☐	☐	☐

☐ Perpendicular to sketch
☐ Edit sketch edges
☐ Edit sketch vertices

SETTING THE SNAPPING ENVIRONMENT

The upper window of the Snapping Environment dialog contains check boxes for the feature parts in each layer. As you digitize a new feature, the cursor snaps to existing features according to which boxes are checked. (Checking either the Vertex or Edge box for a point layer makes the cursor snap to point features.) The cursor snaps when it comes within a specified distance of a feature. To set this snapping tolerance, click the Options command on the Editor menu and click the General tab.

The lower portion of the dialog sets snapping rules that an edit sketch uses on itself. For example, to make sure that you completely close new polygons you digitize, you would check the Edit sketch vertices check box. For more information, click the Contents tab in ArcGIS Desktop Help and navigate to *Editing in ArcMap > Creating new features > Using the snapping environment.*

7 Click the Vertex check boxes for the WaterValves and FireHydrants layers as shown in the following graphic. Close the Snapping Environment dialog.

To digitize the water lines, you will use the Create New Feature tool.

8 Click the Create New Feature tool.

9 Move the mouse pointer over the map display. The cursor changes to a crosshair on a blue circle. Move the cursor toward valve 763.

When you come within the snapping tolerance of the valve, the blue circle moves to it like a magnet.

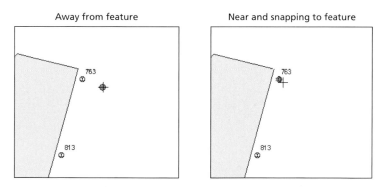

Away from feature

Near and snapping to feature

Now you will digitize the first water line, from valve 763 to valve 813. To draw a line feature, you click once to begin the line, click again for each vertex, and double-click to finish the line. Because the lines don't change direction, you won't need any vertices.

10 With the cursor snapped to valve 763, click to start the first water line.

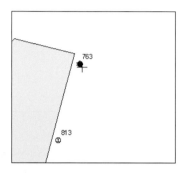

11 Move the cursor toward valve 813. The edit sketch of the line moves with the mouse (an effect known as rubberbanding).

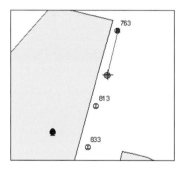

12 Move the cursor over valve 813. When the cursor snaps to it, double-click to end the line. (If you make a mistake, click the Undo button on the Standard toolbar and repeat steps 10 through 12.)

Now you will add a second line connecting valve 813 to valve 831.

13 With the cursor still snapped to valve 813, click to begin a new line. Move the cursor over valve 831. When the cursor snaps to it, double-click to end the line.

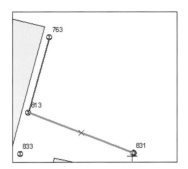

The first line changes from cyan (the default color of edit sketches) to Cretean blue (the color symbolizing water lines in the map). Now, you will digitize the third and final water line, from valve 813 to the fire hydrant.

14 Move the cursor over valve 813 so that the cursor snaps to it. Click to start the line. Move the cursor over the fire hydrant. When the cursor snaps to it, double-click to end the line.

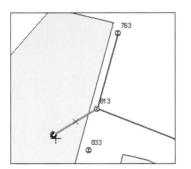

Now you will open the attribute table for the WaterLines layer.

15 In the table of contents, right-click the WaterLines layer and click Open Attribute Table.

OBJECTID*	SHAPE*	SHAPE_Length	Install_Date	Line_Type
37	Polyline	104.563291	<Null>	Main
38	Polyline	148.831584	<Null>	Main
39	Polyline	68.126485	<Null>	Main

Record: 1   Show: All Selected   Records (1 out of 3 Selected.)   Options

The length of each line, in feet, has been calculated in the SHAPE_Length field. (Length and area attributes maintained by the software accurately measure features in the geodatabase, but they do not have legal authority. An official utility database would include an "as-built" length attribute containing the results of field surveys.)

The Install_Date field is <Null> because no attribute values have been entered for it. The Line_Type attribute values have been set to Main for all three water lines, in accordance with the default value for water lines you specified in exercise 14c. The default value isn't right for the last line you digitized, which connects a valve to a hydrant.

16 In the Line_Type field for the third (highlighted) record, click on Main. In the drop-down list that appears, click Hydrant Lateral.

OBJECTID*	SHAPE*	SHAPE_Length	Install_Date	Line_Type
37	Polyline	104.563291	<Null>	Main
38	Polyline	148.831584	<Null>	Main
39	Polyline	68.126485	<Null>	Main

Main
Domestic Lateral
Hydrant Lateral

Record: 3   Show: All Selected   Records (1 out of 3 Selected.)   Options

You are finished digitizing for now and can save your work.

17 Close the attribute table. On the Editor toolbar, click the Editor menu and click Stop Editing. Click Yes to save your edits. Close the Editor toolbar. (If you docked the Editor toolbar, you must undock it, then close it.)

There is no need to save the map document. Your edits were saved to the feature class in the geodatabase. Any map document that contains the WaterLines layer will include the new features.

18 If you are continuing to the next exercise, leave ArcMap open. Otherwise, click the File menu and click Exit. Click No when prompted to save your changes.

Using feature construction tools

In this exercise, you will digitize features representing land parcels. The basic procedure—starting an edit session and setting the snapping environment—is the same as in the previous exercise, but you will use some different tools. ArcMap can set the lengths and angles of edit sketch edges to precise specifications. It also has tools for automatically completing some operations (like finishing a square) once you provide the necessary information.

Exercise 15b

You have left your job with the city and gone to work for a developer who is planning to subdivide a large tract of land. Having obtained parcel data from the city's GIS department, you will use preliminary field measurements to digitize some new parcels in accordance with the developer's proposal. Eventually, your map will go to the city's Planning Department for review. If the design is approved, the developer will commission a licensed survey crew to conduct a legal survey of the parcel boundaries.

1 Start ArcMap. In the ArcMap dialog, click the option to use an existing map. In the list of existing maps, double-click Browse for maps. (If ArcMap is already running, click the File menu and click Open.) Navigate to **C:\GTKArcGIS\Chapter15**. Click **ex15b.mxd** and click Open.

The map shows the parcels displayed against a background image that lets you see what has been built on the parcels. Some have finished houses, some have houses under construction, and some are vacant.

You will zoom in and digitize a new parcel next to parcels 2731 and 2726.

2 Click the View menu, point to Bookmarks, and click First Parcel Site.

3 On the Standard toolbar, click the Editor Toolbar button.

4 On the Editor toolbar, click the Editor menu and click Start Editing.

First, you will set the snapping environment so that boundary lines for the new parcels snap to the vertices of existing parcels.

5 On the Editor toolbar, click the Editor menu and click Snapping. In the Snapping Environment dialog, check the Vertex box for the Parcels layer as shown in the following graphic. Close the Snapping Environment dialog.

The new parcel will share two sides with existing parcels, as shown in the following graphic. A task called Auto Complete Polygon is used to digitize features that share boundaries with existing features. You will digitize the two new sides and ArcMap will finish the polygon.

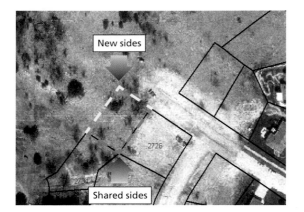

6 On the Editor toolbar, click the Task drop-down arrow and click Auto Complete Polygon. The Target is set to Parcels, the only editable layer in the map.

7 Click the Auto Complete Polygon tool. (The tool name changes to match the task.)

8 In the table of contents, turn off the Subdivision Image layer to see the parcels more clearly.

9 Move the cursor over the northmost corner of parcel 2731 so that the cursor snaps to its vertex. Click to begin the polygon.

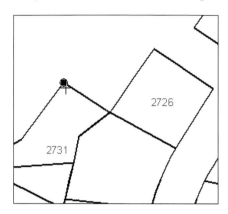

The two boundaries you'll digitize must be aligned with the boundaries of the existing parcels. Your field notes say that the new parcel's northwest boundary should be parallel to the northwest boundary of parcel 2731 and that it should be 118 feet long.

10 Right-click anywhere on the northwest boundary of parcel 2731 to open the context menu. On the context menu, click Parallel. (If you left-click by mistake and add a vertex, click the Undo button on the Standard toolbar.)

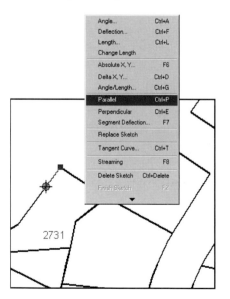

You can use the Escape key on the keyboard to close the context menu without choosing a menu command. The Escape key will also cancel the effect of a menu command.

11 Move the cursor over the map display without clicking. The line is constrained to be parallel to the line segment you just clicked on.

12 With the cursor located anywhere in the display, right-click. On the context menu, click Length. In the Length pop-up box, delete the existing value and type **118** as shown in the following graphic, then press the Enter key. (The graphic shows both the menu and the pop-up box; in reality, the menu disappears when the box displays.)

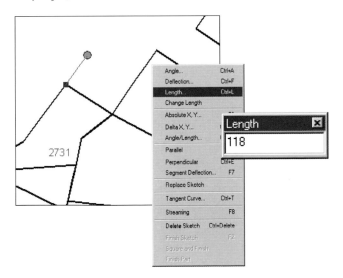

The first side of the new parcel is finished. It is 118 feet long and runs parallel to the boundary of parcel 2731. The cursor moves to anticipate the next line segment. (Yours may move to a different position from the one in the graphic.)

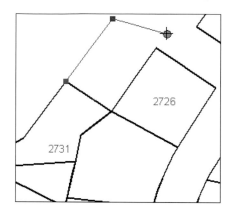

13 Move the cursor over the northmost corner of parcel 2726 so that the cursor snaps to its vertex. Double-click to end the line segment.

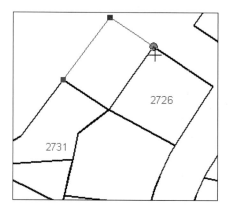

The third and fourth sides of the polygon are completed automatically, using the existing parcel boundaries.

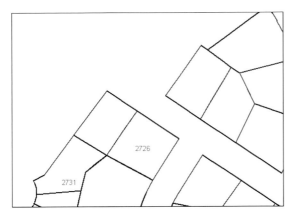

Now you will add a second parcel to a different part of the subdivision.

14 In the table of contents, turn on the Subdivision Image layer. Click the View menu, point to Bookmarks, and click Second Parcel Site. You will digitize the new parcel in the area shown by the yellow box. (The box appears only in the book, not on your screen.)

This time you don't have boundaries to use, so you'll change the task to Create New Feature. Your notes tell you that the new parcel should have a corner at a point exactly 61.1 feet from a corner of parcel 2719 and 119.4 feet from a corner of parcel 2707. You will use the Distance-Distance tool to choose the Point of Beginning for the new parcel.

15 On the Editor toolbar, click the Task drop-down arrow and click Create New Feature. Click the Sketch tool drop-down arrow and click the Distance-Distance tool.

16 In the table of contents, turn off the Subdivision Image layer.

17 Move the cursor over the northwest corner of parcel 2719 and click when the cursor snaps to its vertex. Press the D key on the keyboard once. In the Distance pop-up box, type **61.1**, as shown in the following graphic, then press Enter.

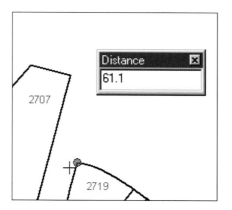

A circle appears on the map. Its center is the vertex you clicked on; its radius is 61.1 feet.

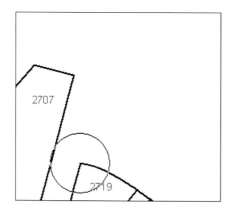

18 Move the cursor over the northeast corner of parcel 2707 and click when the cursor snaps to its vertex. Press the D key on the keyboard once. In the Distance pop-up box, type **119.4**, as shown in the following graphic, then press Enter.

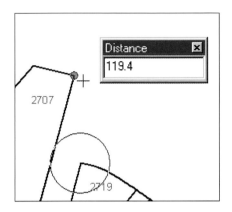

A second circle is drawn, with a radius of 119.4 feet. The circles intersect at two points.

19 Move the cursor back and forth without clicking.

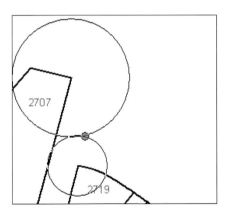

The highlighted dot is constrained to move from one point of intersection to the other. Theoretically, either could be correct. It so happens, however, that the point on the left would start the parcel in the middle of an unbuilt road. The point on the right is the one you want.

Using feature construction tools

20 Move the cursor to the point on the right and click. The circles disappear. Move the cursor slightly away. A red square marks the spot.

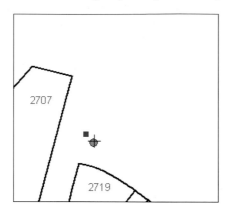

You are now ready to digitize the parcel, using field notes detailing the length and angle of the parcel sides.

21 On the Editor toolbar, click the Sketch tool drop-down arrow and click the Create New Feature tool.

22 Right-click anywhere on the map display. On the context menu, click Angle. In the pop-up box, replace the current value with **73.4**, as shown in the following graphic, then press Enter.

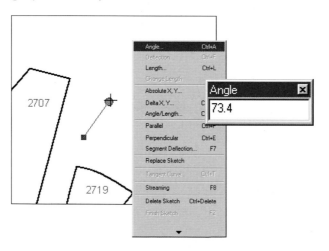

The line is constrained to the angle you set. The Angle command uses east as 0 degrees and measures positive angles counterclockwise. Angles are constrained in either direction along an axis, as you can see by moving the cursor over the display area. For example, an angle value of 45 constrains the angle to 45 degrees in one direction and 225 degrees (45 plus 180) in the other.

23 Right-click anywhere above the starting point. On the context menu, click Length. In the pop-up box, replace the current value with **54.87**, as shown in the following graphic, then press Enter.

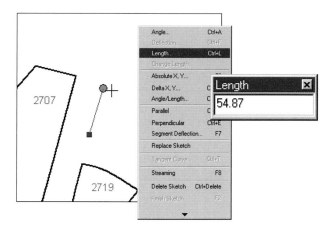

The first side of the parcel is complete. The starting point changes to a green square and the current vertex becomes a red square.

You will now set an angle and a length to create the second line segment.

24 Right-click anywhere to the right of the red vertex. On the context menu, click Angle. In the pop-up box, replace the current value with **-15.72** (note the minus sign), as shown in the following graphic, then press Enter.

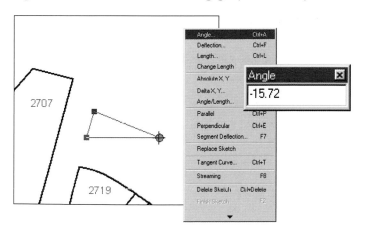

25 Right-click anywhere to the right of the red vertex. On the context menu, click Length. In the pop-up box, replace the current value with **117**, as shown in the following graphic, then press Enter.

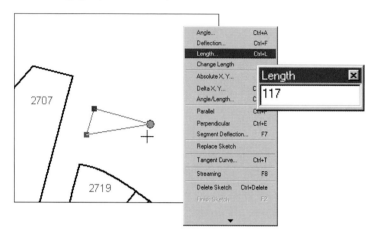

The second side of the parcel is done. To complete the last two sides, you'll use the Square and Finish command, which completes a polygon by drawing a right angle.

26 Right-click anywhere below the red vertex. On the context menu, click Square and Finish.

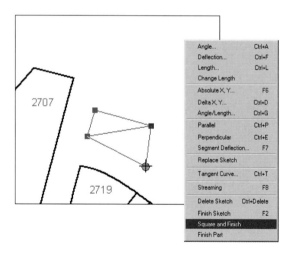

The parcel is drawn to your specifications.

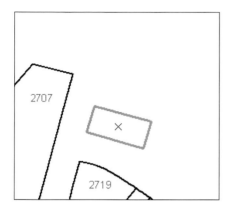

27 On the Editor toolbar, click the Editor menu and click Stop Editing. Click Yes to save your edits. In the table of contents, turn on the Subdivision Image layer.

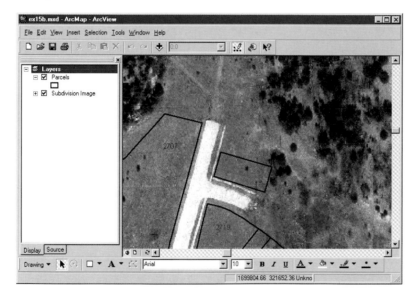

You have added two proposed parcels to the subdivision. The developer has more in mind, but you won't have to digitize them in this book. You don't need to save the map document. Your edits were made directly to the feature class in the geodatabase. When you saved them, the geodatabase was updated.

28 Close the Editor toolbar. If you are continuing to the next chapter, leave ArcMap open. Otherwise, click the File menu and click Exit. Click No when prompted to save your changes.

Editing features and attributes

Deleting and modifying features
Splitting and merging features
Editing feature attribute values

Creating features is one part of maintaining a geodatabase. Another part, equally important, is making changes to existing features.

Features may be edited in several ways. They may be deleted, moved, divided, merged, resized, reshaped, or buffered. In addition to the tasks on the Editor toolbar, there are commands on the Editor menu for changing features.

When features are edited, their attributes often need to be updated as well. Length and area attributes are updated automatically by ArcMap; other attributes must be updated manually. Sometimes attribute values need to be edited even when features don't change—for example, when a land parcel is sold. Sometimes new attributes are added to a table.

With an ArcView license, you can edit personal geodatabases and shapefiles. With an ArcEditor or ArcInfo license, you can also edit coverages and multiuser geodatabases. Files in CAD format cannot be edited directly, but can be converted to an editable format. Editing raster and TIN layers requires the ArcGIS Spatial Analyst and ArcGIS 3D Analyst extensions, respectively.

Deleting and modifying features

To modify a feature, you add, delete, or move vertices on the feature's edit sketch.

Exercise 16a

You are the GIS specialist for the city's planning department. To prepare for a meeting of the City Commission, you will make some changes proposed for parcels in a new subdivision. Since the changes are recommendations only, you will not work with the city's live geodatabase, but with a copy designated for planning use.

Your first task is to delete two parcels on land the city is negotiating to buy back from the subdivision developer. Your second task is to enlarge the boundaries of two parcels to make room for a pond to catch water runoff from a nearby road and sidewalk. The map is simply for discussion, so your edits don't have to be exact. If the proposals are implemented, a licensed survey crew will resurvey the parcels.

1 Start ArcMap. In the ArcMap dialog, click the option to use an existing map. In the list of existing maps, double-click Browse for maps. (If ArcMap is already running, click the File menu and click Open.) Navigate to **C:\GTKArcGIS\Chapter16**. Click **ex16a.mxd** and click Open.

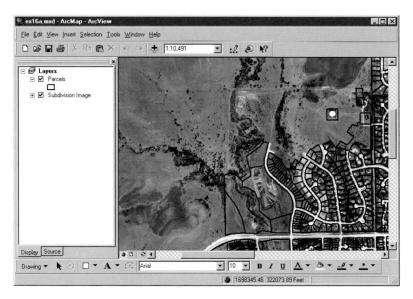

The parcels are outlined in black against an aerial photo of the subdivision. You will zoom in on the parcels to be deleted.

2 Click the View menu, point to Bookmarks, and click First Parcel Site.

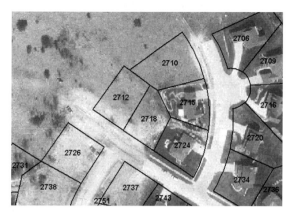

The parcels are labeled with their ID numbers. (The labels are set to display at scales of 1:4,000 and larger.) You will delete parcels 2712 and 2718 in the middle of the display.

3 On the Standard toolbar, click the Editor Toolbar button.

4 On the Editor toolbar, click the Editor menu and click Start Editing.

The target layer is Parcels, the only editable layer in the map. The task is set to Create New Feature. You can delete selected features regardless of which task is set.

5 On the Editor toolbar, click the Edit tool.

6 On the map, click anywhere on parcel 2712. It is outlined in cyan to show that it is selected. Hold down the Shift key and click on parcel 2718 to select it as well.

The small blue "x" in the center of the selected parcels is called a selection anchor. Every selection in an edit session, whether of one feature or many, has one. They are used as reference points for rotating and scaling features, which you won't need to do in this exercise.

7 With parcels 2712 and 2718 selected, click the Delete button on the Standard toolbar.

The selected features are deleted.

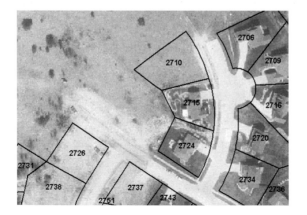

8 On the Editor toolbar, click the Editor menu and click Save Edits.

Now you will modify the shapes of two parcels to accommodate the proposed detention pond. You need to move the parcel edges to a nearby sidewalk. You will add a vertex to one parcel's edit sketch and move another vertex that is shared by two parcels.

9 Click the View menu, point to Bookmarks, and click Second Parcel Site.

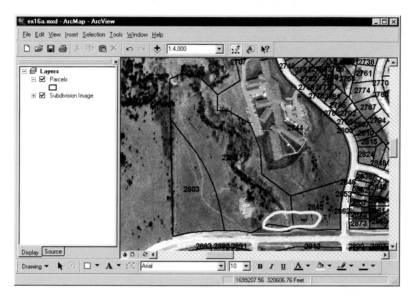

The proposed pond is outlined in yellow in the book (but not on your screen).

The parcels to be edited are 2768 and 2845. The parcels will be extended to the sidewalk at the bottom of the display. The sidewalk appears on the image as a thin white line that runs east–west and lies just north of the road. To make the edits, you will zoom in closer.

10 Click the View menu, point to Bookmarks, and click Proposed Drainage Change.

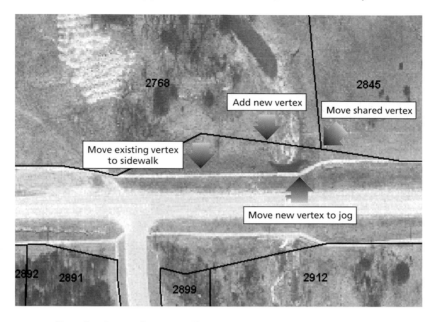

You will make four edits. You'll move an existing vertex in parcel 2768 to the sidewalk, add a new vertex to parcel 2768, and move the new vertex to the point where the sidewalk jogs. Last, you'll move a vertex shared by parcels 2768 and 2845.

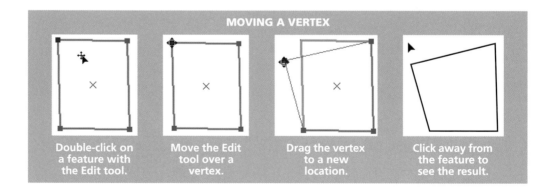

11 On the Editor toolbar, click the Edit tool if necessary.

12 Double-click anywhere on parcel 2768 to select it and display its edit sketch.

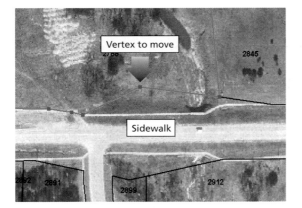

On the edit sketch, the last digitized vertex is a red square; all the rest are green. On the Editor toolbar, ArcMap has automatically changed the task from Create New Feature to Modify Feature.

13 Place the cursor over the first vertex to be moved. The cursor changes to a four-headed arrow.

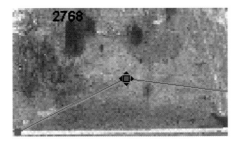

14 Drag the vertex straight down to the sidewalk. Release the mouse button.

The green line shows the new shape of the feature. The highlighted cyan line remains in place as a reference. It will disappear when you unselect the polygon or select another feature.

Now you'll add a new vertex and move it to accommodate the jog in the sidewalk.

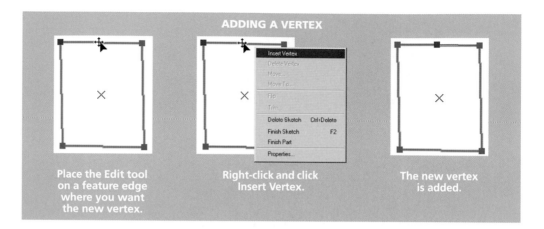

ADDING A VERTEX

Place the Edit tool on a feature edge where you want the new vertex.

Right-click and click Insert Vertex.

The new vertex is added.

15 Right-click on the green line about where the arrow is in the following graphic. On the context menu, click Insert Vertex.

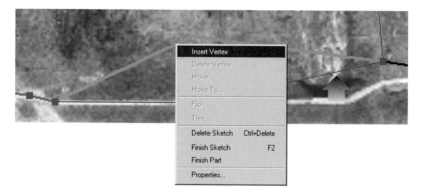

A new vertex is added where you clicked.

16 Place the cursor over the new vertex and drag the vertex to where the sidewalk changes direction. Release the mouse button.

17 Click somewhere outside the polygon to complete the edit.

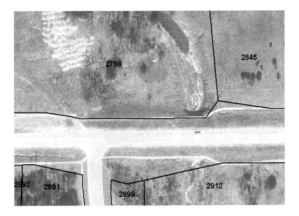

18 On the Editor toolbar, click the Editor menu and click Save Edits.

Now you'll move a shared vertex, one that lies on the boundary of two polygons. If you move a shared vertex with the Edit tool, only one polygon is modified. The result is either a gap or an overlap between the two polygons. If you move a vertex with the Shared Edit tool, the common boundary moves with it and both polygons are modified.

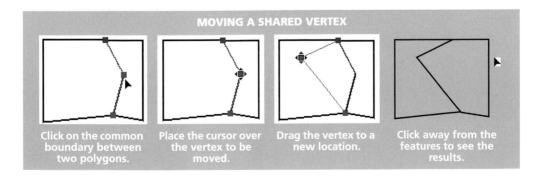

MOVING A SHARED VERTEX

Click on the common boundary between two polygons.

Place the cursor over the vertex to be moved.

Drag the vertex to a new location.

Click away from the features to see the results.

19 On the Tools toolbar, click the Pan tool. Pan the display until you can see the entire common boundary between parcels 2768 and 2845.

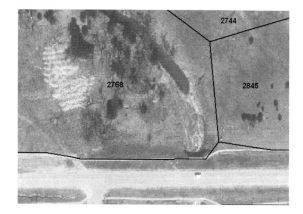

20 On the right side of the Editor toolbar, click the Shared Edit tool.

21 Move the cursor over the map display. The cursor for the Shared Edit tool is the same as for the Edit tool. Double-click anywhere on the shared boundary.

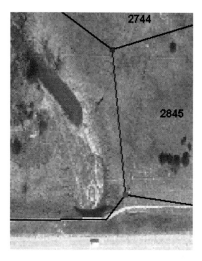

The common boundary is shown in green. The two shared vertices are displayed. (If your boundary is orange, double-click on it again.)

22 Place the cursor over the green (lower) vertex.

23 Drag the vertex to the point where the sidewalk changes direction again. Release the mouse button.

The original boundary remains displayed until you complete the edit.

24 Click somewhere away from the two polygons to complete the edit.

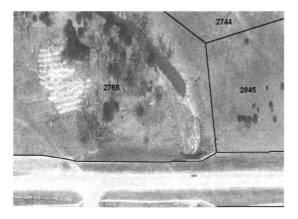

25 On the Editor toolbar, click the Editor menu and click Stop Editing. Click Yes when prompted to save your edits. Close the Editor toolbar.

The map is ready for the City Commission meeting. You don't need to save the map document because your edits were made directly to the feature class in the geodatabase.

26 If you are continuing to the next exercise, leave ArcMap open. Otherwise, click the File menu and click Exit. Click No at the prompt to save your changes.

Splitting and merging features

To split a polygon or a line (create two features from one), you digitize a line across the feature where you want to split it. You can split several features at once.

To merge polygons or lines (create one feature from two or more), you select them and click the Merge command on the Editor menu. The merged features do not have to be spatially connected. For example, you could merge a large polygon representing a country and smaller polygons representing its offshore islands. The country and islands would then exist as a single feature with a single record in the attribute table.

When features in geodatabase feature classes are split or merged, ArcMap updates their Shape_Length and Shape_Area attributes. This is not done for features in other data formats, such as shapefiles. For all feature classes, ArcMap updates the attribute that keeps track of the number of features. In a geodatabase, this is the OBJECTID (OID) attribute. In a shapefile, it is FEATUREID (FID). Changes to other attributes, including user-defined IDs (like parcel numbers) or legal measurements of length and area, must be made manually.

Exercise 16b

The planning department has been notified of two pending property changes. In one case, an owner wants to subdivide her land so that she can sell a piece of it. In the other, the owner of one half of a duplex has bought the other half. Because the duplex had two owners, there was a parcel boundary dividing the house. Now the boundary needs to be removed.

1 Start ArcMap. In the ArcMap dialog, click the option to use an existing map. In the list of existing maps, double-click Browse for maps. (If ArcMap is already running, click the File menu and click Open.) Navigate to **C:\GTKArcGIS\Chapter16**. Click **ex16b.mxd** and click Open.

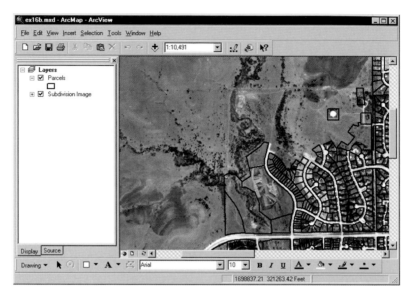

When the map opens, you see the familiar subdivision. You'll zoom in to the parcel to be split.

2 Click the View menu, point to Bookmarks, and click First Parcel Site.

The display zooms in on parcel 2707. The yellow line (which appears in the book but not on your screen) shows where the parcel is to be split. When the parcel is split, ArcMap will update the attribute table with the correct area of the two new parcels. To see this for yourself, you'll check the area of parcel 2707 before you split it.

3 On the Tools toolbar, click the Identify tool and click on parcel 2707.

```
Identify Results                                          ☒
Layers: <Top-most layer>                    ▼
⊟ Parcels        Location: (1699489.786420 321267.088998)
  ⊞ 761          Field         Value
                 OBJECTID      761
                 Shape         Polygon
                 PARCELS_ID    2707
                 Shape_Length  1413.316530
                 Shape_Area    107248.703651
```

The Shape_Area field shows a value of 107,248 square feet before the decimal place.

4 Close the Identify window. In the table of contents, turn off the Subdivision Image layer.

5 On the Standard toolbar, click the Editor Toolbar button.

6 On the Editor toolbar, click the Editor menu and click Start Editing. The target is set to Parcels, the only editable layer. The task is set to Create New Feature.

7 On the Editor toolbar, click the Edit tool.

```
Editor
Editor ▼   ▶  ✎ ▼  Task: Create New Feature    ▼
```

8 Double-click on parcel 2707 to select it and display its edit sketch. You will draw the split line between the vertices indicated by red arrows in the graphic.

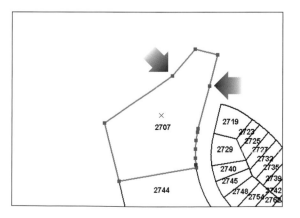

When you double-click to display a feature's edit sketch, the task on the Editor toolbar changes automatically to Modify Feature. Similarly, if you set the task to Modify Feature, you will see the edit sketch of any feature you select. Modify Feature is the only task in which feature vertices are displayed.

Before digitizing the split line, you will set the snapping environment so that the line snaps to vertices.

9 On the Editor toolbar, click the Editor menu and click Snapping. In the Snapping Environment dialog, check the Vertex box for the Parcels layer, as shown in the following graphic. Close the dialog.

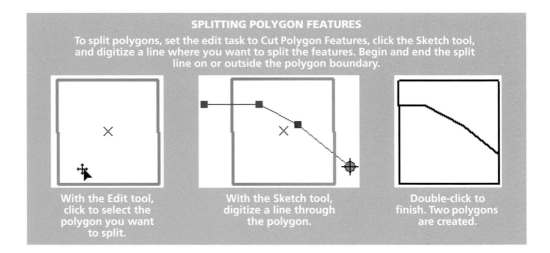

SPLITTING POLYGON FEATURES
To split polygons, set the edit task to Cut Polygon Features, click the Sketch tool, and digitize a line where you want to split the features. Begin and end the split line on or outside the polygon boundary.

With the Edit tool, click to select the polygon you want to split.

With the Sketch tool, digitize a line through the polygon.

Double-click to finish. Two polygons are created.

Next, you will change the task to Cut Polygon Features.

10 On the Editor toolbar, click the Task drop-down list and click Cut Polygon Features. Click the Cut Polygon Features tool.

Although the parcel vertices no longer display when the task is changed, the split line you digitize will still snap to them.

11 On the display, the cursor changes to a crosshair on a blue circle. Move the cursor to the position shown in the following graphic. When it snaps to the vertex, click the left mouse button.

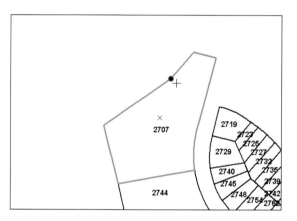

12 Move the cursor over the second vertex. When it snaps to it, double-click to end the split line.

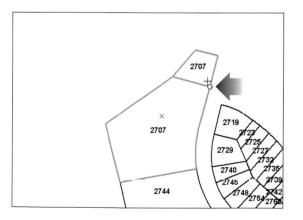

The parcel is split in two. Each parcel is labeled with the same PARCELS_ID of 2707. In the next exercise, you'll update the PARCELS_ID for the smaller parcel.

13 On the Editor toolbar, click the Editor menu and click Save Edits.

14 On the Tools toolbar, click the Identify tool. Click on each of the two new parcels.

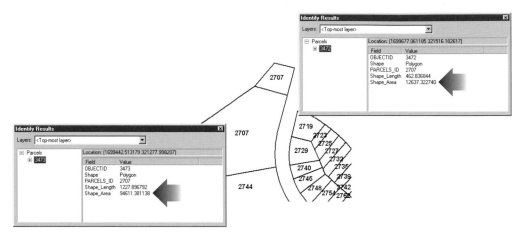

The sum of the areas of the two new parcels equals the area of the original parcel. The PARCELS_ID number, a user-defined attribute, does not change. Both parcels, however, are assigned new OBJECTID numbers.

Your next task is to merge two parcels where the owner of one half of a duplex has bought the other half.

15 Close the Identify window. Click the View menu, point to Bookmarks, and click Second Parcel Site.

16 Turn on the Subdivision Image layer.

In the center of the map display, two parcels—2855 and 2861—are located on a cul-de-sac. The parcel boundary crossing the duplex needs to be removed.

17 On the Editor toolbar, click the Edit tool.

When you merge polygons, it doesn't matter what the toolbar task setting is.

18 Click anywhere on parcel 2855 to select it. Hold down the Shift key and click on parcel 2861 to select it as well.

19 On the Editor toolbar, click the Editor menu and click Merge. The two parcels become one.

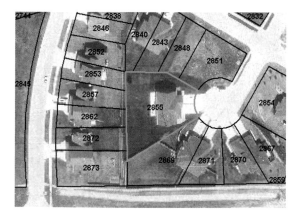

20 In the table of contents, right-click the Parcels layer and click Open Attribute Table. Click Selected at the bottom of the table to display selected records.

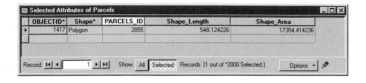

The record that remains is for the first feature you selected, parcel 2855. Its Shape_Length and Shape_Area values are updated.

21 Close the table. On the Editor toolbar, click the Editor menu and click Stop Editing. Click Yes to save your edits. Close the Editor toolbar.

You don't need to save the map document because your edits were made directly to the Parcels feature class in the geodatabase.

22 If you are continuing to the next exercise, leave ArcMap open. Otherwise, click the File menu and click Exit. Click No at the prompt to save your changes.

Editing feature attribute values

In ArcMap, you can change attribute values one at a time by typing new values into the table during an edit session. You can also change values for a selected set of records or for all records in a table with the Field Calculator. The Field Calculator assigns values to a field according to an expression, which may simply be a value, like "101" or "Residential," or may be an expression using math operators. The Field Calculator can be used either in or out of an edit session.

Besides editing attribute values, you can add and delete records or add new fields to a table and define properties for those fields. Records are added and deleted during an edit session. Fields are added and deleted outside an edit session.

Exercise 16c

Having split parcel 2707, you need to assign a new PARCEL_ID number to one of the new parcels. After that, you will add an attribute to the parcels feature class. In a previous meeting with the City Commission, you found that parcel sizes were often given as acres rather than square feet. The Parcels feature class doesn't have an acreage attribute. You will add one and have ArcMap calculate values for it by converting square feet to acres.

chapter

1. Start ArcMap. In the ArcMap dialog, click the option to use an existing map. In the list of existing maps, double-click Browse for maps. (If ArcMap is already running, click the File menu and click Open.) Navigate to **C:\GTKArcGIS\Chapter16**. Click **ex16c.mxd** and click Open.

The map shows the parcels you split in the previous exercise. Both have an ID of 2707.

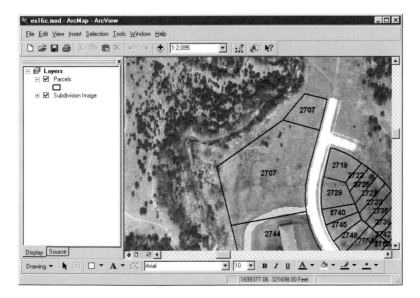

You will assign a new ID number to the smaller parcel.

2 On the Standard toolbar, click the Editor Toolbar button.

3 On the Editor toolbar, click the Editor menu and click Start Editing.

The target layer is Parcels and the task is Create New Feature.

4 On the Editor toolbar, click the Edit tool.

5 Click on the small parcel 2707 to select it.

6 In the table of contents, right-click the Parcels layer and click Open Attribute Table. Click Selected at the bottom of the table.

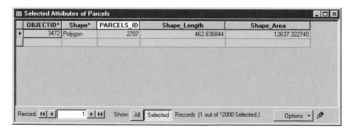

CHAPTER 16 • EDITING FEATURES AND ATTRIBUTES

Field names on gray backgrounds indicate fields that are maintained by ArcMap. They cannot be edited. Names on white backgrounds indicate fields that can be edited.

7 Click in the cell for the PARCELS_ID field. Highlight and delete the existing value of 2707. Type **4001** and press Enter.

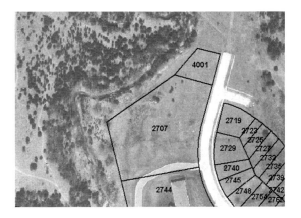

The value 4001 does not duplicate an existing parcel ID. This is the only value you need to edit. If there were other attributes, such as an address or owner name, you would update these as well.

8 On the Editor toolbar, click the Editor menu and click Stop Editing. Click Yes to save your edits. Move the table away from the map display.

When the edit session is finished, there are no longer any selected records in the table or selected features on the map. On the map, the smaller parcel is labeled with its new PARCEL_ID.

Now you will add a field to the table to store parcel size in acres.

9 At the bottom of the Selected Attributes of Parcels table, click All.

Currently, the Shape_Area field contains the square footage of each parcel. After adding the new field, you will write an expression in the Field Calculator to convert square feet to acres.

10 In the table, click the Options menu and click Add Field. (If the Add Field command is disabled, you may not have concluded the edit session in step 8.)

The Add Field dialog opens.

When you add a field to a table, you name it, specify its data type, and set field properties, just as you did in chapter 14.

ADDING FIELDS FROM ARCCATALOG

New fields can be added from ArcCatalog or ArcMap. With an ArcView license, fields can be added only to personal geodatabase or shapefile feature classes. With an ArcEditor or ArcInfo license, fields can also be added to feature classes in coverages and ArcSDE geodatabases. For more information, click the Contents tab in ArcGIS Desktop Help and navigate to *ArcCatalog > Exploring the values in a table > Adding and deleting columns*.

---

11 In the Name text box of the Add Field dialog, type **Acres**. Click the Type dropdown arrow and click Float, as shown in the following graphic. (Float is a numeric field that allows decimal points.) Click OK.

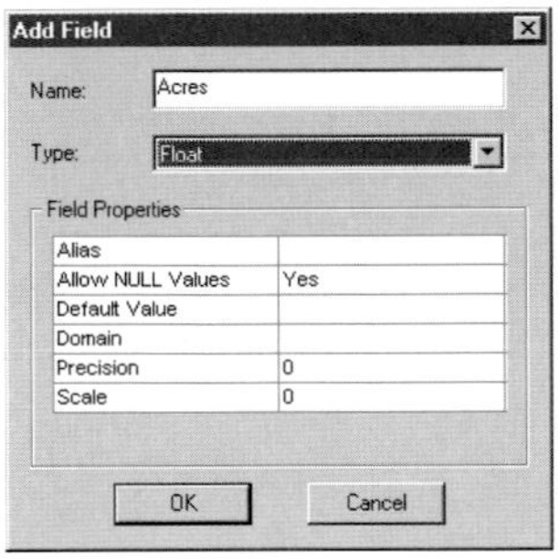

The new field is added to the table. Its values are set to <Null>.

Shape*	PARCELS_ID	Shape_Length	Shape_Area	Acres
Polygon	219	771.272726	34756.355063	<Null>
Polygon	220	951.705862	37783.615299	<Null>
Polygon	222	1094.739692	74870.416576	<Null>
Polygon	221	3841.477939	367909.421562	<Null>
Polygon	223	953.156376	21397.130913	<Null>
Polygon	224	575.903911	17960.900181	<Null>
Polygon	225	714.166729	31394.712774	<Null>
Polygon	241	1309.803923	96184.958256	<Null>

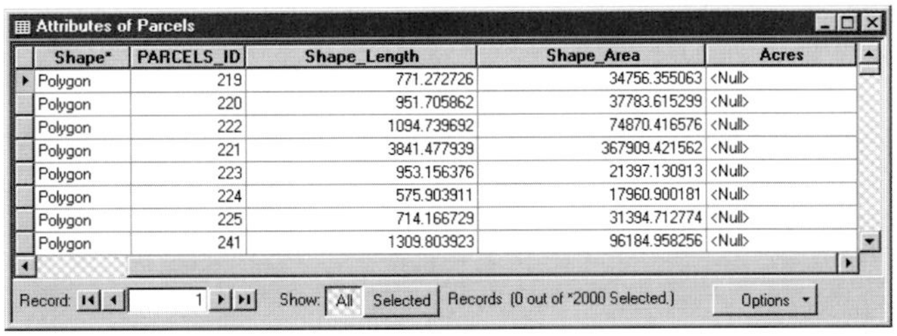

Now you will calculate values for the Acres field, which you can do whether you are in an edit session or not. Field calculations made in an edit session take longer but have an Undo option. Calculations made outside an edit session are faster but can't be undone. (To replace an incorrect calculation, you can make a new one.) For the sake of speed, you will make your calculation without starting an edit session.

12 In the attribute table, right-click the Acres field name and click Calculate Values.

Shape*	PARCELS_ID	Shape_Length	Shape_Area	Acres
Polygon	219	771.272726	34756.355063	<Null>
Polygon	220	951.705862	37783.615299	<Null>
Polygon	222	1094.739692	74870.416576	<Null>
Polygon	221	3841.477939	367909.421562	<Null>
Polygon	223	953.156376	21397.130913	<Null>
Polygon	224	575.903911	17960.900181	<Null>
Polygon	225	714.166729	31394.712774	<Null>
Polygon	241	1309.803923	96184.958256	<Null>

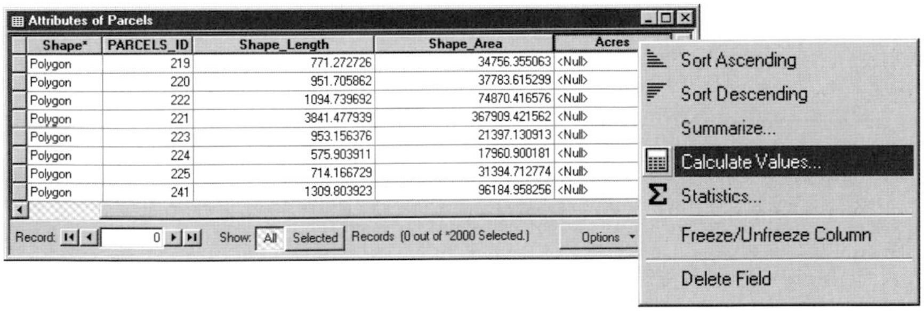

A message appears reminding you that you won't be able to undo your calculation.

13 Click Yes to continue. The Field Calculator dialog opens.

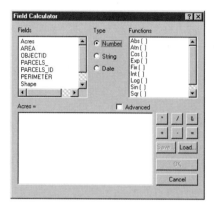

You will create an expression to convert feet to acres. Since 1 acre equals 43,560 square feet, dividing the values in the Shape_Area field by 43,560 will give each parcel's acreage.

14 In the Fields list of the Field Calculator, click on Shape_Area to add it to the expression box. Click the Division (/) button. Type a space and type **43560**. Make sure your dialog matches the following graphic, then click OK.

The values are calculated and written to the Acres field of the table.

Shape*	PARCELS_ID	Shape_Length	Shape_Area	Acres
Polygon	219	771.272726	34756.355063	0.797896
Polygon	220	951.705862	37783.615299	0.867392
Polygon	222	1094.739692	74870.416576	1.718788
Polygon	221	3841.477939	367909.421562	8.446038
Polygon	223	953.156376	21397.130913	0.491211
Polygon	224	575.903911	17960.900181	0.412326
Polygon	225	714.166729	31394.712774	0.720723
Polygon	241	1309.803923	96184.958256	2.208103

Attributes of Parcels

Record: 0 — Show: All Selected — Records (0 out of *2000 Selected.) — Options

ArcMap will not automatically update these values. When you make changes to parcels that affect their size, you'll have to recalculate the Acres field.

You don't need to save the map document. Your edits were made directly to the feature class attributes in the geodatabase.

15 Close the table. Close the Editor toolbar. If you are continuing to the next chapter, leave ArcMap open. Otherwise, click the File menu and click Exit. Click No at the prompt to save your changes.

Geocoding addresses

Creating a geocoding service
Matching addresses
Rematching addresses

In chapter 15, you learned that most spatial data was originally digitized from paper maps. It's also possible to create spatial data—specifically, point features—from information that describes or names a location. The most common kind of information that does this is an address. The process of creating map features from addresses, place names, or similar information is called geocoding.

The value of geocoding is that it lets you map locations from data that is readily available. If you own a business, you can't buy an atlas that has a map of your customers. With a list of your customer addresses, however, you can make this map for yourself.

Geocoding requires that you have an address table—a list of addresses stored as a database table or a text file. You also need a set of reference data, such as streets, on which the addresses can be located.

Address	City	State	Zip
▶ 3387 Arlington Avenue	Riverside	California	92506
5314 Victoria Avenue	Riverside	California	92506
2466 Fairview Avenue	Riverside	California	92506
2464 Arlington Avenue	Riverside	California	92506
2200 Arroyo Drive	Riverside	California	92506

Address table

Reference data

ArcGIS uses address information in the attribute table of the reference data to figure out where to locate address points. The more detailed the reference data, the more accurately addresses can be located.

The same table of addresses is geocoded using two sets of reference data. On the street map of Riverside, California, address points are placed in the correct location on the correct street. On the ZIP Code map of the United States (zoomed in to Southern California), the same address points are placed in the center of the correct ZIP Code. Because all five points have the same location, they look like one point.

Street-level reference data is commercially available. Its attributes include street name, street type (Avenue, Boulevard, and so on), and directional prefixes and suffixes necessary to avoid ambiguity in address location. Each street feature is divided into segments that have beginning and ending addresses, much as you see on neighborhood street signs. This makes it possible to estimate the position of an address along the length of a street segment. There may be separate address ranges for each side of the street, so an address can be placed on the correct side of the street.

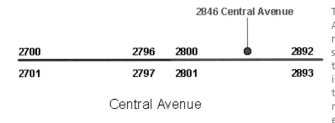

To geocode the address 2846 Central Avenue, ArcGIS examines the reference data and finds the street segment of Central Avenue that has the correct address range. Since 2846 is midway between 2800 and 2892, the address point is placed in the middle of the street segment, on the even-numbered side of the street.

In addition to an address table and reference data, geocoding requires a geocoding service. A geocoding service is a file that specifies the reference data and its relevant attributes, the relevant attributes from the address table, and various geocoding rules and tolerances.

The output of the geocoding process is either a shapefile or a geodatabase feature class of points. The geocoded data has all the attributes of the address table, some of the attributes of the reference data, and, optionally, some new attributes, such as the x,y coordinates of each point.

Creating a geocoding service

Geocoding starts with creating a geocoding service. Geocoding services come in different styles, each appropriate to reference data with different attributes. For example, the style called "Single Field" is used with reference data that contains only a single attribute of geographic information. In a reference map of the United States, for instance, this would probably be a state name field. The data to be geocoded could be located in the correct state, but no more precisely than that.

The geocoding service style called "ZIP" is used with reference data that has a ZIP Code attribute. A table of U.S. addresses could be located within the correct ZIP Codes.

The "US Streets" style is used with street reference data that contains a street name attribute and beginning and ending address ranges for each side of a street. A table of U.S. addresses could be geocoded to their approximate positions along the length of a street and on the correct side of the street.

Each geocoding service style requires that certain attributes be present in the address table as well. For more information about geocoding service styles, click the Contents tab in ArcGIS Desktop Help and navigate to *Geocoding addresses > Preparing reference data for a geocoding service* and *Geocoding addresses > Preparing address data for geocoding.*

Exercise 17a

You work for an online Yellow Pages company that sells advertising—everything from listings and banner ads to interactive storefronts. A new service you plan to offer is a digital map that displays the location of a client's business. Your job is not to create the Internet map service itself (that would require ArcIMS) but rather to test the technology for converting customer addresses to map points. Being inexperienced with geocoding, you'll work with a small sample of your potential customer base.

1 Start ArcMap. In the ArcMap dialog, click the option to use an existing map. In the list of existing maps, double-click Browse for maps. (If ArcMap is already running, click the File menu and click Open.) Navigate to **C:\GTKArcGIS\Chapter17**. Click **ex17a.mxd** and click Open.

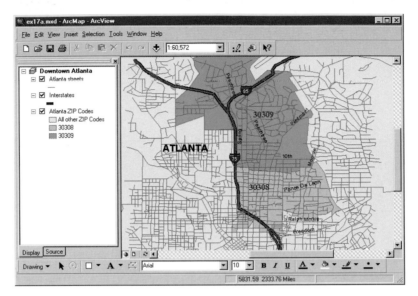

The map shows a portion of downtown Atlanta, Georgia, with layers of streets, interstate highways, and ZIP Codes.

2 At the bottom of the table of contents, click the Source tab.

When the Source tab is selected, the table of contents shows nonspatial tables, such as dBASE® files, that belong to the map document. In this case, you see a table of customers, which contains a sample of your customer database. This is the address table you'll geocode in the next exercise.

The geocoding service style you choose depends on the attributes in your reference layer (the Atlanta streets layer) and in your address table. You'll open the two tables to look at this information.

3 In the table of contents, right-click the Customers table and click Open.

	OID	CUST_ID	NAME	ADDRESS	ZIP	TYPE
►	0	840367	Accessories Inc	725 LAKEVIEW AVE NE	30309	Retail Clothing
	1	291063	Antiques Inc	491 BISHOP ST NE	30308	Retail
	2	520746	Damar Sales	388 7TH ST NE	30308	Car Dealer
	3	197302	Eastern Graphics	150 6TH ST NE	30308	Printing
	4	914582	Gelroy Associates	762 ARGONNE AVE NE	30308	Real Estate
	5	107892	Homes For Sale	500 RANKIN ST NE	30308	Real Estate
	6	308574	Industrial Supply Co	751 JUNIPER	30308	Wholesale
	7	489041	Leonard Associates	555 10TH ST NE	30309	Stockbroker
	8	734173	Lomer-Lockler Beauty College	220 6TH ST NE	30308	Trade School
	9	227309	Oar Clothing Co	400 7TH ST NE	30308	Retail Clothing
	10	197842	Ron's Food Mart	844 MIRTEL ST NE	30308	Retail Food
	11	216438	S and S Industrial Products	711 KENNESAW AVE NE	30308	Wholesale
	12	185628	Shawly and Company	911 MONROE DR NE	30308	Restaurant
	13	913007	Sound Concepts	400 PONCE DE LEON AVE NE	30308	Retail Entertainment
	14	166732	Southern Properties	699 JUNIPER ST NE	30308	Real Estate
	15	318592	J & R Bookkeeping	42 NORTH NE	30308	Bookkeeping

Record: 1 Show: All Selected Records (0 out of 16 Selected.) Options ▼

The attributes include customer ID, name, street address, five-digit ZIP Code, and business type. For geocoding, the relevant attributes are ADDRESS and ZIP.

4 Close the Attributes of Customers table. In the table of contents, right-click the Atlanta streets layer and click Open Attribute Table.

	FID	Shape*	L_F_ADD	L_T_ADD	R_F_ADD	R_T_ADD	PREFIX	PRE_TYPE	NAME	TYPE	SUFFIX	ZIPL	Z
►	0	Polyline	800	898	801	899			Drummond	St	SW	30314	3031
	1	Polyline			173	199			Hunter	St	SW	30303	3030
	2	Polyline	100	128	101	129			Jones	Ave	NW	30313	3031
	3	Polyline	130	158	131	159			Jones	Ave	NW	30313	3031
	4	Polyline	160	166	161	167			Jones	Ave	NW	30313	3031
	5	Polyline	168	214	169	215			Jones	Ave	NW	30314	3031
	6	Polyline	216	262	217	263			Jones	Ave	NW	30314	3031
	7	Polyline	264	324	265	325			Jones	Ave	NW	30314	3031
	8	Polyline	326	372	327	373			Jones	Ave	NW	30314	3031
	9	Polyline	374	402	375	403			Jones	Ave	NW	30314	3031
	10	Polyline	404	452	405	453			Jones	Ave	NW	30314	3031
	11	Polyline	454	478	455	479			Jones	Ave	NW	30314	3031
	12	Polyline	480	528	481	529			Jones	Ave	NW	30314	3031
	13	Polyline	530	588	531	589			Jones	Ave	NW	30314	3031
	14	Polyline	590	634	591	635			Jones	Ave	NW	30314	3031
	15	Polyline	636	688	637	689			Jones	Ave	NW	30314	3031
	16	Polyline	690	738	691	739			Jones	Ave	NW	30314	3031
	17	Polyline	740	798	741	799			Jones	Ave	NW	30314	3031
	18	Polyline	300	322	301	323			Oliver	St	NW	30314	3031

Record: 1 Show: All Selected Records (0 out of 4873 Selected.) Options ▼

The four address range attributes are: L_F_ADD (left "from" address), L_T_ADD (left "to" address), R_F_ADD (right "from" address), and R_T_ADD (right "to" address). These are the beginning and ending street numbers on each side of a street segment.

There are several other address attributes:

- PREFIX is a direction that precedes a street name, like the "N" in 139 N. Larchmont Blvd.
- PRE_TYPE is a street type that precedes a street name, like "Avenue" in 225 Avenue D.
- ZIPL and ZIPR are the ZIP Codes for the left and right sides of a street segment.
- CITYL and CITYR are the city names for the left and right sides of a street segment.
- NAME, TYPE, and SUFFIX direction are also shown in the table.

The attributes in the Atlanta streets table most closely match the "U.S. Streets with Zone" geocoding service style.

5 Close the table. On the Standard toolbar, click the ArcCatalog button.

6 In the catalog tree, click the Geocoding Services folder.

Make sure the Contents tab is active in the display window.

7 In the window, double-click on Create New Geocoding Service. The dialog box that opens contains a complete list of the ArcGIS geocoding styles.

8 Scroll through the list to US Streets with Zone (File) and click on it.

The US Streets with Zone style comes in two versions: (File) for reference data in shapefile format and (GDB) for geodatabase format. The Atlanta streets layer is a shapefile.

9 Click OK.

The New US Streets with Zone (File) Geocoding Service dialog opens.

You've already chosen a geocoding style; now you'll specify the reference data that will be used with it.

10 In the Name text box, highlight the name New Geocoding Service and type **Atlanta customers**.

11 On the Primary table tab, click the Browse button next to the Reference data box.

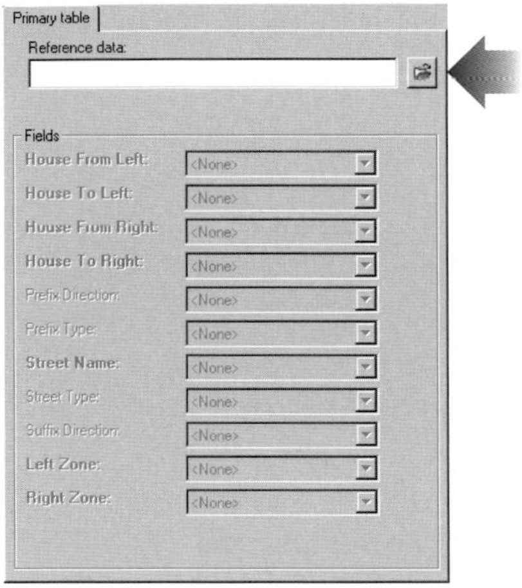

12 In the Choose Reference Data dialog, navigate to **C:\GTKArcGIS\Chapter17 \Ex17aData** and click on **streets.shp**. (Streets.shp is the file name of the Atlanta streets layer.) Make sure your dialog matches the following graphic, then click Add.

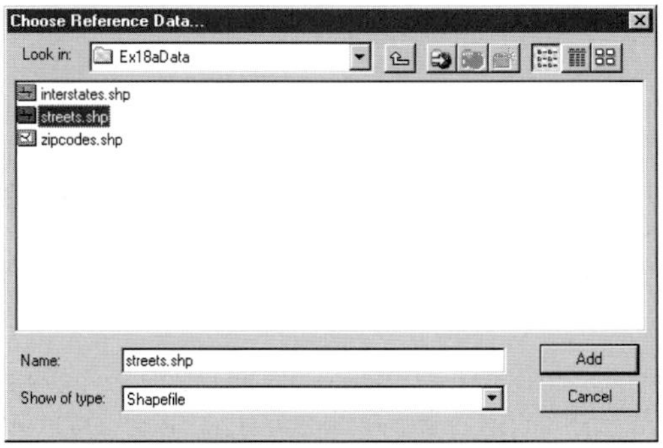

The path to the reference data is added to the Reference data box.

The Fields list shows the types of address information in the reference data that the geocoding style can use. Required information is boldfaced. The values in the corresponding drop-down lists show the reference data attributes that contain this information. In each case, ArcGIS has already selected the correct field name. If it hadn't, you could use the drop-down arrows to choose the right fields.

In the Input Address Fields frame, you specify the fields from the address table (Customers) that contain address information.

The box on the left lists the two kinds of input address information required by the geocoding style: Street (for the street address) and Zone (for the ZIP Code). The box on the right lists the field names that, by default, ArcGIS recognizes as containing this information.

In step 3, you saw that the street address information in the Customers table is contained in a field called ADDRESS. You'll keep this field name and delete the other two. (If your customer street address information was stored in a field with an unrecognized name, such as Cust_Addr, you would click Add to include it.)

13 In the window on the right, click on Addr and click Delete. Make sure that the Street field name is highlighted and click Delete again.

14 In the window on the left, click on Zone.

In the Customers table, the zone information is contained in a field called ZIP. Again, you'll delete the unnecessary field names.

15 In the window on the right, click on Zipcode and click Delete. Delete the City and Zone field names as well.

You'll accept the default settings in the rest of the dialog.

16 Make sure your dialog matches the following graphic, then click OK.

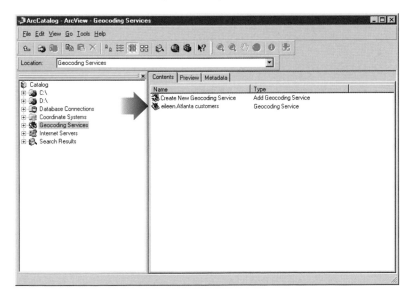

ArcGIS creates the new geocoding service.

The name of the geocoding service is prefixed by the user name on your computer, so (unless your name is Eileen) yours will be different.

In the next exercise, you'll add the Atlanta customers geocoding service to ArcMap and use it to match addresses.

17 Make sure ArcCatalog is the active application. Click the File menu and click Exit.

18 If you're continuing with the next exercise, leave ArcMap open. Otherwise, click the ArcMap File menu and click Exit. Click No when prompted to save your changes.

Matching addresses

Now that you've created a geocoding service, you're ready to geocode. Geocoding is also called address matching because it compares a table of addresses to reference data attributes and looks for matches.

The first step in address matching is standardizing the addresses in the address table; that is, dividing them into their component parts. This is done by the geocoding service. For example, the address "500 Rankin Street NE" has four parts: the street number (500), the street name (Rankin), the street type (Street), and a suffix (NE). The reference data is already standardized—each address part is a separate attribute.

ArcGIS takes each standardized address from the address table and looks for features in the reference data with matching parts. For each address, it generates a list of probable or possible matching locations, called candidates, in the reference data. Each candidate gets a score that rates its likelihood of being the correct location. For ArcGIS to make a match and create a point feature, a candidate's score must reach a certain level. You can choose both the score that defines a location as a candidate and the score that defines a candidate as a match. By default, the minimum candidate score is 10, on a scale of 100, and the minimum match score is 60.

When ArcGIS has made as many matches as it can, it creates a new data set, which has a point feature for each address, whether matched or not. Features that have unmatched addresses are not assigned spatial coordinates, and therefore do not display. You can adjust the geocoding options and try to find matches for unmatched addresses.

Most of the time, geocoding is done from a table of addresses, but as long as you have created a geocoding service, you can also geocode by typing address information into the Find dialog. Geocoding this way does not create new features, but will flash a matching location on the map or place a graphic there. It's useful in situations where you need to locate a single address or a few addresses quickly—for example, to make immediate deliveries.

Exercise 17b

Before geocoding your customer table, you'll test the geocoding service by locating the address of the Ace Market, a downtown Atlanta business.

1 Start ArcMap. In the ArcMap dialog, click the option to use an existing map. In the list of maps, double-click Browse for maps. (If ArcMap is already running, click the File menu and click Open.) Navigate to **C:\GTKArcGIS\Chapter17**. Click **ex17b.mxd** and click Open.

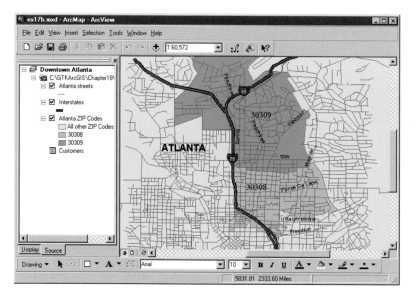

The map shows the layers of Atlanta streets, interstate highways, and ZIP Codes. The Customers table is at the bottom of the table of contents. You'll add the geocoding service to the map document.

2 Click the Tools menu, point to Geocoding, and click Geocoding Services Manager.

3 Click Add. In the Add Geocoding Service browser, navigate to the top of the catalog structure and double-click Geocoding Services. Click on the Atlanta customers geocoding service. Make sure your dialog matches the following graphic (except for the name prefix), then click Add.

The name of the geocoding service and a description of the style appear in the Geocoding Services Manager dialog.

4 Make sure your dialog matches the following graphic, then click Close.

Now that the geocoding service has been added to the map document, you can find addresses on the map.

5 On the Tools toolbar, Click the Find button.

6 In the Find dialog, click the Addresses tab. The Atlanta customers geocoding service should be displayed in the Choose a geocoding service drop-down list. If it isn't, click the drop-down arrow and select it.

7 In the Street or Intersection box, type **1171 Piedmont Ave NE**, the address of the Ace Market. Make sure your dialog matches the following graphic, then click Find.

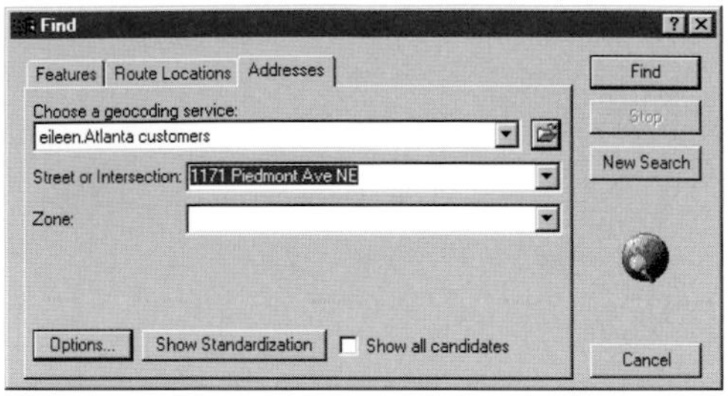

One candidate appears at the bottom of the dialog. Its score is 66.

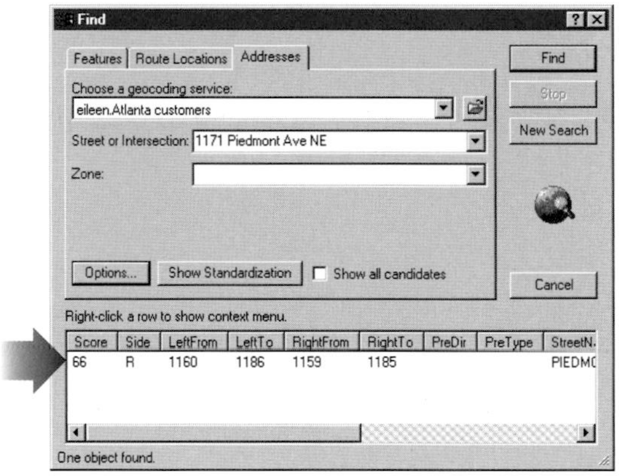

By default, only the candidate with the highest score is displayed. If you wanted, you could display additional candidates by checking the Show all candidates check box.

8 Scroll across the dialog and look at the candidate's address information.

The address range for odd street numbers, RightFrom and RightTo, is correct because it includes the street number 1171. The street name, street type, and suffix directions are also correct.

It seems as if the candidate should have scored higher, but, as you may recall from the previous exercise, your geocoding service needs an address and a zone for input. When you typed the Ace Market address, you didn't include its ZIP Code.

9 In the Find dialog, click in the Zone box and type **30309**. Click Find. The candidate now gets a perfect score.

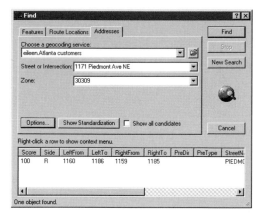

10 Right-click anywhere on the candidate. On the context menu, click Add as Graphic(s) to Map. Close the Find dialog.

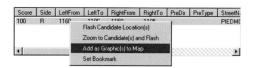

ArcGIS places a large black dot on the map at the location of the candidate.

Since you geocoded the Ace Market only to make sure that the geocoding service was working, you can now delete the graphic.

11 On the Tools toolbar, click the Select Elements tool.

12 Click on the graphic to select it. (Blue selection handles appear.) Right-click on it and click Delete.

Now you'll geocode the customer table.

13 In the table of contents, with the Source tab still selected, right-click on the Customers table and click Geocode Addresses.

In the Choose a geocoding service to use dialog, the Atlanta customers service is highlighted.

14 Click OK to open the Geocode Addresses dialog.

Geocoding creates a point feature for every address. The points can be saved as a shapefile or as a geodatabase feature class. Your Atlanta data is in shapefile format, so you'll save the address points as a shapefile, too.

15 Click the Browse button next to the Output shapefile or feature class box.

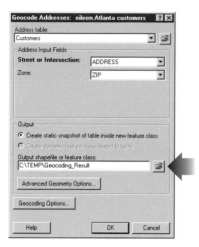

16 In the Saving Data dialog, navigate to **C:\GTKArcGIS\Chapter17\MyData**. Click the Save as type drop-down arrow and click Shapefile. In the Name box, highlight the default name of Geocoding_Result.shp and type **Geocode1.shp**. Make sure that your dialog matches the following graphic, then click Save.

The Geocode Addresses dialog updates with the new path.

17 Make sure your dialog matches the following graphic, then click OK.

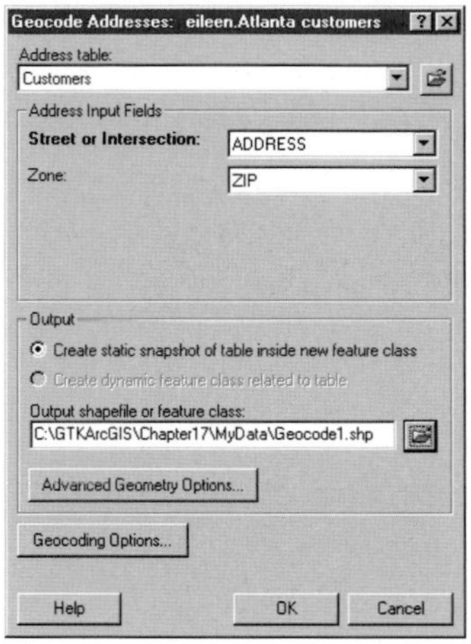

ArcMap geocodes the addresses and creates the output shapefile. When the geocoding process is done, the Review/Rematch Addresses dialog displays.

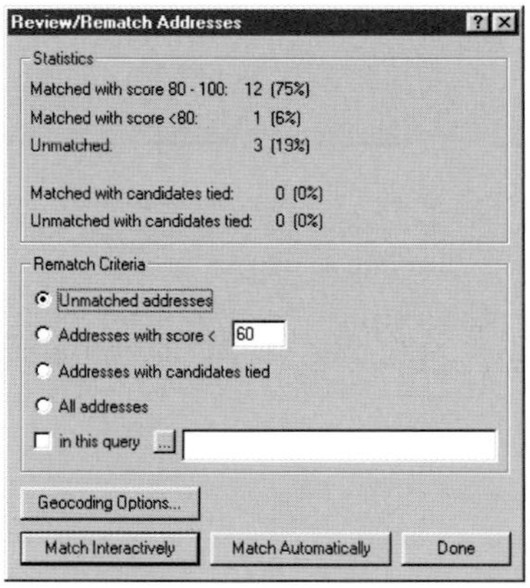

Of the sixteen addresses in the Customers table, twelve were matched with a score from 80 to 100. One was matched with a score less than 80. Three addresses are unmatched. You'll match the unmatched addresses in the next exercise. For now, you'll look at the attributes of the geocoded shapefile.

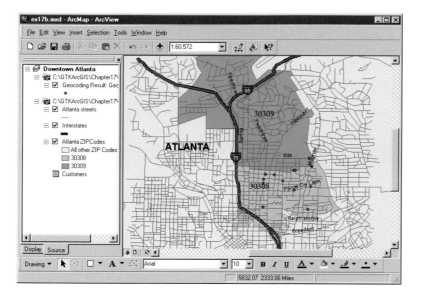

18 In the Review/Rematch Addresses dialog, click Done.

The Geocoding_Result: Geocode1 layer is listed at the top of the table of contents. There are thirteen point features displayed on the map, representing the locations of the matched addresses.

19 In the table of contents, right-click the Geocoding_Result: Geocode1 layer and click Open Attribute Table.

FID	Shape	Status	Score	Side	ARC_Street	ARC_Zone	CUST_ID	
0	Point	U	0		725 LAKEVIEW AVE NE	30309	840367	Acce
1	Point	M	100	R	491 BISHOP ST NE	30308	291063	Antiq
2	Point	M	100	L	388 7TH ST NE	30308	520746	Dama
3	Point	M	100	L	150 6TH ST NE	30308	197302	Easte
4	Point	M	100	L	762 ARGONNE AVE NE	30308	914582	Gelro
5	Point	M	100	L	500 RANKIN ST NE	30308	107892	Home
6	Point	M	61	R	751 JUNIPER	30308	308574	Indus
7	Point	M	100	R	555 10TH ST NE	30309	489041	Leon
8	Point	M	100	L	220 6TH ST NE	30308	734173	Lome
9	Point	M	100	L	400 7TH ST NE	30308	227309	Oar D
10	Point	U	0		844 MIRTEL ST NE	30308	197842	Ron's
11	Point	M	100	R	711 KENNESAW AVE NE	30308	216438	S and
12	Point	M	100	R	911 MONROE DR NE	30308	185628	Shaw
13	Point	M	100	L	400 PONCE DE LEON AVE NE	30308	913007	Soun
14	Point	M	100	R	699 JUNIPER ST NE	30300	188732	South
15	Point	U	0		42 NORTH NE	30308	318592	J & R

The table contains sixteen records, one for each address in the Customers table. The Status attribute tells you whether or not each address was matched (M), unmatched (U), or tied (T) with another address for the highest score. Point geometry is created only for features with the status M. The Score attribute contains the match score and the Side attribute tells you whether an address is on the right or left side of the street.

The next two attributes, ARC_Street and ARC_Zone, contain the information from the ADDRESS and ZIP fields in the Customers table. The remaining attributes are the same as those in the Customers table.

Although ARC_Street and ARC_Zone contain the same values as ADDRESS and ZIP, the attributes serve a different purpose. When you rematch unmatched addresses, you can edit the values in ARC_Street and ARC_Zone to make matches. You would do this, for example, if you found mistakes in the Customers table. The ADDRESS and ZIP attributes, on the other hand, preserve the original information from the Customers table.

20 Close the table. You have already saved the geocoded shapefile. There is no need to save the map document.

21 If you're continuing with the next exercise, leave ArcMap open. Otherwise, click the File menu and click Exit. Click No when prompted to save your changes.

Rematching addresses

When you geocode at the street address level, it's common to have addresses that aren't matched. Occasionally, this is the result of reference data that has errors or is incomplete. For instance, an address may belong to a subdivision that is newer than the reference data. More often, there is a mistake, such as a spelling error, in the address table. In some cases, the problem is with the way ArcGIS has standardized an ambiguous address.

Unmatched addresses can be rematched automatically (ArcGIS does all of them at once) or interactively (you do them one at a time). If you rematch automatically, you need to adjust the matching options, particularly the minimum match score and the spelling sensitivity, or your results won't change. If you rematch interactively, you have additional options. You can edit the way ArcGIS has standardized an address and you can match a candidate with a score below the minimum match score.

Exercise 17c

So far, the geocoding service has found matches for thirteen addresses in the Customers table, leaving three unmatched. In this exercise, you'll match these three. First, you'll modify the geocoding service's settings to generate more candidates. Then you'll interactively match each address.

chapter

14
15
16
17

1 Start ArcMap. In the ArcMap dialog, click the option to use an existing map. In the list of maps, double-click Browse for maps. (If ArcMap is already running, click the File menu and click Open.) Navigate to **C:\GTKArcGIS\Chapter17**. Click **ex17c.mxd** and click Open.

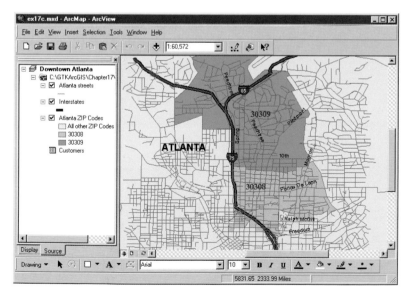

The map layers include the familiar streets, interstate highways, and ZIP Codes of downtown Atlanta. You'll add the layer of geocoded addresses you created in the previous exercise.

2 On the Standard toolbar, click the Add Data button.

3 In the Add Data dialog, navigate to **C:\GTKArcGIS\Chapter17\MyData**. Click Geocode1.shp as shown in the following graphic, then click Add.

The Geocode1 layer is added to the table of contents. It is symbolized with the default ArcMap point symbol in a random color. If you like, you can change the symbol to make it easier to see. In the following graphics, the point symbol has been set to Circle2, Fire Red, 7 points.

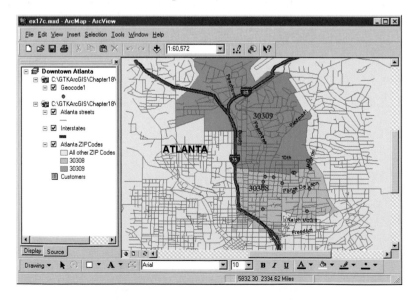

Now you'll rematch the unmatched addresses.

4 Click the Tools menu, point to Geocoding, point to Review/Rematch Addresses, and click Geocode1. The Rematch Addresses dialog prompts you to start editing.

> **Rematch Addresses** ☒
>
> This operation requires that you be editing this workspace. Would you like to start editing?
>
> [Yes] No

5 Click Yes. The Review/Rematch Addresses dialog opens.

> **Review/Rematch Addresses** ☐❔☒
>
> **Statistics**
> Matched with score 80 - 100:   12 (75%)
> Matched with score <80:   1 (6%)
> Unmatched: 3 (19%)
>
> Matched with candidates tied: 0 (0%)
> Unmatched with candidates tied: 0 (0%)
>
> **Rematch Criteria**
> ○ Unmatched addresses
> ○ Addresses with score < 60
> ○ Addresses with candidates tied
> ○ All addresses
> ☐ in this query ⋯ [   ]
>
> [Geocoding Options...]
> [Match Interactively] [Match Automatically] [Done]

In the Statistics frame, you see the results from the last exercise. The Rematch Criteria frame has options for specifying which addresses you want to rematch. You'll accept the default option of Unmatched addresses.

On the first try, ArcGIS failed to match three addresses. You'll lower the spelling sensitivity to make it easier to find a match. (Because ZIP Codes in address matching are treated as text strings, a wrong digit is a misspelling.)

6 At the bottom of the dialog, click Geocoding Options. The Geocoding Options dialog opens.

7 Drag the Spelling sensitivity slider to 60, as shown in the following graphic, then click OK.

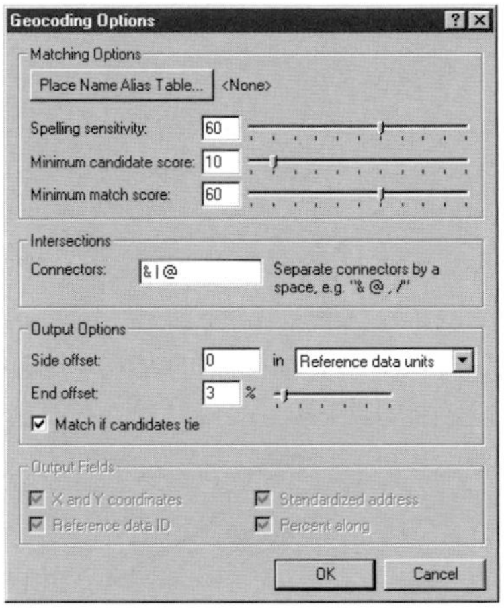

You return to the Review/Rematch Addresses dialog.

8 At the bottom of the dialog, click Match Interactively. The Interactive Review dialog opens.

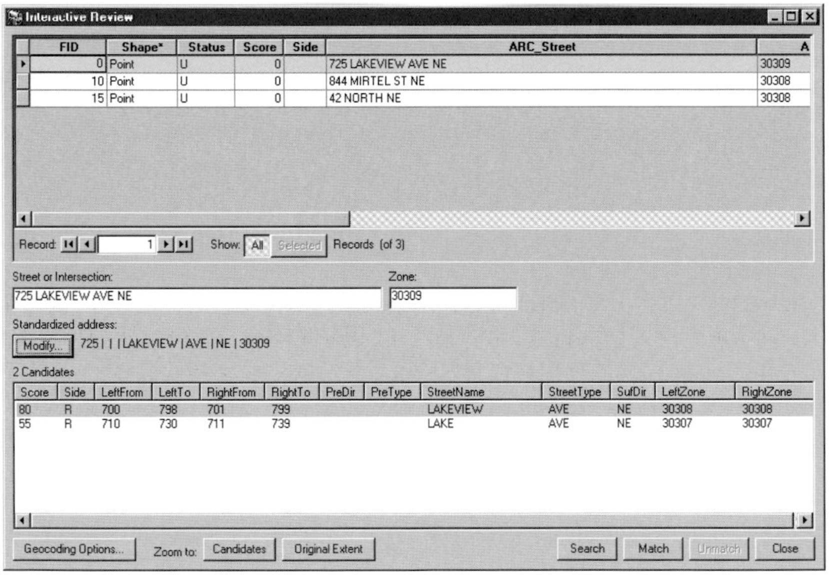

The top of the dialog displays the three unmatched records. The first one is highlighted in blue. In the middle of the dialog, the Street or Intersection box and the Zone box contain the current address information for the highlighted record. Edits to this information will be written to the ARC_Street and ARC_Zone fields of the Geocode1 table.

The Standardized address field shows how ArcMap has divided the address into parts. The bottom of the dialog displays match candidates for the highlighted record.

The first of the two candidates for 725 LAKEVIEW AVE NE has a score of 80. It has the correct address range because 725 falls between the RightFrom of 701 and the RightTo of 799. The street name, street type, and suffix direction all match. Only the ZIP Code is different. The second candidate has a score of 55. For this candidate, neither the street name nor the ZIP Code match.

9 At the bottom of the Interactive Review dialog, click Zoom to: Candidates. Move the dialog away from the map. The map is zoomed to the extent of the two candidates.

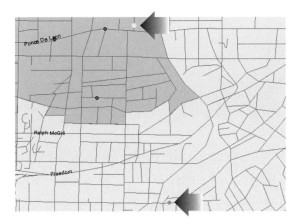

The candidate that is highlighted in the dialog is yellow, the other candidate is cyan. Common sense suggests that the candidate on Lakeview Avenue is the correct address location and that the wrong ZIP Code was entered in the Customers table.

10 At the bottom of the Interactive Review dialog, click Zoom to: Original Extent. In the Zone box, highlight the value 30309 and type **30308**. Press Enter.

The edit changes the candidate's match score to a perfect 100.

11 At the bottom of the dialog, make sure the first candidate is highlighted in gray. Click Match.

The candidate is matched. The record's Status attribute changes from U to M and its ARC_Zone attribute changes from 30309 to 30308. (Its ZIP attribute remains 30309.)

Now you'll rematch the other two addresses.

12 At the top of the Interactive Review dialog, click the gray tab to the left of the second record to select it.

Again, there are two match candidates. For the top candidate, all address information matches except the spelling of the street name. It's likely that a spelling error was made when this address was entered in the Customer table.

13 In the Street or Intersection box, highlight MIRTEL and type **MYRTLE**. Press Enter.

The scores of the two original candidates are adjusted and two new candidates are added. The top candidate now has a score of 100.

14 At the bottom of the dialog, make sure that the top candidate is highlighted in gray. Click Match.

FID	Shape*	Status	Score	Side	ARC_Street	A
0	Point	M	100	R	725 LAKEVIEW AVE NE	30308
10	Point	M	100	L	844 MYRTLE ST NE	30308
15	Point	U	0		42 NORTH NE	30308

The record's status changes from U to M and its name is changed in the ARC_Street field.

Finally, you'll rematch the third address.

15 At the top of the Interactive Review dialog, click the gray tab to the left of the third record to select it.

This time, there are no candidates. You could try lowering the spelling sensitivity still further, but the problem appears to be something else. It looks like the address, 42 NORTH NE, has been incorrectly standardized. The street name (NORTH) has been interpreted as a prefix direction (N) and the suffix direction (NE) has been taken for the street name.

42 | N | | NE | | | 30308

16 Next to the standardized address, click Modify. The Edit Standardization dialog opens.

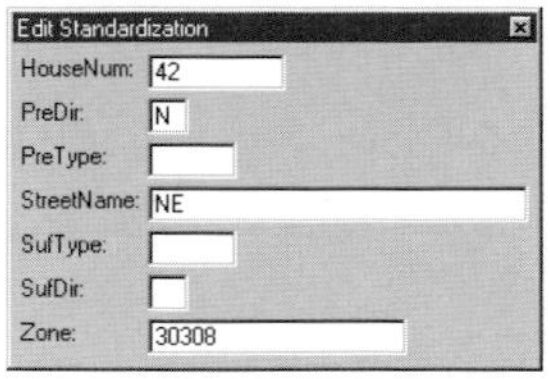

17 In the PreDir box, highlight the value N and press Delete on your keyboard. In the StreetName box, highlight the value NE and type **NORTH**. Click in the SufDir field and type **NE**. (In the SufDir box, you only see one letter at a time.) Be sure to press Enter.

18 Make sure your dialog matches the following graphic, then close the dialog.

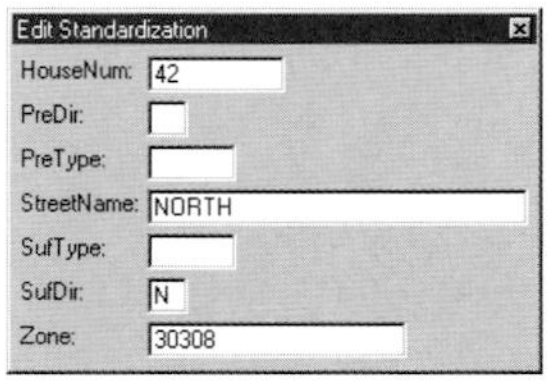

The Standardized address is updated and eleven candidates appear.

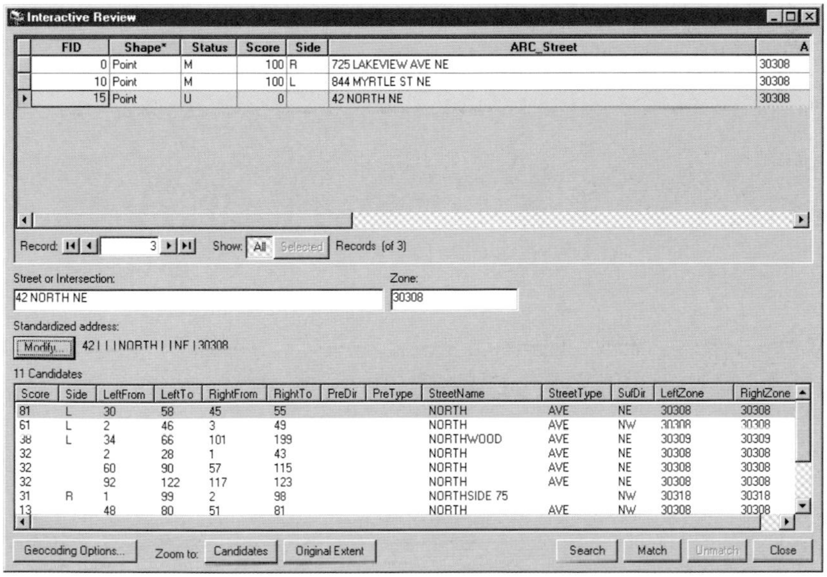

Most of the candidates have a street type (AVE), but there is no street type in the record to be matched. When an address component is missing from either the address or the candidate, it isn't possible to get a match score of 100.

You could add AVE to the Street or Intersection box and improve the candidate match scores (the top candidate would then score 100), but instead you'll simply match the top candidate with its current score.

19 Make sure that the top candidate, with a score of 81, is highlighted. Click Match.

	FID	Shape*	Status	Score	Side	AHC_Street	A
	0	Point	M	100	R	725 LAKEVIEW AVE NE	30308
	10	Point	M	100	L	844 MYRTLE ST NE	30308
▶	15	Point	M	81	L	42 NORTH NE	30308

The candidate is matched. The record's status changes from U to M. You've matched all the addresses in your customer table.

20 At the bottom of the Interactive Review dialog, click Close to return to the Review/Rematch Addresses dialog.

The Statistics frame shows you that fifteen addresses were matched with scores of 80 or better. One was matched with a score of less than 80.

21 In the Review/Rematch Addresses dialog, click Done.

On the map there are now sixteen geocoded points.

22 In the table of contents, right-click the Geocode1 layer and click Zoom to Layer.

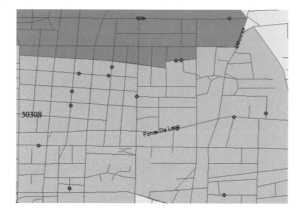

23 In the table of contents, right-click the Geocode1 layer and click Open Attribute Table.

FID	Shape*	Status	Score	Side	ARC_Street	ARC_Zone	CUST_ID
1	Point	M	100	R	491 BISHOP ST NE	30308	291063
2	Point	M	100	L	388 7TH ST NE	30308	520746
3	Point	M	100	L	150 6TH ST NE	30308	197302
4	Point	M	100	L	762 ARGONNE AVE NE	30308	914582
5	Point	M	100	L	500 RANKIN ST NE	30308	107892
6	Point	M	61	R	751 JUNIPER	30308	308574
7	Point	M	100	R	555 10TH ST NE	30309	489041
8	Point	M	100	L	220 6TH ST NE	30308	734173
9	Point	M	100	L	400 7TH ST NE	30308	227309
11	Point	M	100	R	711 KENNESAW AVE NE	30308	216438
12	Point	M	100	R	911 MONROE DR NE	30308	185628
13	Point	M	100	L	400 PONCE DE LEON AVE NE	30308	913007
14	Point	M	100	R	699 JUNIPER ST NE	30308	166732
0	Point	M	100	R	725 LAKEVIEW AVE NE	30308	840367
10	Point	M	100	L	844 MYRTLE ST NE	30308	197842
15	Point	M	81	L	42 NORTH NE	30308	318592

Record: ◄ ◄ 1 ► ►◄ Show: All Selected Records (0 out of 16 Selected.) Options ▼

All the records have the value M in the Status field. Edits that you made during rematching ("Mirtel" to "Myrtle" for example) are reflected in the ARC_Street and ARC_Zone fields. The field names are white because you are still in an edit session.

Now that you know how to geocode addresses, the project to offer digital maps as one of your company's advertising services can move forward.

24 Close the table.

25 To end the editing session, click the Editor Toolbar button on the Standard toolbar.

26 On the Editor toolbar, click the Editor menu and click Stop Editing. When prompted to save your edits, click Yes. Close the Editor toolbar.

27 If you want to save your work, click the File menu and click Save As. Navigate to **C:\GTKArcGIS\Chapter17\MyData**. Rename the file **my_ex17c.mxd** and click Save.

28 If you are continuing to the next chapter, leave ArcMap open. Otherwise, click the File menu and click Exit. Click No when prompted to save your changes.

Making maps quickly

Opening a map template

Adding x,y data to a map

Drawing graphics on a map

Using Geography Network with ArcMap

Making a map that's accurate, informative, and nice to look at usually takes time, as you'll see in the next chapter. Sometimes, however, you have to make a professional-quality map on short notice. ArcMap comes with a number of templates to help you do this. In a template, the map elements you need (data frames, legend, title, north arrow, background color, and so on) are already in place. All you do is add data and the map is ready to print.

You may not even need to add data—many ArcMap templates already contain layers for the world and the United States. A single template may be all you need, or you may want to use a template as a basemap and add your own layers to it.

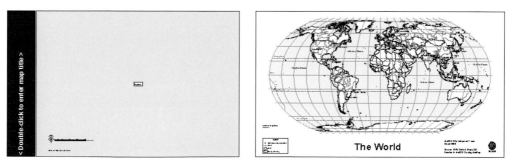

The LandscapeClassic template (left) has layout elements but no data. The WorldRobinson template (right) has countries, cities, rivers, and lakes in a Robinson projection.

Finding the data you want for a map is becoming an easy matter. A huge amount of data is available over the Internet—the only problem has been knowing where to find it. Now there's Geography Network, a Web site sponsored by ESRI, which offers data, online maps, and other geographic services. With an Internet connection, you can access a vast number of online maps in ArcMap, work with them using ArcMap tools, and combine them with your own data layers.

Opening a map template

By default, every ArcMap document uses a template called the normal template. When you open a new document and switch to layout view, the layout page (or *virtual* page) is blank and has a single data frame. This is the appearance prescribed by the normal template.

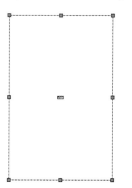

In the course of making a map, you may add data to this data frame, resize it, insert more data frames, and add such elements as legends and scale bars. When you save the map, you save it not as a template but as a map document, or .mxd file. That way, the template does not change. Then, when you create a new ArcMap document, you start again with a blank page.

Rather than designing your own layout, you can open a custom template (that is, a template other than the normal template). Again, any changes you make are saved as a map document, so the template is not affected.

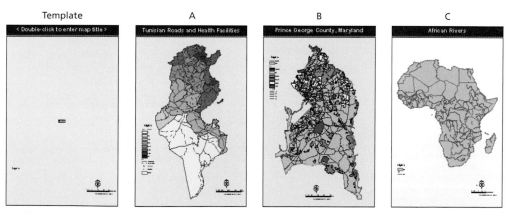

| Template | A | B | C |

On the left is the PortraitClassic template. On the right are three maps that use it, each with different data. In map A, a title has been specified but the template is otherwise unchanged. In map B, the legend, north arrow, and scale bar have been moved from their default positions. In map C, the background color has been changed.

You can also create new templates. If you've made an arrangement of map elements and data frames (with or without data) that you want to use again, click Save As on the File menu and set the Save as type drop-down list to ArcMap templates. This will save the file with a .mxt extension. ArcMap custom templates are saved in the **C:\arcgis\arcexe81\Bin\Templates** folder. You can add your own templates to this folder or to any folder you choose. You can also modify existing templates. For more information, click the Contents tab in ArcGIS Desktop Help and navigate to *ArcMap > Getting started with ArcMap > Saving a map and exiting ArcMap* and *Customizing ArcMap and ArcCatalog > Saving your customizations*.

Exercise 18a

It's early June 1999. As the information officer for the Philippine Atmospheric Geophysical and Astronomical Services Administration, you've been asked to talk to a group of journalists about Typhoon Maggie, also known as Etang.

Typhoon Etang was first spotted off the coast of Samar, an island in the east central part of the Philippines. It has since traveled northwest, and is currently about 250 kilometers off the northeast coast of Luzon, where the capital, Manila, is located. The typhoon will probably pass harmlessly north of Luzon, through open ocean, but should it strike land it could be devastating.

The presentation is scheduled for tomorrow, but you weren't told about the briefing until today. Now it's 11:00 P.M. and you're trying to create a PowerPoint® slide presentation and still have time for a little sleep.

You want to show the path of the typhoon and its current location on a map of the country with rivers, populated places, and other useful geography. You'll use an ArcMap template for the basemap and draw the typhoon path yourself.

1 Start ArcMap. In the ArcMap dialog, click the option to use a template, then click OK. (If ArcMap is already running, click the File menu and click New.)

The New dialog opens. All the templates that come with ArcGIS can be found here. Instead of using one of these, however, you'll use a template that was specially created for this exercise.

2 Click the Browse button near the bottom of the dialog.

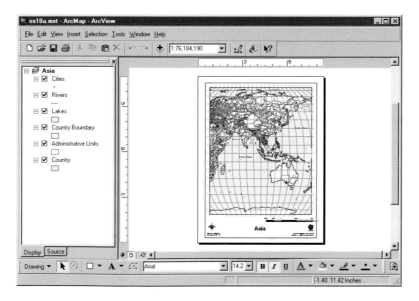

3 In the Open dialog, navigate to **C:\GTKArcGIS\Chapter18**. Click on **ex18a.mxt** and click Open.

The template opens in layout view and shows the countries of Asia. The blue lines of latitude and longitude covering the map are called a graticule.

With the entire map displayed, you can't read the text and labels. This is because the page in the window (the virtual page) is smaller than the printed page would be. The layout toolbar shows you the size of the virtual page relative to the actual page. Your percentage may be different.

4 On the Layout toolbar, click the Zoom to 100% button.

The layout zooms to actual size and you see the map at the resolution it would have on a printed page. You can no longer see the entire layout. The display scale of the data has not changed.

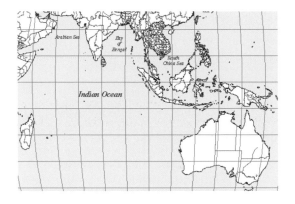

5 On the Layout toolbar, click the Pan tool.

6 Pan to the lower left corner of the map.

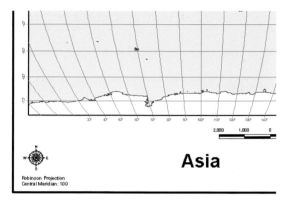

At 100 percent, map elements and text are legible, as they would be on the printed page. (The numbers on your scale bar may differ from those in the graphic.)

7 On the Layout toolbar, click the Zoom Whole Page button.

The layout returns to full view.

The zoom buttons on the Layout toolbar do not affect the display scale of data in a data frame. The data frame shows all of Asia, but you are only interested in the Philippines. You'll use a bookmark to zoom in on the data you want to see.

8 Click the View menu, point to Bookmarks, and click Philippines.

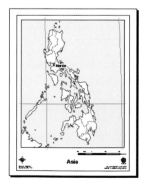

The map zooms in on the Philippines. The graticule, with its relatively wide intervals of 10 degrees, will not help the journalists describe the typhoon's location. You'll reduce the size of the intervals to make the map more informative.

9 In the table of contents, double-click on the Asia data frame to open the Data Frame Properties dialog. Click the Grids tab.

10 On the Grids tab, click Properties.

11 In the Reference System Properties dialog, click the Intervals tab.

12 In the Interval frame, replace the X Axis Interval value of 10.000000 with **5** and the Y Axis Interval of 10.000000 with **5**, as shown in the following graphic. Click OK, then click OK in the Data Frame Properties dialog.

The graticule intervals are changed.

13 On the Tools toolbar, click the Select Elements tool.

14 Click outside the data frame to unselect the graticule.

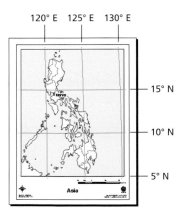

The graticule is now divided into intervals of 5 degrees. Parallels and meridians are labeled on the layout, but the labels are too small to see when you are zoomed to the whole virtual page.

If you want to add a graticule to a data frame that doesn't have one, open the Data Frame Properties dialog, click the Grids tab, and click New Grid to start the Grids and Graticules wizard. (Graticules use curved lines to mark latitude and longitude coordinates. Grids use straight lines to mark projected coordinates.)

You now have your basemap. In the next exercise, you'll display points that mark Etang's progress.

15 If you want to save your work, click the File menu and click Save As. Navigate to **C:\GTKArcGIS\Chapter18\MyData**. Rename the file **my_ex18a.mxd** and click Save.

Although you opened a map template (.mxt), you are saving a map document (.mxd).

16 If you are continuing with the next exercise, leave ArcMap open. Otherwise, click the File menu and click Exit. Click No if prompted to save your changes.

Adding x,y data to a map

As you know from the previous chapter, ArcMap can turn geographic information from a table into points on a map. When the information consists of street addresses, the process is fairly elaborate. If, however, you have a table of coordinate values (obtained from a Global Positioning System device or other source), ArcMap can create point data with little preparation.

A table of coordinates must contain two fields, one for the x-coordinate and one for the y-coordinate. The values may be in any geographic or projected coordinate system.

Exercise 18b

As part of your presentation to the press, you want to show the location, speed, and path of Typhoon Etang. You have been given a text file of latitude–longitude coordinates showing where the typhoon has been at different times. You'll add this file to the map document and display the coordinates as points on the map.

1 Start ArcMap. In the ArcMap dialog, click the option to use an existing map. In the list of existing maps, double-click Browse for maps. (If ArcMap is already running, click the File menu and click Open.) Navigate to **C:\GTKArcGIS\Chapter18**. Click **ex18b.mxd** and click Open.

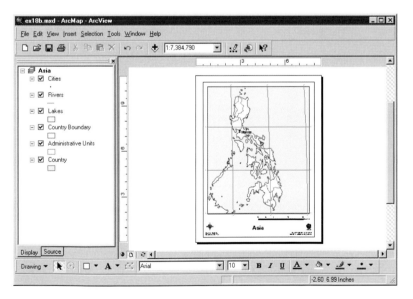

The map document opens in layout view. It looks as it did at the end of the previous exercise, with graticule intervals of 5 degrees.

You'll add the file of latitude–longitude coordinates to the map document.

2 On the Standard toolbar, click the Add Data button.

3 In the Add Data dialog, navigate to **C:\GTKArcGIS\Chapter18\Data**. Click on latlong_etang.txt, as shown in the following graphic, and click Add.

The text file is added to the table of contents and displayed on the Source tab.

4 In the table of contents, right-click on latlong_etang.txt and click Open.

Latitude	Longitude	Date_	Time_	Speed_kph
15.5	129	June03	6:00 am	105
15.8	128.4	June03	12:00 pm	120
16.8	127.9	June03	6:00 pm	120
17.3	127.1	June04	12:00 am	145
17.4	126.4	June04	6:00 am	160
17.5	126	June04	12:00 pm	160
18.1	125.3	June04	6:00 pm	160
18.9	124.5	June05	12:00 am	170

The table shows the typhoon's position and speed over the course of two days.

Although latitude and longitude are measured in degrees, minutes, and seconds, the values in the table have been converted to *decimal degrees* so that ArcMap can store and process them efficiently. Decimal degrees represent minutes and seconds as fractions. For example, the value 30° 15′ is 30.25 decimal degrees because 15 minutes is a quarter of a degree.

5 Close the table. In the table of contents, right-click on latlong_etang.txt and click Display XY Data.

ArcMap has correctly picked Longitude and Latitude as the fields containing coordinate values. Below this, in the Spatial Reference frame, the description is set to Unknown Coordinate System. If you knew which geographic coordinate system the latitude–longitude values were based on, you could click Edit and select it. Since you don't know, you'll let ArcMap assign a default geographic coordinate system. (Even if it's not the right one, the error will be too small to matter for your map.)

6 Click OK in the Display XY Data dialog to display the points on the map.

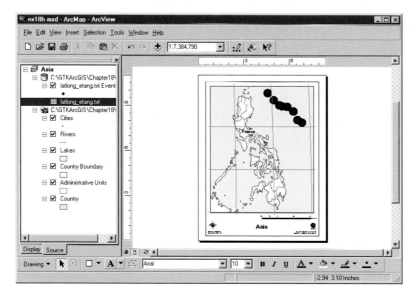

A layer called latlong_etang.txt Events is added to the table of contents. ("Events" is a technical term for points created from x,y coordinate values.) You'll give the layer a simpler name, then resymbolize the points with a symbol for typhoons.

7 In the table of contents, double-click the latlong_etang.txt Events layer. In the Layer Properties dialog, click the General tab.

8 Replace the layer name with **Etang,** as shown in the following graphic, then click OK.

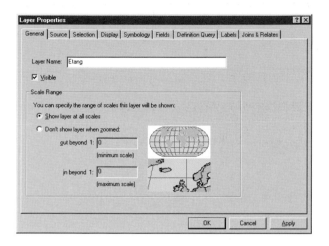

9 In the table of contents, click the symbol for the Etang layer. The Symbol Selector dialog opens.

10 In the Symbol Selector, click More Symbols. Click Weather to load symbols from the Weather style.

11 Scroll to the bottom of the symbol list and click the Typhoon symbol. Change its size from 18 points to **4**. Make sure that your dialog matches the following graphic, then click OK.

The points are resymbolized on the map.

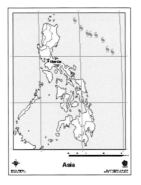

You'll save the typhoon points as a layer file.

12 In the table of contents, right-click on the Etang layer and click Save As Layer File.

13 In the Save Layer dialog, navigate to **C:\GTKArcGIS\Chapter18\MyData**. Accept the default name of Etang.lyr, as shown in the following graphic, then click Save.

Save Layer	✕
Look in: 🗀 MyData ▾

| Name: | Etang.lyr | Save |
| Save as type: | Layer files (*.lyr) ▾ | Cancel |

In the next exercise, you'll draw a line along the typhoon's path.

14 If you want to save your work, click the File menu and click Save As. Navigate to **C:\GTKArcGIS\Chapter18\MyData**. Rename the file **my_ex18b.mxd** and click Save.

15 If you are continuing with the next exercise, leave ArcMap open. Otherwise, click the File menu and click Exit. Click No if prompted to save your changes.

chapter

18
19

Adding x,y data to a map

Drawing graphics on a map

With the tools on the Draw toolbar, you can add graphics and text to a layout. Since graphics don't change size as you zoom in or out on data, wait to do this until you're satisfied with the display scale. A graphic box that encloses a feature at one display scale, for instance, may not enclose it at another.

Exercise 18c

Now that you have added the point locations of Typhoon Etang to your map, you'll draw the typhoon's path by connecting the symbols. Then you'll add some descriptive text and change the map title. When your map is ready, you'll export it in a format that PowerPoint supports so you can include it in your presentation.

1 Start ArcMap. In the ArcMap dialog, click the option to use an existing map. In the list of existing maps, double-click Browse for maps. (If ArcMap is already running, click the File menu and click Open.) Navigate to **C:\GTKArcGIS\Chapter18**. Click **ex18c.mxd** and click Open.

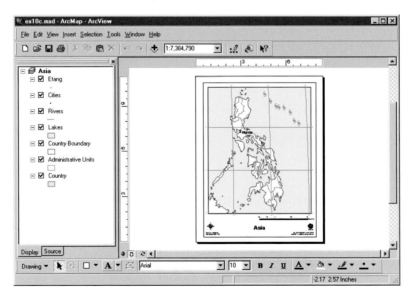

The map looks as it did at the end of the previous exercise. You'll zoom in on the layout to draw a line connecting the typhoon symbols.

2 On the Layout toolbar, click the Zoom In tool.

3 Drag a zoom rectangle as shown in the following graphic.

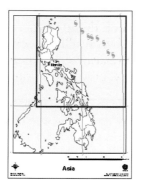

The layout zooms in to the area of the storm's path.

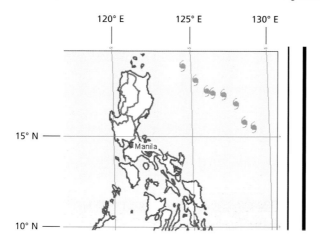

4 On the Draw toolbar, click the drop-down arrow by the New Rectangle tool and click the New Curve tool.

5 Draw the typhoon path on the map. Start by clicking on the symbol farthest to the east. Click on each symbol to draw a line connecting them. Double-click on the last symbol to end the line. If you make a mistake, end the line, press the Delete key, and start again.

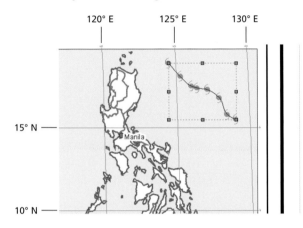

6 With the graphic selected, move the mouse pointer over the line and right-click. On the context menu, click Properties.

7 In the Properties dialog, click the Symbol tab if necessary. Click the color square. On the color palette, click Electron Gold, as shown in the following graphic. Click OK in the dialog.

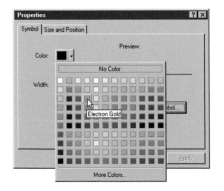

The new color is applied to the line.

8 Click outside the data frame to unselect the line.

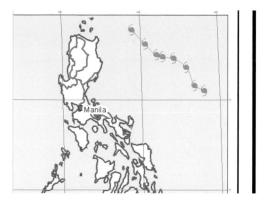

Now you'll add text to show the typhoon's time and speed at its last recorded position.

9 On the Tools toolbar, click the Identify tool.

10 Click the symbol at the last recorded position of Etang.

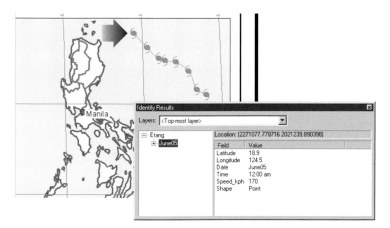

The time was 12 A.M. on June 5. The typhoon's speed was 170 kilometers per hour.

11 Close the Identify Results window. On the Draw toolbar, click the drop-down arrow by the New Text tool and click the Callout tool.

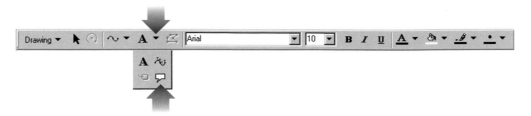

12 Click again on the same typhoon symbol. In the pop-up text box, type **June 5 12:00 am - 170kph** and press the Enter key.

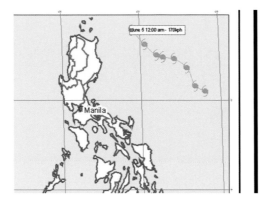

The text is added to the map and the text box is selected.

13 On the Draw toolbar, click the Font Size drop-down arrow and click 14.

14 Drag the callout text to the right of the typhoon symbol. Click outside the data frame to unselect the text.

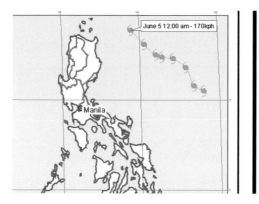

Since the map is no longer a map of Asia, you need to change its title.

15 On the Layout toolbar, click the Zoom Whole Page button.

16 Double-click on the title Asia at the bottom of the map.

17 In the Properties dialog, on the Text tab, replace Asia with **Path of Typhoon Etang**, as shown in the following graphic. Click OK.

18 Click outside the page to unselect the title.

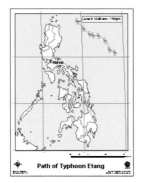

Finally, you'll export an image of the map in .emf format for your PowerPoint slide presentation. EMF files can be added to common Windows applications such as Power-Point and Microsoft Word and resized without distortion. To learn more about the many graphic file formats ArcMap supports, click the Contents tab in ArcGIS Desktop Help and navigate to *ArcMap > Laying out and printing maps > Exporting a map.*

19 Click the File menu and click Export Map.

20 In the Export dialog, navigate to **C:\GTKArcGIS\Chapter18\MyData**. If necessary, click the Save as type drop-down arrow and click EMF (*.emf). Replace the default file name with **etang**, as shown in the following graphic, then click Export.

In this chapter, you zoomed in on the basemap data you needed in an ArcMap template. You added latitude–longitude coordinates from a table and displayed them as points. In the next exercise, you'll see how Geography Network can bring maps straight from the Internet into ArcMap.

21 If you want to save your work, click the File menu and click Save As. Navigate to **C:\GTKArcGIS\Chapter18\MyData**. Rename the file **my_ex18c.mxd** and click Save.

22 If you are continuing with the next exercise, leave ArcMap open. Otherwise, click the File menu and click Exit. Click No if prompted to save your changes.

Using Geography Network with ArcMap

Geography Network, at www.geographynetwork.com, is a resource for online maps, downloadable data, GIS services such as geocoding and driving directions, and links to other geographic information sites.

You can connect to Geography Network from your Web browser, from ArcCatalog, or from ArcMap. You can display online maps (called map services) in ArcMap, zoom and pan them, add your own layers, and export or print the result.

To find the map service you want, you use a custom browser called Geography Network Explorer. Once you've found the service, you can add it to ArcMap by clicking a button.

In this exercise, you'll add a map service to ArcMap, then apply a template to the map. Because the map service is delivered over the Internet, performance will vary according to the speed of your connection.

Geography Network is evolving, so the steps for this exercise are online, where they can be updated as needed. If you print the exercise and work from the printout, you'll have more room on your screen for ArcMap and Geography Network Explorer.

Exercise 18d

Your presentation will emphasize that it looks as if Typhoon Etang will pass north of Luzon. Nevertheless, you want to discuss some of the physical features and infrastructure of the island so that the journalists understand what might happen and what could be done if the typhoon did make landfall.

A mountain range along the eastern coast of Luzon, while not especially high (about 1,400 meters), offers protection against storm surge. The mountains can also be a buffer against winds and rain. Fortunately, all of the larger cities in northern Luzon are located west of the mountains in the central valley. The fact that most major roads on the island are near rivers is a potential problem—it means that roads might be flooded before people could be evacuated. Flooded roads would also complicate relief operations. Most emergency relief would be based in Manila, but it might make sense to locate shelters and other services on the west coast in case the major north–south roads became unusable.

It's now past midnight, and the data you want—topography, roads, cities—isn't at hand. You'll see if you can find it on Geography Network.

To begin the exercise, open your Web browser and point it to **www.esri.com/ esripress/gtkarcgis.html**. Click the **Exercise 18d** link.

Making maps for presentation

Laying out the page
Adding a title
Adding a north arrow, a scale bar, and a legend
Adding final touches and setting print options

A good map should inform, reveal, clarify, or convince. The elements for accomplishing these purposes include carefully prepared and symbolized data, a legend to explain the symbols, a descriptive title, projection information, and a source statement. A north arrow and scale bar often help to orient the map reader.

Maps should be tailored to their audience. A map meant for a group of scientists, for example, might use symbols and abbreviations unfamiliar to the general public. Maps should also be tailored to their uses. A map for a researcher in the field might be designed to fold rather than lie flat and might be less elegant than a map meant to hang on a wall.

In this chapter, you'll create the map shown below of proposed tiger conservation areas in India.

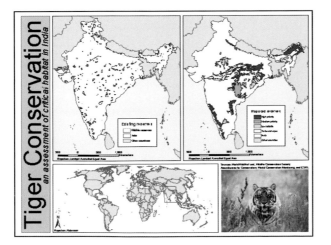

Laying out the page

The amount of space on which elements can be arranged may be anything from a letter-sized sheet of paper to a wall poster 44 by 34 inches. The orientation may be vertical (portrait) or horizontal (landscape). Choosing the dimensions and the orientation of the map before you start makes the layout process easier.

ArcMap has rulers, guides, and a grid to help you arrange map elements on a page. You can also align, nudge, distribute (space evenly), rotate, and resize selected elements to place them where you want.

Exercise 19a

You are a research associate for the World Wildlife Fund and have just finished an analysis of tiger populations in India. Loss of habitat is bringing wild tigers to the edge of extinction as forest lands are claimed for residential, commercial, and industrial use. Though poaching is not common in reserves or other protected areas, it is a problem in areas where there is little threat from the law.

Present wildlife reserves in India have been of some help, but are too small and scattered to maintain existing populations. After studying the data, you have developed a plan to connect existing reserves along vegetation corridors, consolidating them into larger areas that can better support the tigers.

The plan identifies the priority of proposed reserves as high, medium, or low. Reserves with higher priority have a better chance of sustaining a large tiger population for many years. The plan also identifies potential reserves for which research has yet to be completed.

You will create a map as part of a proposal to the United Nations Environment Program seeking support for the tiger conservation project.

1 Start ArcMap. In the ArcMap dialog box, click the option to use an existing map. In the list of existing maps, double-click Browse for maps. (If ArcMap is already running, click the File menu and click Open.) Navigate to **C:\GTKArcGIS\Chapter19**. Click **ex19a.mxd** to highlight it and click Open.

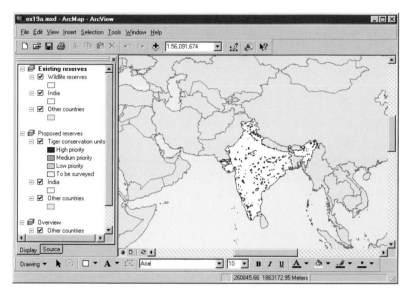

The map document contains three data frames: Existing reserves, Proposed reserves, and Overview. Existing reserves is active. Reserves are symbolized with purple outlines.

All three data frames will be part of your map layout. You'll show existing reserves next to proposed reserves. For orientation, you'll include a map of the world with India framed on it.

2 Click the View menu and click Layout View.

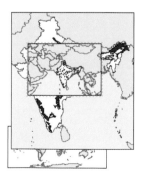

The data frames are stacked on the virtual page according to their order in the table of contents. It will be easier to see what you're doing if you make the ArcMap application window as large as possible.

3 In the ArcMap application title bar, click the middle button in the upper right corner to maximize the application window.

The ArcMap application fills your screen.

4 On the Layout toolbar, click the Zoom Whole Page button.

The virtual page is enlarged within the layout window. At the moment, its orientation is portrait.

5 Click the File menu and click Page Setup.

6 In the Map Size frame of the Page Setup dialog, click Landscape as shown in the following graphic. Click OK.

In the layout, the orientation changes.

To help you place data frames exactly, you'll turn on guides. Guides are cyan lines originating from arrows on the layout rulers. They help you align and position elements but do not themselves appear on the printed map. In this exercise, some guides have already been set for you.

7 Click the View menu and click Guides.

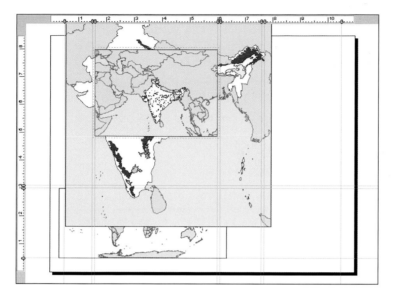

The guides display on the layout.

8 Place the mouse pointer over the vertical ruler. Click to add a guide at 8 inches as shown in the following graphic.

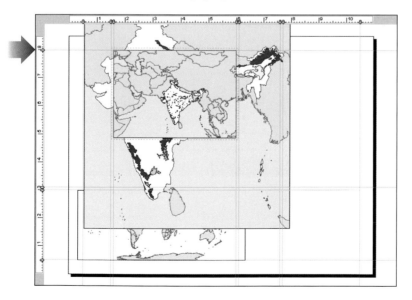

The guides will be more useful if map elements snap (automatically align) to them.

9 Right-click on an empty part of the virtual page. On the context menu, point to Guides and click Snap to Guides.

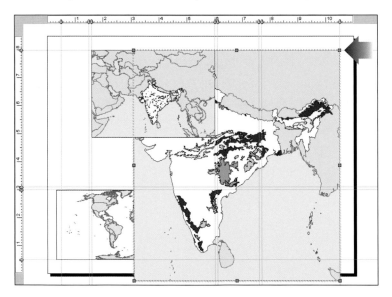

Now you'll resize and arrange the data frames on the page, beginning with Proposed reserves (the largest data frame).

10 Click on the Proposed reserves data frame to select it.

Once selected, it is outlined with a dashed blue line and marked with blue selection handles.

11 Move the mouse pointer over the data frame. The cursor has a four-headed arrow. Drag the frame so that its upper right corner snaps to the guides at 8 inches (on the vertical ruler) and 10.5 inches (on the horizontal ruler).

You'll make the data frame smaller by dragging a selection handle.

When you resize a data frame, ArcMap automatically adjusts the map extent and view scale. (If you want to make sure one or the other stays the same, you can set a fixed scale or extent on the Data Frame tab of the Data Frame Properties dialog.)

12 Place the mouse pointer over the selection handle at the lower left corner of the data frame. The cursor changes to a two-headed arrow. Drag the corner of the data frame until it snaps to the guides at 3.1 inches (vertical ruler) and 6.1 inches (horizontal ruler).

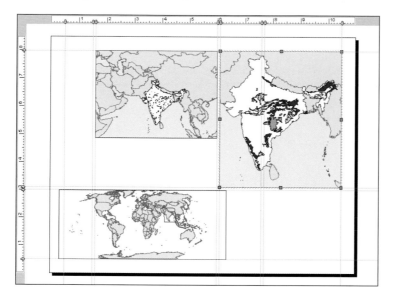

The view scale, shown on the Standard toolbar, should be somewhere around 1:28,000,000. Make a note of it. Later, you'll use this number to set the scale of the Existing reserves data frame.

Next, you'll move the Overview data frame, which shows the map of the world with India marked by a red rectangle.

13 Click on the Overview data frame to select it. Drag the frame so that its upper left corner snaps to the guides at 3 inches (vertical ruler) and 1.6 inches (horizontal ruler).

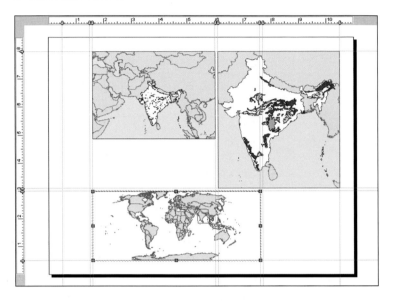

Now you'll resize the Existing reserves data frame to match the Proposed reserves data frame.

14 Click on the Existing reserves data frame to select it. Put the mouse pointer over the selection handle at the bottom center of the data frame. The cursor changes to a two-headed arrow. Drag the data frame until its bottom edge snaps to the guide at 3.1 inches (vertical ruler).

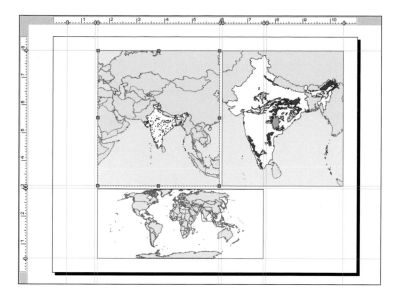

The data frames now have their final sizes and positions. (Another way to resize a data frame is with the Size and Position tab on the Data Frame Properties dialog. The tab lets you set a height and width for the data frame and move a corner, midpoint, or the center of the frame to a page position you specify.)

In the Existing reserves data frame, India is displayed at a smaller scale than in the Proposed reserves frame. You'll change its view scale to match the Proposed Reserves frame.

15 Make sure that the Existing reserves data frame is still selected. On the Standard toolbar, highlight the current view scale and replace it with the scale value of the Proposed reserves data frame. (If you didn't make a note of the value in step 12, type **28000000**.) Press Enter.

The display scale changes appropriately (your scale may be different). India, however, is not centered in the data frame.

16 On the Tools toolbar, click the Pan tool.

17 Pan the data so that India is similarly positioned in both data frames.

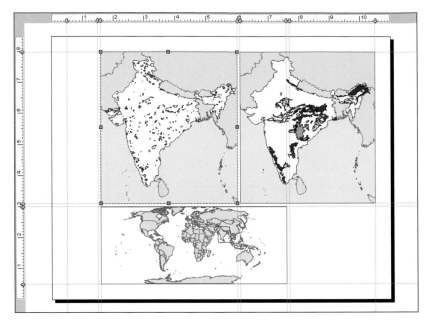

18 On the Tools toolbar, click the Select Elements tool.

19 Click on an empty part of the virtual page to unselect the data frame.

In the next exercise, you'll add a title to the map.

20 If you want to save your work, click the File menu and click Save As. Navigate to **C:\GTKArcGIS\Chapter19\MyData**. Rename the file **my_ex19a.mxd** and click Save.

21 In the ArcMap application title bar, click the middle button in the upper right corner to restore the application window to its former size.

22 If you are continuing with the next exercise, leave ArcMap open. Otherwise, click the File menu and click Exit. Click No if prompted to save your changes.

Adding a title

All maps have titles, and many have subtitles as well. A good title helps the reader understand what to look for in the map.

Exercise 19b

Now that you have laid out the three data frames, you'll add a title to convey the subject of the map—tiger conservation—and a subtitle to convey the specific focus—suitable habitat.

1 Start ArcMap. In the ArcMap dialog box, click the option to use an existing map. In the list of existing maps, double-click Browse for maps. (If ArcMap is already running, click the File menu and click Open.) Navigate to **C:\GTKArcGIS\Chapter19**. Click **ex19b.mxd** and click Open.

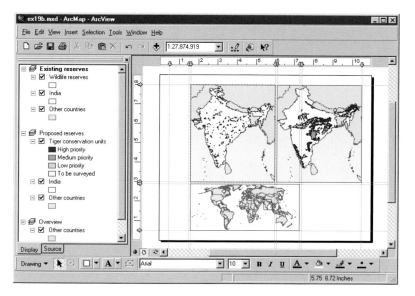

The map opens in layout view. It looks as it did at the end of the previous exercise.

2 In the ArcMap application title bar, click the middle button in the upper right corner to maximize the application window.

If your application window is already maximized, don't worry—it just means that you didn't restore it to its former size at the end of the previous exercise.

3 On the Layout toolbar, click the Zoom Whole Page button.

Now you'll insert the title.

4 Click the Insert menu, and click Title.

A text box is added to the page. The default title is the name of your ArcMap document, ex19b.

5 In the text box, type **Tiger Conservation** and press Enter.

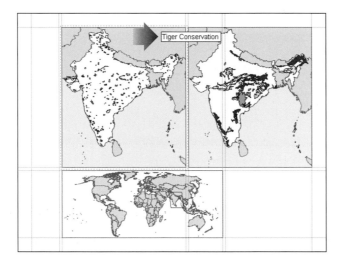

If you make a mistake and need to change the text after pressing Enter, double-click on the title to open its text properties.

The title is too small. You can change its font, size, style, or color on the Draw toolbar.

6 On the Draw toolbar, in the Font size window, highlight the current value and replace it with **62**. Press Enter.

The title size changes to 62 points. Before positioning the title, you'll add a subtitle.

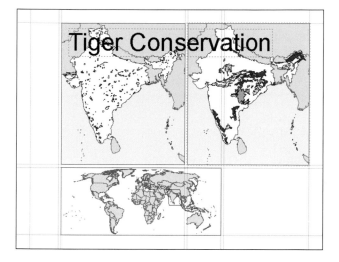

7 Click the Insert menu and click Title.

A text box is added to the page. Again, the default title is the map document name.

8 In the text box, type **an assessment of critical habitat in India** and press Enter.

You'll change the font and style of the subtitle.

9 On the Draw toolbar, click the Font Size drop-down arrow and click 22. Click the Italic button.

The subtitle is changed on the map.

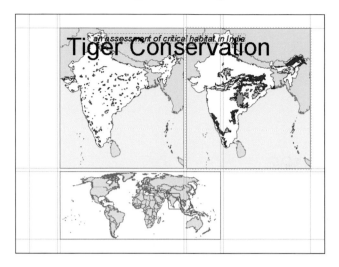

You'll position the two elements, then group them.

10 Drag the subtitle directly below the title, close but not touching. Position it so that the first word in the subtitle, "an," is underneath the "r" in "Tiger." Use the following graphic as a guide.

Tiger Conservation
an assessment of critical habitat in India

The subtitle needs to be very close to the title to fit in the space prepared for it.

11 Right-click on the subtitle. On the context menu, point to Nudge and click Nudge Up. (You can also press 8 on your keyboard's numeric keypad.) Keep nudging until the subtitle is as close as possible to the title without touching it.

If you go too far, you can use Nudge Down (or press 2 on your numeric keypad). You can also delete the subtitle and try again.

12 With the subtitle selected, hold down the Shift key and click on the title. Both elements are selected. Right-click on either title. On the context menu, click Group.

Tiger Conservation
an assessment of critical habitat in India

Anything you do to the grouped title, such as changing the font size or color, will affect both elements. (To ungroup an element, select it, right-click on it, and click Ungroup on the context menu.)

Now you'll rotate the grouped title and move it to the left side of the page.

13 With the grouped title selected, right-click on it. On the context menu, point to Rotate or Flip and click Rotate Left.

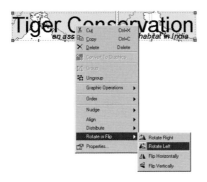

It will be easier to put the title in the right place if it snaps to the guides.

14 Right-click on an empty part of the virtual page. On the context menu, point to Guides and click Snap to Guides.

15 Drag the title to the left side of the virtual page so that the upper left corner snaps to the guides at 8 inches (vertical ruler) and 0.5 inches (horizontal ruler).

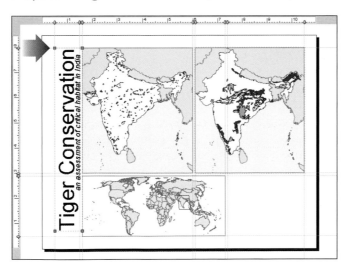

16 Click on an empty part of the virtual page to unselect the grouped title.

Your title is not quite complete. You'll add a background rectangle to frame it.

17 On the Draw toolbar, click the New Rectangle tool.

18 Drag a rectangle that snaps to the guides around the title. The upper left corner should snap to 8 inches (vertical ruler) and 0.5 inches (horizontal ruler). The lower right corner should snap to 0.5 inches (vertical ruler) and 1.5 inches (horizontal ruler).

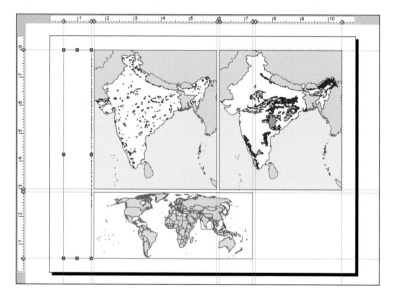

By default, the rectangle is pale yellow. You'll change its color and move it behind the title.

19 Make sure the rectangle is selected. On the Draw toolbar, click the Fill Color drop-down arrow. On the color palette, click More Colors.

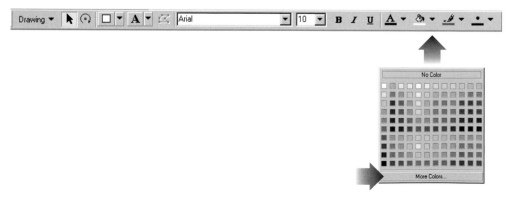

20 On the Color Selector dialog, click the Color tab if necessary. Replace the R (red) value with **176**. Press the Tab key on your keyboard. Replace the G (green) value with **204** and press Tab again. Replace the B (blue) value with **204**. The custom color is previewed in the lower left corner of the dialog. Make sure your dialog matches the following graphic, then click OK.

The rectangle color changes to a blue-gray.

21 Right-click on the selected rectangle, point to Order, and click Send to Back.

Finally, you'll center the title within the rectangle. Because ArcMap aligns elements in relation to the last selected element, you'll select the title first.

22 Click on the title. Make sure the title, not the rectangle, is selected.

23 Hold down the Shift key and click on the bottom of the rectangle, outside the title's selection box.

Both the grouped title and the rectangle should be selected. The rectangle's selection color is blue, indicating that it is the last selected element. The title's selection color changes to green.

24 Right-click on either selected element, point to Align, and click Align Vertical Center.

25 Right-click on either selected element, point to Align, and click Align Center.

The title is centered vertically and horizontally within the rectangle.

26 Right-click once more on either selected element and click Group, then click on an empty part of the virtual page to unselect the grouped element.

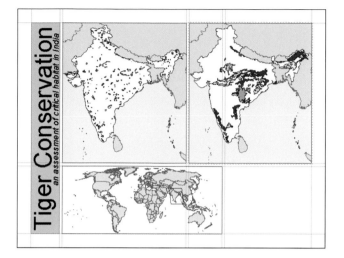

In the next exercise, you'll add a north arrow, a scale bar, and a legend to the Proposed reserves data frame.

27 If you want to save your work, click the File menu and click Save As. Navigate to **C:\GTKArcGIS\Chapter19\MyData**. Rename the file **my_ex19b.mxd** and click Save.

28 In the ArcMap application title bar, click the middle button in the upper right corner to restore the application window to its former size.

29 If you are continuing with the next exercise, leave ArcMap open. Otherwise, click the File menu and click Exit. Click No if prompted to save your changes.

Adding a north arrow, a scale bar, and a legend

North arrows, scale bars, and legends are associated with the data frame that is active when they are inserted. A scale bar changes when the display scale of its data frame changes. A legend is updated when layers in its data frame are deleted or resymbolized. Although these elements can be moved anywhere on a map layout, it is usually best to keep them within the data frame they belong to.

ArcMap has many different styles for north arrows, scale bars, and legends and allows you to customize them.

Exercise 19c

The people who review the proposal and your map will be familiar with the geography of India. Still, legends are necessary for interpreting any map, while scale bars and north arrows provide geographic orientation.

1 Start ArcMap. In the ArcMap dialog box, click the option to use an existing map. In the list of existing maps, double-click Browse for maps. (If ArcMap is already running, click the File menu and click Open.) Navigate to **C:\GTKArcGIS\Chapter19**. Click **ex19c.mxd** and click Open.

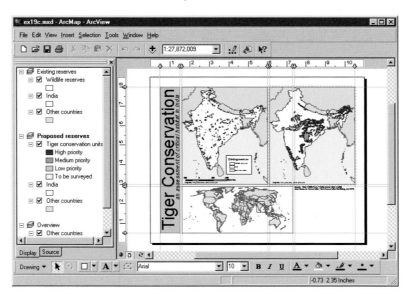

The map opens in layout view. It looks as it did at the end of the previous exercise but has a few additional elements, such as the legend and scale bar in the Existing reserves data frame. You'll insert these elements in the Proposed reserves data frame as well, but first you'll add a north arrow to the Overview data frame.

2 In the ArcMap application title bar, click the middle button in the upper right corner to maximize the application window.

3 On the Layout toolbar, click the Zoom Whole Page button.

4 Click the Overview data frame to select it.

5 Click the Insert menu and click North Arrow. In the dialog, click on ESRI North 3, as shown in the following graphic, and click OK.

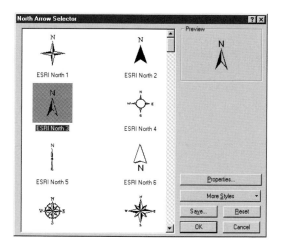

The north arrow is added to the map.

6 Drag the north arrow to the lower left corner of the Overview data frame. Leave a little bit of room beneath it.

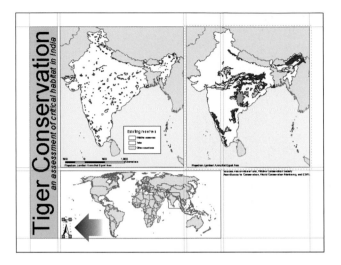

Now you'll add a scale bar to the Proposed reserves data frame. Scale bars allow you to measure the sizes of map features and the distances between them.

7 Click on the Proposed reserves data frame to select it.

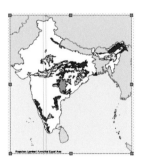

8 Click the Insert menu, and click Scale Bar.

In the Scale Bar Selector dialog, click Alternating Scale Bar 1, as shown in the following graphic, and click OK.

The scale bar is added to the virtual page. Before moving it, you'll change some of its properties to match the scale bar in the Existing reserves data frame.

10 Right-click on the scale bar and click Properties. If necessary, click the Scale and Units tab.

The scale bar currently has four divisions. The left-most division itself has four subdivisions. The scale units are meters.

11 In the middle of the dialog, click the When resizing drop-down arrow and click Adjust width.

This will make the width of the scale bar change if the display scale of the data frame changes.

ADJUSTING SCALE BARS

A scale bar changes as you zoom in or out on its data frame. If the scale bar is adjusted by division value, the distance represented by a scale bar division is variable. As you zoom in, it represents less distance; as you zoom out, it represents more. If the scale bar is adjusted by the number of divisions, the distance represented by a division stays the same, but there are fewer divisions as you zoom in and more as you zoom out. If the scale bar is adjusted by width, the distance represented by a division and the number of divisions stays the same, but the entire scale bar grows wider as you zoom in and narrower as you zoom out. (If a scale bar is adjusted by width, you cannot widen it by dragging; its width changes only with the display scale.)

---

12 In the Division value box at the top of the dialog, replace the current value with **500**.

13 Click the Number of divisions down arrow and change the value to **3**. Click the Number of subdivisions down arrow and change its value to **2**.

14 Check Show one division before zero.

15 In the lower portion of the dialog, click the Division Units drop-down arrow. Scroll up and click Kilometers. Make sure that your dialog matches the following graphic, then click OK.

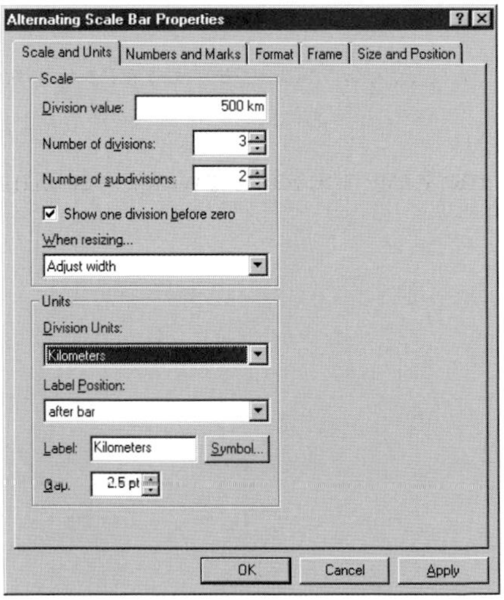

In the layout, the scale bar reflects the new properties you set.

16 Drag the scale bar to the lower left corner of the Proposed reserves data frame, just above the projection information.

You'll change its height to match the other scale bar.

17 With the scale bar selected, hold down the Shift key and click on the scale bar in the Existing reserves data frame.

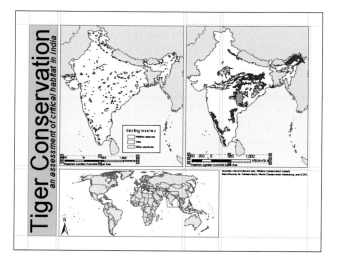

Both scale bars are selected. The Existing reserves scale bar, selected last, is outlined in blue.

18 Right-click on either scale bar. On the context menu, point to Distribute and click Make Same Height.

19 Right-click again on either scale bar. On the context menu, point to Align and click Align Bottom.

The two scale bars now look the same and have the same property settings.

Next, you'll add a legend to the Proposed reserves data frame.

20 Click on the Proposed reserves data frame to select it. Click the Insert menu and click Legend to open the Legend Wizard.

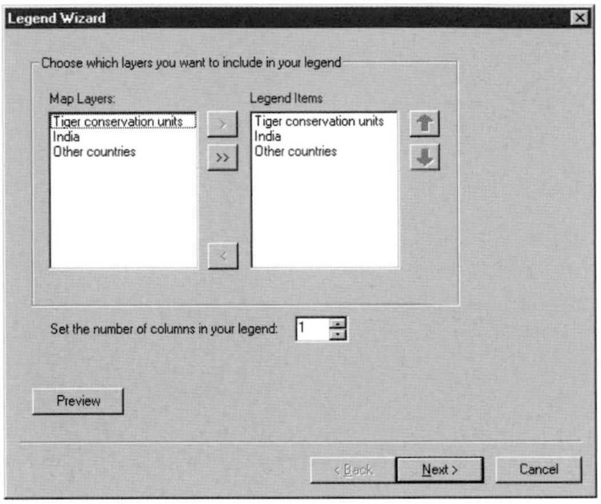

By default, the legend includes all layers from the map. The number of legend columns is set to one. Click Next to accept the defaults.

In the second panel, you'll change the legend title.

21 Replace the default title with **Proposed reserves**, as shown in the following graphic. Click Next.

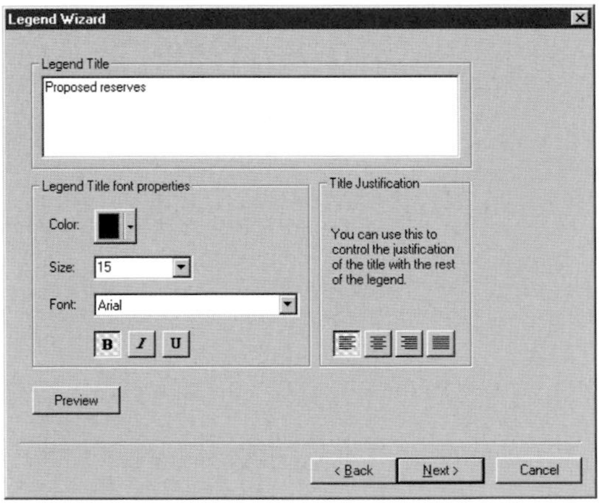

In the third panel, you'll add a border to the legend.

22 Click the Border drop-down arrow and click 1.0 Point. Click the Background drop-down arrow, scroll to the bottom of the list, and click White.

The next two panels set symbols and spacing for the legend, but you will not change these. Clicking Preview at any time displays the legend on the map in its current form and allows you to exit the wizard or return and make further changes.

23 On the wizard panel, click Preview. If necessary, move the wizard away from the map.

The legend is added to the map and the wizard remains open.

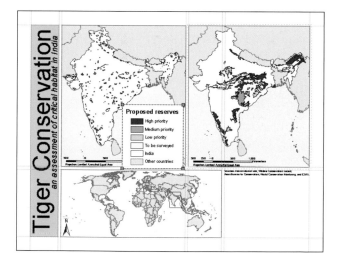

24 On the wizard panel, click Finish.

Finally, you'll resize and move the legend.

25 Drag the legend somewhere over the Proposed reserves data frame. Place the mouse pointer over any selection handle, drag the legend to about half its original size, and position it as shown in the following graphic. When finished, click on an empty part of the virtual page to unselect the legend.

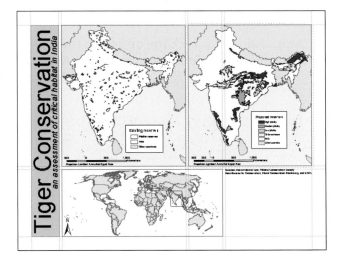

In the next exercise, you'll add a few more map elements and prepare to print your map.

26 If you want to save your work, click the File menu and click Save As. Navigate to **C:\GTKArcGIS\Chapter19\MyData**. Rename the file **my_ex19c.mxd** and click Save.

27 In the ArcMap application title bar, click the middle button in the upper right corner to restore the application window to its former size.

28 If you are continuing with the next exercise, leave ArcMap open. Otherwise, click the File menu and click Exit. Click No if prompted to save your changes.

Adding final touches and setting print options

Before sending a map to print, you should check your page setup options and preview the map in ArcMap.

Exercise 19d
The map is almost ready. You'll add a picture and a neatline, preview the map, and send it to a printer.

1 Start ArcMap. In the ArcMap dialog box, click the option to use an existing map. In the list of existing maps, double-click Browse for maps. (If ArcMap is already running, click the File menu and click Open.) Navigate to **C:\GTKArcGIS\Chapter19**. Click **ex19d.mxd** and click Open.

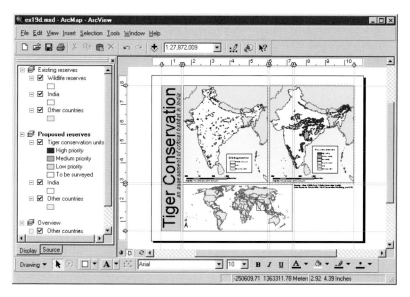

The map opens in layout view. It looks as it did at the end of the previous exercise.

2 In the ArcMap application title bar, click the middle button in the upper right corner to maximize the application.

3 On the Layout toolbar, click the Zoom Whole Page button.

4 Click the Insert menu and click Text.

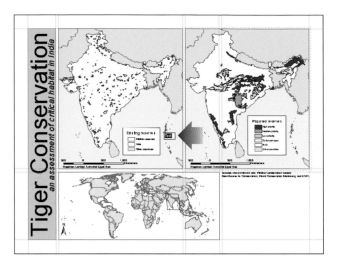

The text box appears in the middle of the virtual page with the word "Text" highlighted.

5 In the text box, type **Projection: Robinson** and press Enter. The text is selected.

6 On the Draw toolbar, highlight the value in the Font Size drop-down list and replace it with **6.53**. Press Enter.

Drawing ▾ | ▸ ⊙ □ ▾ A ▾ ☒ | Arial | ▾ | 6.53 ▾ | B *I* U | A ▾ | ◇ ▾ | ◢ ▾ | ⬤ ▾

7 Drag the text to the lower left corner of the Overview data frame and place it beneath the north arrow.

You'll add a photograph of a tiger. Who could resist a picture of such a magnificent animal?

8 Click the Insert menu and click Picture.

9 In the Open dialog, navigate to **C:\GTKArcGIS\Chapter19\Data.** Click on tiger.jpg, as shown in the following graphic, and click Open.

The tiger image is added to the map.

10 Right-click on an empty part of the virtual page. On the context menu, point to Guides and click Snap to Guides.

11 Place the mouse pointer over the image and drag it so that its lower right corner snaps to the guides at 0.5 inches (vertical ruler) and 10.5 inches (horizontal ruler).

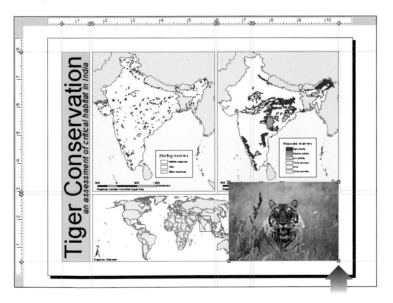

12 Place the mouse pointer over the selection handle in the upper left corner of the graphic. Drag to resize the image so that its left edge snaps to the guide at 7.4 inches (horizontal ruler). Click on an empty part of the virtual page to unselect the image.

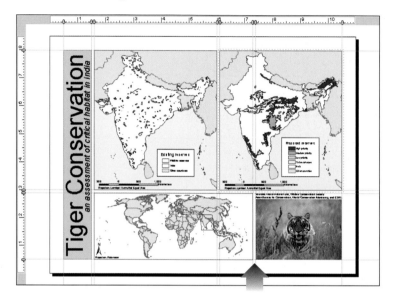

The map is almost finished. The last element you add will be a neatline, a bounding line that frames the other elements.

13 Click the Insert menu and click Neatline.

14 In the Neatline dialog, make sure the option to place the neatline around all elements is selected. Click the Border drop-down arrow and click 2.5 Point.

15 Click the Background drop-down arrow. Scroll up and click None. Make sure that your dialog matches the following graphic, then click OK.

16 Click on an empty part of the virtual page to unselect the neatline.

Before you print a map, you should make sure that your map size and printer setup specifications match. Otherwise, your map may be cut off or misaligned.

17 Click the File menu and click Page Setup.

In exercise 19a, you changed the map page orientation from Portrait to Landscape. Now you'll change your Printer Setup options, too.

18 In the Printer Setup frame, click the Landscape option. If necessary, click the Name drop-down arrow and click the printer you want to use. Accept the default printer page size (Letter) and printer engine (Windows Printer). Make sure that your dialog matches the following graphic, except for the printer name. Click OK.

You are ready to preview your map. The preview shows you how the map will look on the printed page, so you can correct any mistakes in advance.

19 Click the File menu and click Print Preview.

Edge of page ——

Neatline ——

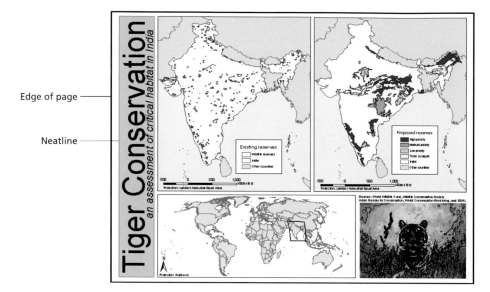

You should be mainly concerned with the alignment of elements on the page. Your alignment will depend on the type of printer you are connected to and its configuration. If the map elements overlap the page edge, you'll correct this problem in a moment.

Don't worry that the quality of the tiger image is poor in the preview—it will be fine when it prints.

20 Click Print to open the Print dialog.

21 If the map looked good in the print preview, click OK to print it.

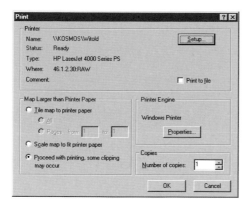

22 If the map went over the edge of the page, click the Scale map to fit printer paper option, then click OK.

You have finished the map and you have finished this book.

23 If you want to save your work, click the File menu and click Save As. Navigate to **C:\GTKArcGIS\Chapter19MyData**. Rename the file **my_ex19d.mxd** and click Save.

24 In the ArcMap application title bar, click the middle button in the upper right corner to restore the application window to its former size.

25 Click the File menu and click Exit. Click No if prompted to save your changes.

Data license agreement

Important:
Read carefully before opening the sealed media package

ENVIRONMENTAL SYSTEMS RESEARCH INSTITUTE, INC. (ESRI), IS WILLING TO LICENSE THE ENCLOSED DATA AND RELATED MATERIALS TO YOU ONLY UPON THE CONDITION THAT YOU ACCEPT ALL OF THE TERMS AND CONDITIONS CONTAINED IN THIS LICENSE AGREEMENT. PLEASE READ THE TERMS AND CONDITIONS CAREFULLY BEFORE OPENING THE SEALED MEDIA PACKAGE. BY OPENING THE SEALED MEDIA PACKAGE, YOU ARE INDICATING YOUR ACCEPTANCE OF THE ESRI LICENSE AGREEMENT. IF YOU DO NOT AGREE TO THE TERMS AND CONDITIONS AS STATED, THEN ESRI IS UNWILLING TO LICENSE THE DATA AND RELATED MATERIALS TO YOU. IN SUCH EVENT, YOU SHOULD RETURN THE MEDIA PACKAGE WITH THE SEAL UNBROKEN AND ALL OTHER COMPONENTS TO ESRI.

ESRI License Agreement

This is a license agreement, and not an agreement for sale, between you (Licensee) and Environmental Systems Research Institute, Inc. (ESRI). This ESRI License Agreement (Agreement) gives Licensee certain limited rights to use the data and related materials (Data and Related Materials). All rights not specifically granted in this Agreement are reserved to ESRI and its Licensors.

Reservation of Ownership and Grant of License: ESRI and its Licensors retain exclusive rights, title, and ownership to the copy of the Data and Related Materials licensed under this Agreement and, hereby, grant to Licensee a personal, nonexclusive, nontransferable, royalty-free, worldwide license to use the Data and Related Materials based on the terms and conditions of this Agreement. Licensee agrees to use reasonable effort to protect the Data and Related Materials from unauthorized use, reproduction, distribution, or publication.

Proprietary Rights and Copyright: Licensee acknowledges that the Data and Related Materials are proprietary and confidential property of ESRI and its Licensors and are protected by United States copyright laws and applicable international copyright treaties and/or conventions.

Permitted Uses:
Licensee may install the Data and Related Materials onto permanent storage device(s) for Licensee's own internal use.

Licensee may make only one (1) copy of the original Data and Related Materials for archival purposes during the term of this Agreement unless the right to make additional copies is granted to Licensee in writing by ESRI.

Licensee may internally use the Data and Related Materials provided by ESRI for the stated purpose of GIS training and education.

Uses Not Permitted:
Licensee shall not sell, rent, lease, sublicense, lend, assign, time-share, or transfer, in whole or in part, or provide unlicensed Third Parties access to the Data and Related Materials or portions of the Data and Related Materials, any updates, or Licensee's rights under this Agreement.

Licensee shall not remove or obscure any copyright or trademark notices of ESRI or its Licensors.

Term and Termination: The license granted to Licensee by this Agreement shall commence upon the acceptance of this Agreement and shall continue until such time that Licensee elects in writing to discontinue use of the Data or Related

Materials and terminates this Agreement. The Agreement shall automatically terminate without notice if Licensee fails to comply with any provision of this Agreement. Licensee shall then return to ESRI the Data and Related Materials. The parties hereby agree that all provisions that operate to protect the rights of ESRI and its Licensors shall remain in force should breach occur.

Disclaimer of Warranty: THE DATA AND RELATED MATERIALS CONTAINED HEREIN ARE PROVIDED "AS-IS," WITHOUT WARRANTY OF ANY KIND, EITHER EXPRESS OR IMPLIED, INCLUDING, BUT NOT LIMITED TO, THE IMPLIED WARRANTIES OF MERCHANTABILITY, FITNESS FOR A PARTICULAR PURPOSE, OR NONINFRINGEMENT. ESRI does not warrant that the Data and Related Materials will meet Licensee's needs or expectations, that the use of the Data and Related Materials will be uninterrupted, or that all nonconformities, defects, or errors can or will be corrected. ESRI is not inviting reliance on the Data or Related Materials for commercial planning or analysis purposes, and Licensee should always check actual data.

Data Disclaimer: The Data used herein has been derived from actual spatial or tabular information. In some cases, ESRI has manipulated and applied certain assumptions, analyses, and opinions to the Data solely for educational training purposes. Assumptions, analyses, opinions applied, and actual outcomes may vary. Again, ESRI is not inviting reliance on this Data, and the Licensee should always verify actual Data and exercise their own professional judgment when interpreting any outcomes.

Limitation of Liability: ESRI shall not be liable for direct, indirect, special, incidental, or consequential damages related to Licensee's use of the Data and Related Materials, even if ESRI is advised of the possibility of such damage.

No Implied Waivers: No failure or delay by ESRI or its Licensors in enforcing any right or remedy under this Agreement shall be construed as a waiver of any future or other exercise of such right or remedy by ESRI or its Licensors.

Order for Precedence: Any conflict between the terms of this Agreement and any FAR, DFAR, purchase order, or other terms shall be resolved in favor of the terms expressed in this Agreement, subject to the government's minimum rights unless agreed otherwise.

Export Regulation: Licensee acknowledges that this Agreement and the performance thereof are subject to compliance with any and all applicable United States laws, regulations, or orders relating to the export of data thereto. Licensee agrees to comply with all laws, regulations, and orders of the United States in regard to any export of such technical data.

Severability: If any provision(s) of this Agreement shall be held to be invalid, illegal, or unenforceable by a court or other tribunal of competent jurisdiction, the validity, legality, and enforceability of the remaining provisions shall not in any way be affected or impaired thereby.

Governing Law: This Agreement, entered into in the County of San Bernardino, shall be construed and enforced in accordance with and be governed by the laws of the United States of America and the State of California without reference to conflict of laws principles. The parties hereby consent to the personal jurisdiction of the courts of this county and waive their rights to change venue.

Entire Agreement: The parties agree that this Agreement constitutes the sole and entire agreement of the parties as to the matter set forth herein and supersedes any previous agreements, understandings, and arrangements between the parties relating hereto.

Installing the data and software

Getting to Know ArcGIS Desktop includes two CDs, one with exercise data and one with ArcView 8 software. The exercise data takes up about 215 megabytes of hard disk space, the software about 700 megabytes.

If you install the data and the software, the entire process will take about thirty-five minutes.

If you already have a licensed copy of ArcView, ArcEditor, or ArcInfo installed on your computer (or accessible through a network), do not install the software CD. Use your licensed software to do the exercises in this book.

Installing the data

Follow the steps below to install the exercise data. Do not copy the files directly from the CD to your hard drive.

1 Put the data CD in your computer's CD drive. In your file browser, click on the icon for your CD drive to see the folders on the CD. Double-click the Setup.exe file to begin.

Name	Size	Type	Modified
GTKArcGIS		File Folder	5/21/01 5:23 PM
inst32i.ex	292KB	EX_ File	10/2/98 7:15 PM
_ISDel.exe	27KB	Application	10/27/98 1:06 PM
_Setup.dll	34KB	Application Extension	9/29/98 5:34 PM
_sys1.cab	172KB	WinZip File	5/21/01 5:20 PM
_sys1.hdr	4KB	HDR File	5/21/01 5:20 PM
_user1.cab	2KB	WinZip File	5/21/01 5:20 PM
_user1.hdr	5KB	HDR File	5/21/01 5:20 PM
Data.tag	1KB	TAG File	5/21/01 5:20 PM
data1.cab	103,132KB	WinZip File	5/21/01 5:21 PM
data1.hdr	48KB	HDR File	5/21/01 5:20 PM
lang.dat	5KB	DAT File	9/18/98 3:12 PM
layout.bin	1KB	BIN File	5/21/01 5:21 PM
os.dat	1KB	DAT File	7/27/98 6:41 PM
Setup.exe	70KB	Application	10/2/98 7:04 PM
Setup.ini	1KB	Configuration Settings	5/21/01 5:20 PM
setup.ins	56KB	Internet Communication Settings	5/21/01 5:20 PM
setup.lid	1KB	LID File	5/21/01 5:20 PM

e: 0 bytes]

2 Read the Welcome.

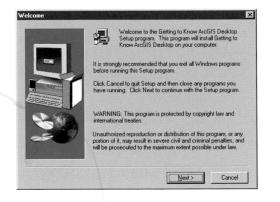

3 Click Next. Accept the default installation folder or navigate to the drive where you want to install the data.

4 Click Next. The exercise data is installed on your computer in a folder called GTKArcGIS. When the installation is finished, you see the following message:

5 Click Finish.

If you have a licensed copy of ArcView, ArcEditor, or ArcInfo installed on your computer, you are ready to start *Getting to Know ArcGIS Desktop*. Otherwise, follow the instructions below to install and register the software.

Installing the software

Please read the important information provided below before installing the software.

The ArcView software included on this CD–ROM is intended for educational purposes only. Once installed and registered, the software will run for 180 days. The software cannot be reinstalled nor can the time limit be extended. It is recommended that you uninstall this software when it expires. You must uninstall it before installing any other copies of ArcView, ArcEditor, or ArcInfo (Version 8.x). You do not need to uninstall versions of ArcView GIS 3.x before installing ArcView 8; both can be used simultaneously.

Before you install the software, print out the readme.txt file included on the software CD. This file gives you step-by-step instructions for installing and registering the software components that you will need to complete the exercises in this book.

The procedure outlined in the readme.txt file installs all programs included with the standard installation of ArcView 8 with the exception of Seagate Crystal Reports. You may optionally register and evaluate the ArcGIS extensions ArcGIS 3D Analyst, ArcGIS Spatial Analyst, ArcGIS Geostatistical Analyst, and/or ArcPress for ArcGIS when you install ArcView. The ArcGIS StreetMap extension is not available for evaluation. Please note that the ArcGIS tutorial data included on the software CD uses about 125 megabytes of space and is not the data you will use with this book. If you need to conserve disk space, you can uncheck the ArcGIS tutorial Data check box during the installation.

Allow about thirty-five minutes to install and register ArcView 8. Actual time will vary depending on processor, hard drive, and CD drive speeds. If Microsoft Windows Installer and Microsoft Internet Explorer (IE) 5.0 (or higher) are not currently installed on your computer, you will be prompted to install them from this CD, which adds about twenty minutes to the installation. (Installing IE on your system in no way obligates you to use it as your Internet browser. You may continue using the browser of your choice.)

ESRI PROVIDES NO TECHNICAL SUPPORT FOR THIS COMPLIMENTARY CD. IF YOU HAVE QUESTIONS OR ENCOUNTER PROBLEMS DURING THE INSTALLATION PROCESS, REFER TO THE COMPLETE INSTALLATION GUIDE INCLUDED ON THE CD OR GO TO THE ESRI ONLINE SUPPORT CENTER AT *support.esri.com*.

Uninstalling the data and software

To uninstall the exercise data or software from your computer, open your operating system's control panel and click the Add/Remove Programs icon. In the Add/Remove Programs Properties dialog, select whichever of the following entries you want to uninstall and follow the prompts to remove them:

* Getting to Know ArcGIS Desktop
* ArcView 8.1 (Demo Edition)
* ArcGIS Tutorial Data

ESRI Press publishes books about the science, application, and technology of GIS. Ask for these titles at your local bookstore or order by calling 1-800-447-9778. You can also read book descriptions, read reviews, and shop online at www.esri.com/esripress. Outside the United States, contact your local ESRI distributor. ESRI Press titles are distributed to the book trade by the Independent Publishers Group (800-888-4741 in the United States, 312-337-0747 outside the United States).

ESRI PRESS
380 NEW YORK STREET, REDLANDS, CALIFORNIA 92373-8100
www.esri.com/esripress

Getting to Know ArcGIS Desktop: Basics of ArcView, ArcEditor, and ArcInfo
Book design, production, and copyediting by Michael Hyatt
Image editing by Jennifer Galloway
Cover design and production by Amaree Israngkura
Printing coordination by Cliff Crabbe